JUST TRANSPORTATION

JUST TRANSPORTATION

Dismantling Race and Class
Barriers to Mobility

Edited by
Robert D. Bullard and
Glenn S. Johnson

NEW SOCIETY PUBLISHERS

Cover design by David Lester.

Printed in the U.S.A. on partically recycled paper using soy-based inks by Capital City Press, Montpelier, Vermont.

Inquiries regarding requests to reprint all or part of *Just Transportation* should be addressed to New Society Publishers at the address below.

Paperback ISBN: 0-86571-357-X
Hardback ISBN: 0-86571-356-1

To order directly from the publisher, please add $3.00 to the price of the first copy, and $1.00 for each additional copy (plus GST in Canada). Send check or money order to:

New Society Publishers,
P.O. Box 189, Gabriola Island, B.C. V0R 1X0, Canada

New Society Publishers aims to publish books for fundamental social change through nonviolent action. We focus especially on sustainable living, progressive leadership, and educational and parenting resources. Our on-line catalog is available for browsing at: http://www.newsociety.com

NEW SOCIETY PUBLISHERS
Gabriola Island, BC and Stony Creek, CT

This book is dedicated to
Cynthia Wiggins and Rosa Parks

Table of Contents

Acknowledgments

There are a number of persons and organizations we wish to thank for making this book possible. We are especially grateful to Anthony Romero of the Ford Foundation, Dana Alston of the Public Welfare Foundation, and Peter Bahouth of the Turner Foundation who supported the work of the Environmental Justice Resource Center and our research. We offer special thanks to the contributors who endured the constant nagging about deadlines from our two graduate research assistants, Chris Weldon and April Allen. Thanks, Chris and April, for a job well done. Finally, our hats go off to Chris Plant of New Society Publishers for his patience and hard work in bringing this project to completion.

About the Contributors

Susana R. Almanza is a co-founder of People Organized in Defense of the Earth and Her Resources (PODER), an Austin-based grassroots environmental justice group.

Raul R. Alvarez is a co-founder of People Organized in Defense of the Earth and Her Resources (PODER), an Austin-based grassroots environmental justice group.

Robert D. Bullard is the Ware Professor of Sociology and director of the Environmental Justice Resource Center at Clark Atlanta University. His most recent books include Unequal Protection: Environmental Justice and Communities of Color (Sierra Club Books, 1996), and Residential Apartheid: The American Legacy (UCLA Center for Afro-American Studies Publication, 1994).

Michael Cameron is a staff researcher with the Environmental Defense Fund based in Oakland, California.

Don Chen works for the Surface Transportation Policy Project in Washington, D.C.

Sid Davis is Professor of Management at Southern College of Technology located in Marietta, Georgia.

Charles Haines is Professor of Environmental Sciences at Haskell Indian Nations University in Lawrence, Kansas.

Henry Holmes is the director of the Transportation Project of the San Francisco-based Urban Habitat Program.

Glenn S. Johnson is an assistant professor of sociology and research associate in the Environmental Justice Resource Center at Clark Atlanta University.

Bill Lann Lee is the lead attorney for the NAACP Legal Defense and Education Fund's western regional office located in Los Angeles.

John Lewis is a long-time civil rights activist and U.S. congressman from Georgia's Fifth District.

Eric Mann is executive director of the Los Angeles-based Labor/Community Strategy Center. His most recent book is Los Angeles' Lethal Air.

David G. Oedel is a professor of law at Mercer University in Macon, Georgia.

Fern L. Shepard is a staff attorney with the Washington, D.C. office of the Sierra Club Legal Defense Fund.

Paul K. Sonn is an assistant counsel with the NAACP Legal Defense and Education Fund in New York City.

Beverly H. Wright is an environmental sociologist at Xavier University of Louisiana and directs the Deep South Center for Environmental Justice.

Foreword

Congressman John Lewis

Three decades ago, I first went to Washington, D.C. as a twenty-one year-old student to begin a historic journey called the Freedom Rides. The Supreme Court had just issued a decision prohibiting discrimination in interstate travel. I was one of a group of young people who set out to test that decision by traveling by bus from Washington through the Deep South, and into Louisiana. The bus we rode on symbolized freedom — freedom to travel as first-class American citizens.

Despite the new law, barriers that had denied African-Americans freedom to travel were still in place. When we rode across the South, I saw the signs that divided the world into two classes of citizens: black and white. The signs read: White Men, Colored Men; White Women, Colored Women; White Waiting, Colored Waiting. As we traveled and challenged those signs, we were intimidated, attacked, and beaten.

Just Transportation clearly illustrates that our struggle is not over. Today, those physical signs are gone, but the legacy of "Jim Crow" transportation is still with us. Even today, some of our transportation policies and practices destroy stable neighborhoods, isolate and segregate our citizens in deteriorating neighborhoods, and fail to provide access to jobs and economic growth centers.

Neighborhoods in every major city in America still post invisible signs that say: "Poor people and people of color are not welcome." The signs may be invisible, but the message is real. We must find ways to tear down these barriers and build bridges to an inclusive future. Sadly, even after passage of the Civil Rights Act of 1964, the Voting Rights Act of 1965 and the Fair Housing Act of 1968, the scars and stains of racism are still deeply embedded in American society.

We have come a great distance, but we are still a society divided by race and class. From New York to Los Angeles, segregated housing, discriminatory land-use planning and unjust transportation policies keep poor people and minorities separate and apart. Suburban road construction programs expand while urban transit systems are underfunded and fall into disrepair. Service jobs go unfilled in suburban malls and retail centers because public transit too often does not link urban job seekers with suburban jobs.

Even in a city like Atlanta, Georgia — a vibrant city with a modern rail and public transit system — thousands of people have been left out and left behind because of discrimination. Like most other major American cities, Atlanta's urban center is worlds apart from its suburbs. The gulf between rich and poor, minorities and whites, the "haves" and "have-nots" continues to widen.

We need to rededicate ourselves to provide necessary transportation services to all Americans. With the same discipline, moral urgency, and righteous indignation that empowered us during the 1960s and the civil rights movement, we must say "no" to the new forms of segregation that permeate public transportation today.

In the same way that we fought for the right to vote, we must now battle against discrimination in transportation services. When we remove invisible race and class barriers that divide our society, only then will we have just transportation for all Americans.

Preface

Why write a book about transportation? First, transportation affects every aspect of our lives and daily routine — where we live, work, play, shop, go to school, etc. Second, transportation issues appear to have dropped off the radar screens of many mainstream civil rights and social justice organizations. It is time to refocus attention on the role transportation plays in shaping human interaction and human settlement patterns. Third, 1996 marked the 100th anniversary of Plessy v. Ferguson, the U.S. Supreme Court decision that codified "separate but equal" as the law of the land. Despite Brown v. Board of Education and subsequent court rulings and civil rights laws, many aspects of our society remain separate and unequal — along race and class lines.

American society has never been classless or color-blind. Both race and class have always mattered. Millions of Americans are resigned to economically depressed and deteriorating central cities — by neither choice nor chance. Government policies, including transportation policies, have aided, and in some cases subsidized, separate and unequal economic development, segregated housing, and spatial layout of our central cities and suburbs.

Rosa Parks and the Montgomery Bus Boycott of the 1950s were about just transportation and human dignity. The young John Lewis and his Freedom Riders of the 1960s defined Just Transportation as freedom to travel without fear of intimidation. The Los Angeles-based Bus Riders Union, our modern-day freedom fighters of the 1990s, understand that Just Transportation can only be realized if poor people and people of color receive their fair share of transit services and investments.

Road, highways freeways and mass transit systems do not spring up out of thin air. They are planned. Someone makes a conscious decision to locate freeways, bus stops, and train stations where they are built. It is neither just nor fair for our children to die, as Cynthia Wiggins of Buffalo, New York died, crossing a seven-lane highway, because someone decided not to build a city bus stop at a suburban shopping mall. Zoning and other practices of exclusion result in limited mobility for poor people and those concentrated in central cities.

Grassroots community groups all over the country are banding together to put an end to transportation discrimination in freeway construction, transit services and investments, and facility siting. Whether intended or unintended, transportation discrimination hurts the community by depriving its residents of valuable resources, investments, and mobility.

Many of these grassroots groups do not work exclusively on transportation issues. Most have adopted the Principles of Environmental Justice as a working model for organizing. The groups highlighted in this book represent a small but significant part of the environmental justice movement. More important, they represent an emerging new leadership base that is redefining transportation as an environmental, civil rights, and social justice issue.

Introduction

Robert D. Bullard and Glenn S. Johnson

For more than a century, people of color have struggled to end transportation discrimination, linking unequal treatment on buses and trains with violation of constitutionally guaranteed civil rights. History has shown that the stakes are high. In 1896, the U.S. Supreme Court upheld Louisiana's segregated "white" and "colored" seating on railroad cars in Plessy v. Ferguson, ushering in the infamous doctrine of "separate but equal." Plessy not only codified apartheid on transportation facilities, but also served as the legal basis for racial segregation in education until it was overturned by the 1954 court case, Brown v. Board of Education of Topeka.

The modern civil rights movement has its roots in transportation. From the legendary Rosa Parks to the Montgomery Bus Boycott to the Freedom Riders, all roads pointed to a frontal attack on racist transportation policies and practices. Today, transportation is no less a civil rights and quality of life issue. All communities are still not created equal. Some communities accrue benefits from transportation development projects, while other communities bear a disproportionate burden and pay the cost in diminished health. Generally, benefits are more dispersed, while costs or burdens are more localized. Having a seven-lane freeway next door is not a benefit to someone who does not even own a car.

Historically, transportation development policies did not emerge in a race- and class-neutral society. Institutional racism influences local land use, allocation of funds, enforcement of environmental regulations, facility siting, and where people of color live, work, and play.[1] Discrimination is a manifestation of institutional racism and causes life to be very different for whites and people of color.[2] Transportation racism is not an invention of radical social justice activists. It is just as real as the racism found in the housing industry, educational institutions, employment arena, and judicial system.

Racism refers to any policy, practice, or directive that differentially affects or disadvantages (whether intended or unintended) individuals, groups, or communities, based on race or color. Racism combines with public policies and industry practices to provide benefits for whites while shifting costs to people of color.[3] Racism is reinforced by government, legal, economic, political, and military institutions. In a sense, "every state institution is a racial institution." [4]

1

Transportation and social equity concerns extend to disparate outcomes in planning, operation and maintenance, and infrastructure development. Disparate transportation outcomes can be subsumed under three broad categories of inequity: procedural, geographic, and social.

Procedural Inequity Attention is directed to the process by which transportation decisions may or may not be carried out in a uniform, fair, and consistent manner with involvement of diverse public stakeholders. Here the question is: Do the rules apply equally to everyone?

Geographic Inequity Transportation decisions may have distributive impacts (positive and negative) that are geographic and spatial such as rural versus urban versus central city. Some communities are physically located on the "wrong side of the tracks" and often receive substandard services. Environmental justice concerns revolve around the extent that transportation systems address outcomes (diversity and quality of services, resources and investments, facilities and infrastructure, access to primary employment centers, etc.) that disproportionately favor one geographic area or spatial location over another.

Social Inequity The distribution of transportation benefits and burdens are not randomly distributed across population groups. Generally, transportation amenities (benefits) accrue to the wealthier and more educated segment of society, while transportation disamenities (burdens) fall disproportionately on people of color and individuals at the lower end of the socioeconomic spectrum.

Such disamenities result from: transportation infrastructure that physically isolates communities; inequitable distribution of environmental "nuisances" such as maintenance and refueling facilities (air pollution), airports (noise); lack of sufficient mitigation measures to correct inequitable distribution of negative impacts such as noise or displacement of homes, parks, and cultural landmarks; diverse means to access key economic activity and employment locations; age and condition of the transit fleet; availability and condition of facilities and services at transit stations such as information kiosks, seating, cleanliness, and rest rooms; condition of the roadways that service low-income and people-of-color communities; and major transportation investment projects and community economic development spillover effects.

Environmental problems are endangering the health of communities all across this nation. A big contributor to this health threat is pollution from automobiles. Is clean air a right? A growing number of activists are saying yes to this question.

This book attempts to capture the growing grassroots activism around transportation, social equity, and civil rights. The question of who pays and who benefits from the current transportation policies is central to our analysis. There are a number of underlying assumptions that guide our research:

- In light of reversals in key civil rights gains of the earlier decades, it is clear that this country needs to revisit the social equity and environmental justice implications of contemporary transportation policies and decisions.
- Transportation is basic to many other quality of life indicators such as health, education, employment, economic development, access to municipal services, residential mobility, and environmental quality.

- Federal commitment to public transportation in urban areas appears to have reached an all-time low.
- Persisting residential segregation of people of color and the poor from emerging suburban job centers (where public transit is inadequate or nonexistent) may signal a new urban crisis and a new form of "urban apartheid."
- Transportation investments, enhancements, and financial resources advantage some communities and disadvantage others.
- Tax dollars should not be used to promote discrimination (intended or unintended) in any form.
- The public has every right to be involved in decision-making, including issues of costs, investments, and impacts.
- Transit-oriented development and transportation investments can and should play an important part in rebuilding urban America.

Several government initiatives are currently underway in the U.S. Department of Housing and Urban Development's Empowerment and Enterprise Zones, Environmental Protection Agency's Brownfield and Urban Revitalization, Health and Human Services' "Healthy People 2000," and the Department of Commerce's "Sustainable Development" efforts. None of these initiatives can achieve success without addressing transportation.

This book is written in clear language to reach an interdisciplinary audience ranging from grassroots activists, urban planners, and government officials to college undergraduate and graduate students. This audience participates in university-based transportation centers, transportation courses offered in colleges and universities across the country, state departments of transportation, metropolitan planning organizations, and interest groups working on environmental justice, civil rights, social equity, healthy communities, sustainable development, urban enterprise and empowerment zones. For example, the National Association for the Advancement of Colored People (NAACP) has 2,000 chapters across the nation where transportation-related issues raised in our analysis might be used as organizing tools to galvanize local chapters.

The authors are an interdisciplinary team representing grassroots activists, academics, educators, social scientists, planners, and lawyers. Chapter 1 is written by sociologists Robert D. Bullard and Glenn Johnson, who present a socio-historical overview of the civil rights struggles embedded in transportation. The authors place in context the transportation struggles from Plessy v. Furguson and Rosa Parks to the modern-day challenges of unjust, unfair, and illegal transportation practices. They also illustrate how federal transportation policies are linked to and affected by other governmental policies such as housing, residential patterns, spatial layout of cities (i.e., urban sprawl), and environmental protection.

Chapter 2, written by San Francisco-based environmentalist Henry Holmes, discusses a conceptual framework for understanding the link between transportation policy, sustainable communities, and environmental justice. He emphasizes that although we are nearing the end of the twentieth century, we have not achieved true freedom, justice and equity for everyone. He maintains that transportation systems can help achieve the goals of healthy and sustainable communities.

In Chapter 3, Don Chen, a staff analyst with the Washington, D.C.-based Surface Transportation Policy Project, explores the interaction of social equity, environment, land use, economic development, and transportation in promoting livable communities. Mr. Chen also examines the distributive impact of transportation investments on communities and their social equity implications; the efficacy of transportation investments in promoting community-based planning, community and people-oriented design, neighborhood enhancements, business vitality, and economic growth; and the impact of the Intermodal Surface Transportation Efficiency Act in promoting just, healthy, and livable communities.

Chapter 4 was written by two lawyers, Fern L. Shepard (Sierra Club Legal Defense Fund) and Paul K. Sonn (NAACP Legal Defense and Education Fund), whose clients include two communities that are fighting transportation construction projects. One case study analyzes the Washington, D.C. Anacostia neighborhood's dispute with the Federal Highway Administration over the proposed Barney Circle Freeway. The other case study chronicles the tiny, historic James City's longstanding disputes with the North Carolina Department of Transportation's road construction program.

As the attorney of record, Ms. Shepard's case study focuses on the combined community and legal efforts to prevent the Barney Circle Freeway from being built. If constructed, the freeway would cut through the heart of a low-income African American community, excavate over 70,000 tons of hazardous waste, increase noise, pave over and bisect scarce park land, lower property values, and cost some $200 million in federal funds to construct. She concludes that there are clear winners (suburban commuters and interstate truckers) and losers (southeast District of Columbia residents and tax payers who must foot the bill).

Mr. Sonn discusses an administrative justice complaint he filed with the Federal Highway Administration on behalf of the residents of James City, North Carolina, a small African-American city of 800 founded by freed slaves in 1862. He shows that James City has been negatively impacted by highway construction dating back to the 1950s and 1970s. The most recent assault on James City residents is a continuation of past injustices.

Environmental Defense Fund staffer Michael Cameron wrote Chapter 5. In this chapter, he discusses some of the transportation issues unique to southern California. He considers the degree to which efficiency and equity can be pursued at the same time, and examines efficiency reforms such as congestion pricing. He concludes that the impact of efficiency fees on equity will be significant, but if one keeps explicit equity issues in mind, efficiency could improve mobility for all people.

Chapter 6 was written by Eric Mann who directs the Los Angeles-based Labor Community Strategy Center. The author discusses a class action, civil rights suit filed by the Labor/Community Strategy Center, the Korean Immigrant Workers' Advocates and the Southern Christian Leadership Conference; the suit challenged the use of federal funds in building an expensive rail system. Mr. Mann discusses how his organization and its grassroots allies are challenging the allocation of public funds in Los Angeles' two-tiered (buses versus rail) public transit system. He explains that although 90 percent of Los Angeles transit riders use the bus system, the bulk of the dollars are now being expended to build a rail system.

He questions the expenditure of over $700 million on the newly opened Green Line, a line the community has dubbed "the train to nowhere," since it does not go all the way to Norwalk or the airport. Finally, he explains how the Labor Community Strategy Center organized the Bus Riders Union to empower local residents, which later resulted in a settlement with the Los Angeles Metropolitan Transit Authority.

Chapter 7 was written by long-time Atlanta resident and professor Sid Davis. Professor Davis contrasts the different ridership levels among blacks and whites, and men and women in Atlanta. He discusses the Metropolitan Atlanta Rapid Transit Authority (MARTA), and its relationship to the lives of many African-Americans in the Atlanta Metro area. African-Americans disproportionately account for ridership on MARTA, contends the author. And it was African-Americans who originally forced MARTA into being as accessible as it is today. Professor Davis also finds that income is a major factor in transportation inequity.

Mercer University Law professor, David G. Oedel, wrote Chapter 8. This chapter examines the transportation systems in Macon and Bibb County, Georgia. First, he reviews and provides insights into statistical comparisons between the public transportation system and the highway services in Macon. The data supports a class-action lawsuit he filed on behalf of Macon residents under the Intermodal Surface Transportation Efficiency Act. Macon's population is evenly divided between African-Americans and white; however, 90 percent of the bus riders in Macon are African- American. Over 28 percent of Macon's African-American households are carless compared to only 6 percent of the city's whites.

Using several parameters, the author discusses whether or not the level of service and funding are adequate for the majority of the residents in the areas. He concludes that a disproportionate share of public transportation dollars in Macon-Bibb County go to road construction and maintenance at the expense of the bus system. His analysis also shows that no federal monies are accepted to support the bus system, while the bulk of federal dollars received by Macon-Bibb County go to support road construction.

Chapter 9 was written by two Austin-based environmental justice activists, Susana R. Almanza and Raul R. Alvarez. Their chapter discusses in detail the work of People Organized Defense of the Earth and Her Resources around transportation and environmental justice. The authors address the grassroots organization's efforts toward achieving community empowerment through a better understanding of transportation equity issues. They maintain that if the community better understands the role of transportation in their lives and its impact on their community, then the residents have a better chance of becoming empowered.

In Chapter 10, environmental sociologist Beverly Wright details the legacy of freeway construction and neighborhood destruction in her home city of New Orleans. She chronicles the historical development of New Orleans, which is older than the United States, and illustrates how many of our transportation policies have severely destabilized once-thriving African-American business corridors and neighborhoods in the "Cresent City."

Chapter 11, written by environmental science professor Charles Haines, explores the plan by the Kansas Department of Transportation to build a highway through Haskell Indian Nation University (located in Lawrence, Kansas) and its environmental, socioeconomic, and cultural impacts on the surrounding Native American community. He also examines the justice and equity implications of the road construction plan under the National Environmental Policy Act.

The final chapter, Chapter 12, was written by Los Angeles-based NAACP Legal Defense Fund attorney, Bill Lann Lee. Mr. Lee outlines the legal theory and remedies of Title VI of the 1964 Civil Rights Act and its application in transportation. A legal practitioner, the author outlines several of the Title-VI transportation cases he has handled, including the Labor Community Strategy Center's lawsuit against the Metropolitan Transit Authority, the Oakland Cypress Freeway case, and the Los Angeles/El Soreno/Long Beach Freeway case. He uses the El Soreno lawsuit as a case study in transportation discrimination, and provides a practical guide for those interested in pursuing civil rights litigation in transportation.

The individual authors assembled for this volume come from diverse racial, ethnic, and class backgrounds and represent different stakeholder groups. Whether activist or academic, lawyer or client, planner or resident, transportation touches all of our daily lives. Finally, more and more people are challenging unjust, unfair, and unhealthy transportation policies and practices because safe, clean, efficient, affordable, and equitable transportation should be a right of all Americans. It is cost-effective and it is just.

I don't think this is true. I don't think these things can be guaranteed as rights.

Rights:
→ Dignity → need to define it.
→ Opportunity
→ Accessibility

Even safety isn't a right. Nor is cleanliness, efficiency, affordability, or equity.

Right: If I am allowed to travel, you should be allowed to travel.

Just Transportation

*Robert D. Bullard and
Glenn S. Johnson*

Introduction

Transportation touches nearly every aspect of our lives, including where we live, work, and play. Most Americans use some form of motorized travel in carrying out their daily routine, whether it be shopping, visiting friends, attending church or going to the doctor. The decision to build highways, expressways, and beltways has far-reaching effects on land use, energy policy, and the environment. Transportation also profoundly affects residential and industrial growth, and physical and social mobility. Some of us have cars, while millions of urban Americans use mass transit as the primary mode of travel. Americans drive over 2 billion miles each year, and most of these trips — over 86 percent— involve the automobile. Three-fourths of all commuting cars carry only one person.

Over the past seventy-five years, automobile production and highway construction have multiplied, while urban mass transit systems have been dismantled or allowed to fall into disrepair. The American automobile culture was spurred on by massive government investments in roads (3 million miles) and interstate highways (45,000 miles). Just 20 percent of the gasoline tax goes to mass transit, while 80 percent goes to highways. The end result has meant more pollution, traffic congestion, wasted energy, urban sprawl, residential segregation, and social disruption.

All communities have not received the same benefits from transportation advancements and investments. Some of our governmental policies in housing, land use, environment, and transportation may have even contributed to and exacerbated social inequities. For example, federal housing policies have played a key role in the development of spatially differentiated metropolitan areas where African Americans and other people of color are often segregated from whites, and the poor from the more affluent citizens. Federal Housing Administration and Veterans Administration subsidies contributed to the uneven development among central cities, suburbs, and rural areas, fueled the exodus to the suburbs, and accelerated the abandonment of many central cities.

Federal tax dollars subsidized the construction of the automobile-oriented freeways. Many of these construction and infrastructure projects cut wide paths through low-income and people-of-color neighborhoods physically

Represents a small %age of construction activities. ?

isolated residents from their institutions and businesses, disrupted once-stable communities, displaced thriving businesses, contributed to urban sprawl, subsidized infrastructure decline, created traffic gridlock, and subjected residents to elevated risks from accidents, spills, and explosions from vehicles carrying hazardous chemicals and other dangerous materials.

Federal subsidies were necessary and essential ingredients in the development of urban mass transit systems. For millions of inner-city residents, public transportation is the only means of getting around. For them, there is no question that energy efficient public transportation is needed for easy access to child care services, shopping, job centers, and health care services. Cutbacks in mass transit subsidies have the potential of isolating the poor in inner-city neighborhoods away from areas of job growth.

Transportation has a profound impact on residential patterns, industrial growth, and physical and social mobility. Many of our transportation policies are rooted in civil rights and social justice. In 1896, for example, the U.S. Supreme Court wrestled with this question of different treatment accorded blacks and whites. In Plessy v. Ferguson, the Supreme Court examined the constitutionality of Louisiana laws that provided for the segregation of railroad car seating by race.[1] The Court upheld the "white section" and "colored section" Jim Crow seating law, contending that segregation did not violate any rights guaranteed by the U.S. Constitution. *New to me.*

In 1953, nearly four decades after the Plessy decision relegated blacks to the back of the bus, African Americans in Baton Rouge, the capital of Louisiana, staged the nation's first successful bus boycott. African Americans accounted for the overwhelming majority of Baton Rouge bus riders and two-thirds of the bus company's revenue.[2] Their economic boycott effectively disrupted the financial stability of the bus company, costing it over $1,600 a day. The successful Baton Rouge bus boycott occurred two years before the famous 1954 Brown v. Board of Education of Topeka U.S. Supreme Court decision declared "separate but equal" unconstitutional.

On December 1, 1955, a black woman in Montgomery, Alabama ignited the modern civil rights movement. Rosa Parks refused to give up her bus seat to a white man in defiance of local Jim Crow laws. Her action sparked new leadership around transportation and civil rights. Mrs. Parks summarized her feelings about resisting Jim Crow in an interview with sociologist Aldon Morris in 1981: "My resistance to being mistreated on the buses and anywhere else was just a regular thing with me and not just that day."[3]

Transportation was a central theme in the Freedom Riders' campaign in the early 1960s. John Lewis and the young Freedom Riders exercised their constitutional right of interstate travel at the risk of death. Greyhound buses were attacked and some burned in 1961. Nevertheless, the Freedom Riders continued their quest for social justice on the nation's roads and highways.

Birth of a New Movement

The environmental justice movement is rooted in the transport and illegal disposal of toxic waste along roadways in the North Carolina. In 1978, oil laced with highly toxic PCB (polychlorinated biphenyl) was illegally dumped along 210 miles of roadways in fourteen North Carolina counties — the largest PCB spill ever recorded in the United States. When the roadways were cleaned up in 1982, a disposal site was needed for 30,000 cubic yards of PCB-contaminated soil. Warren County, a poor and mostly African-American county, was selected.

Over 500 people were arrested for protesting "Hunt's Dump" (named after the then Governor James Hunt), including District of Columbia delegate Walter Fauntroy (chairman of the Congressional Black Caucus), Reverend Benjamin F. Chavis, Jr., (Commission for Racial Justice), and Reverend Joseph Lowery (Southern Christian Leadership Conference). This marked the first time Americans had been jailed protesting the siting of a waste facility.

The protesters were unsuccessful in blocking the PCB landfill. Nevertheless, they brought national attention to siting inequities and galvanized African-American church leaders, civil rights organizers, and grassroots activists around environmental justice issues.

The demonstrations against the PCB landfill prompted Delegate Fauntroy to request a U.S. General Accounting Office investigation of hazardous was facility siting in Environmental Protection Agency's (EPA) Region IV — eight states in the South (Alabama, Florida, Georgia, Kentucky, Mississippi, North Carolina, South Carolina, and Tennessee). The 1983 GAO report discovered that three of the four offsite hazardous waste landfills in the region were located in predominately African-American communities. African Americans made up about one-fifth of the population in EPA's Region IV. Today, all of the offsite commercial hazardous waste landfills in the region are located in predominately African-American communities.

The events in Warren County also prompted the United Church of Christ Commission for Racial Justice to produce its 1987 Toxic Wastes and Race study. This widely-quoted study documented that three out of five African Americans live in communities with abandoned toxic waste sites; 60 percent of African Americans (15 million) live in communities with one or more waste sites; and three of the five largest commercial hazardous waste landfills are located in predominately African-American or Latino communities, and account for 40 percent of the nation's total hazardous waste landfill capacity in 1987.

In addition to Toxic Wastes and Race, the publication of Dumping in Dixie: Race, Class and Environmental Quality in 1990 chronicled environmental justice struggles of rural, urban, and suburban African-American communities in the South. Other books and reports point to clear signs that all communities are not created equal. Some communities get protected, while others are promised protection. If a community happens to be poor, inner city, or inhabited by people of color, chances are it will receive less environmental protection than an affluent, suburban, white community.[4] Grassroots groups sprang up all over the country to combat these unequal, unjust, and illegal practices.

Mobilizing Across Cultural Boundaries

In 1991, the First National People of Color Environmental Leadership Summit advanced environmental justice beyond its anti-toxics focus to embrace more global issues of public health, cultural survival and sovereignty of native and indigenous peoples, land rights, land use, economic justice, community empowerment, sustainability, energy, transboundary waste trade, and transportation. The summit was held in Washington, D.C. and attracted over 1,000 persons from all fifty states, including Alaska and Hawaii. Delegates came from as far away as Puerto Rico, Mexico, the Marshall Islands, and several African nations.

Summit delegates dealt with diverse issues ranging from environmental protection, health, housing, energy and transportation, sustainable development, and grassroots empowerment. On October 27, 1991 the Summit delegates adopted the Principles of Environmental Justice to take back to their respective communities and serve as a guide in grassroots organizing.

Urban environmental inequities, especially urban air pollution, were documented more than two decades ago in a Council on Environmental Quality report.[5] However, it took more than two decades for equity concerns to register on the national radar screen. People of color and low-income communities bear a disproportionate share of the nation's environmental and health problems. Such disparities include:

- distributive impacts of public policy, quality and quantity of services;
- land use and facility siting;
- investments, enhancements, pricing, and social equity;
- transport of hazardous and radioactive materials;
- public access to services, planning, and decision-making;
- health assessments and community impacts;
- air quality and health risks;
- childhood lead poisoning;
- childhood asthma;
- pesticide poisoning; and
- occupational accidents and illnesses.

Issues to consider regarding disparate outcomes include the following: Is the decision-making process fair? Do the rules apply equally to everyone? Do decisions have distributive and regressive impacts? Are some locations favored over others (cities versus suburbs versus rural areas)? Who benefits and who pays? Who makes the decisions and for whom?

The 1969 National Environmental Policy Act (NEPA) sets policy goals for the protection, maintenance, and enhancement of the environment. NEPA's goal is to assure for all Americans a safe, healthful, productive, and aesthetically and culturally pleasing environment. NEPA requires federal agencies to prepare a detailed statement on the effects of proposed federal actions that significantly affect the human environment.

Congress passed the Intermodal Surface Transportation Efficiency Act (ISTEA) of 1991 to improve "public transportation necessary to achieve national goals for improved air quality, energy conservation, international competitiveness, and mobility for elderly persons, persons with disabilities, and economically disadvantaged persons in urban and rural areas of the country." ISTEA also promised to build intermodal connections between people to jobs, goods and markets, and neighborhoods.

ISTEA mandates that improvements comply with the Clean Air Act, whereby priorities be given to projects that would clean up polluted air. ISTEA also requires transportation plans to comply with Title VI of the Civil Rights Act of 1964, which prohibits discrimination in the use of federal funds, investments, and transportation services.

Improvements in transportation investments and air quality are of special significance to low-income persons and people of color who are more likely to live in areas with reduced air quality compared to whites and affluent people. A 1990 National Argonne Laboratory study discovered that 57 percent of whites, 65 percent of African Americans, and 80 percent of Latinos lived in the 437 counties that failed to meet at least one of the EPA ambient air quality standards; a total of 33 percent of whites, 50 percent of African Americans, and 60 percent of Latinos live in the 136 counties in which two or more air pollutants exceed standards; and 12 percent of whites, 20 percent of African Americans, and 31 percent of Latinos live in the 29 counties with three or more pollutants.[6]

A Framework for Action

What started out as local community-based grassroots struggles against toxins, facility siting, transport of hazardous material, highways and freeways, fare hikes, and disparate services has now blossomed into a national environmental justice movement. Environmental Justice refers to equal enforcement of our laws, policies, and regulations; identifying and addressing discriminatory practices, policies, and guidance; elimination of disproportionately high and adverse human health and environmental impacts on low-income and minority populations; and involving affected communities in decision-making.[7]

Environmental justice embraces the principle that all people and communities are entitled to equal protection of our environmental, health, employment, housing, transportation, and civil rights laws. The U.S. EPA's Office of Environmental Justice defines environmental justice as follows:

"The fair treatment and meaningful involvement of all people regardless of race color, national origin, or income with respect to the development, implementation, and enforcement of environmental laws, regulations and policies. Fair treatment means that no group of people, including racial, ethnic, or socio-economic group should bear a disproportionate share of the negative environmental consequences resulting from industrial, municipal, and commercial operations or the execution of federal, state, local, and tribal programs and policies."[8]

The environmental justice framework rests on an analysis of strategies to eliminate unfair, unjust, and inequitable conditions and decisions. The framework attempts to uncover the underlying assumptions that may contribute to and produce differential exposure and health threats. It also brings to the surface the ethical and political questions of "who gets what, when, why, and how much." Some general characteristics of this framework are the following:

- incorporates the principle of the right of all individuals to be protected from environmental degradation;
- adopts a public health model of prevention as the preferred strategy.

For example, the framework offers a solution to the childhood lead problem by shifting the primary focus from treatment to prevention of the problem;

- shifts the burden of proof to polluters/dischargers who may do harm, who may discriminate, or who do not give equal protection to minorities, low-income persons, and other "protected" classes;

- allows disparate impact and statistical weight or an "effect" test, as opposed to "intent," to infer discrimination; and
- redresses disproportionate impact through targeted action and targeted resources. This strategy targets resources where environmental and health problems are greatest (as determined by some ranking scheme but not limited solely to quantitative risk assessment).

Environmental justice advocates have defined environment to include everything: where we live, where we work, where we play, and where we go to school. Major elements of environmental justice include:

- equal enforcement of laws and regulations;
- identifying and eliminating discriminatory practices and policies;
- addressing environmental, health, and socioeconomic disparities;
- pollution prevention and right-to-know;
- occupational safety and health of workers;
- community empowerment; and
- involving impacted populations in decision-making.

In response to growing public concern, President Clinton on February 11, 1994 issued Executive Order 12898: Federal Actions to Address Environmental Justice in Minority Populations and Low-Income Populations. This order is not a new law but is an attempt to address environmental injustice within existing federal laws and regulations.

The executive order restates the provisions found in the three-decade old Civil Rights Act of 1964, Title VI. The act prohibits discriminatory practices in programs receiving federal funds. The executive order also refocuses attention on NEPA, a twenty-five-year-old law that set policy goals for the protection, maintenance, and enhancement of the environment. NEPA's expressed goal is "to ensure for all Americans a safe, healthful, productive, and aesthetically and culturally pleasing environment." NEPA requires federal agencies to prepare a detailed statement on the environmental effects of proposed federal actions that significantly effect the quality of human health.

The executive order calls for improved methodologies for assessing and mitigating impacts, health effects from multiple and cumulative exposure, collection of data on low-income and minority populations who may be disproportionately at risk, impacts on subsistence fishers and wildlife consumers, and encourages participation of the affected populations in the various phases of the NEPA process, including scoping, data gathering, alternatives, analysis, mitigation, and monitoring.

Embedded in the environmental justice impact assessment are a set of important questions that need to be addressed by transportation analysts as they conduct assessments. That is, analysts should examine how differing impacts relate to each other, understanding direct and indirect impacts as well as the cumulative or counterbalancing impacts of various effects. Indirect impacts are caused by direct impacts. Indirect impacts often occur later in time or further in distance than direct project impacts. On the other hand, cumulative impacts represent incremental impacts of an action added to other past, present, or reasonably foreseeable future actions. All three types of impacts, especially cumulative impacts, have special significance for minority and low-income communities where a disproportionately large share of locally unwanted land uses are located.

The U.S. Department of Transportation's Community Impact Assessment reference guide outlines some important questions that can guide an environmental justice impact assessment.[9] Community impacts are often interconnected. Some of the categories used to assess community impacts might include social and psychological, physical, land use, economic conditions, mobility and access, provision of public services, safety, and displacement features.

Social and Psychological Impacts Will the project cause redistribution of the population or an influx or loss of population? How will the project affect interaction among persons and groups? How will it change social relationships and patterns? Will minority and low-income persons be set apart from others? Will the project cause a change in social values? What is the perceived impact on quality of life?

Physical Impacts Is a wall or barrier effect created (such as from noise walls or fencing)? Will noise or vibrations increase? Will dust or odor increase? Will there be a shadowing effect on property? Will the community's aesthetic character be changed? Is the design of the project compatible with community goals? Has aesthetics surfaced as a community concern?

Land-use Impacts Will there be a loss of farmland? Does it open up new areas for development? Will it induce changes in land use and density? What changes might be expected? Is the project consistent with local land-use plans and zoning?

Economic Impacts Will the proposed action encourage businesses to move to the area, relocate to other locations within the area, close, or move outside the area? What is the impact on both the region and individual communities? How is the local economy affected by construction activities? Are there both positive (jobs generated) and negative (increase in truck traffic, gridlock, detours and loss of access) impacts? Will the proposed action alter business visibility to traffic-based businesses? How will visibility and access changes alter business activity? What is the effect on the tax base (changes in property values, changes in business activity)? What is the likely effect on property values caused by relocation or changes in land use?

Mobility and Access Impacts How does the action affect non-motorist access to businesses, public services, schools, and other facilities? Does the project impede or enhance access between residences and community facilities and businesses? Does it shift traffic? How does the project affect access to public transportation? How does the project affect short- and long-term vehicular access to businesses, public services, and other facilities? Does it affect parking availability?

Public Services Impacts Will the proposed action lead to or help alleviate overcrowding of public facilities (i.e., schools and recreation facilities)? Will it lead to or help alleviate underuse? How will it affect the ability to provide adequate services? Will the project result in relocation or displacement of public facilities or community centers (i.e., places of worship)?

Safety Impacts Will the proposed action increase or decrease the likelihood of accidents for non-motorists? Will the proposed action increase or decrease crime? Will there be changes in emergency response time (i.e., fire, police, and emergency medical)?

Displacement What are the effects on the neighborhood from which people move and into which people are relocated? How many residents will be displaced? What type(s) of dwellings: multi-units homes, single family, rural residences, others? Are there residents with special needs (disabled, minority, elderly residents)? How many businesses and farms will be displaced, and what type(s)? Do they have unique characteristics such as specialty products or a unique customer base? Are there available sites to accommodate those displaced?

Urban Case Studies

Grassroots groups are challenging local, metropolitan, state, and federal transportation agencies to strengthen intermodal options that contribute to the development of just, healthy, and sustainable communities with benefits to all sectors. These groups are demanding that planners and policy-makers think beyond mode, cars, roads, and trains, and make transportation a bridge as opposed to a barrier to opportunity.

In 1996, for example, students from Haskell Indian Nation University (Lawrence, Kansas) challenged the Kansas Department of Transportation and the Federal Highway Administration proposal to build a road through their campus. In a March 20, 1996 meeting, representatives from the environmental justice community, including leaders from Haskell Indian Nation University, expressed their dissatisfaction with the limited progress departments of transportation have made in integrating elements of Executive 12898 into the NEPA process, especially Title VI of the 1964 Civil Right Act. Communities of color, as in the case of Haskell, continue to be routinely treated as "invisible" communities by state departments of transportation (DOT) and metropolitan planning organizations (MPO).

From New York to Los Angeles, grassroots community groups are organizing themselves into a movement to create just, healthy, sustainable, and livable communities. Cities such as Atlanta, Washington, D.C., Chicago, New York, Los Angeles, San Francisco, and Oakland offer fertile ground for grassroots transportation organizing. Some grassroots groups have organized to block freeway construction, bus facility siting, while other groups are demanding energy efficient and cleaner burning public transit vehicles, fair share of transportation investments, services, and benefits that accrue to transit-oriented development.

Atlanta, GA The civil rights legacy is clearly embedded in many of today's transportation concerns. Nowhere is this more apparent than in Atlanta, Georgia — the capital of the New South. African-Americans comprised over 66 percent of the Atlanta's population in 1990. The city had a population of 394,000 in 1990, down from 425,000 in 1990, a 7.3-percent decrease. The Atlanta metropolitan area is the nation's twelfth largest with over 2.8 million people.

Atlanta has long been associated with the struggle for civil rights. It is the birth- place and resting place of Dr. Martin Luther King, Jr. As Atlanta grew, the freeway system displaced or disrupted whole communities. In the 1960s, the Metropolitan Atlanta Rapid Transit Authority (MARTA) was hailed as the solution to metro Atlanta's growing traffic and pollution problem. However, some suburban areas resisted MARTA for fear it would bring blacks and the poor from the city to outlying suburbs. But Atlanta became one of the few southern cities with a modern rail system. MARTA operates thirty-nine miles of rail with 469,000 passengers riding the bus or rail system daily.

Just how far MARTA lines would extend proved to be a thorny issue. Some Metro Atlanta counties opted not to join MARTA. This decision was tinged with racial overtones. Today, local residents are still questioning where MARTA lines go and where they do not go. Even who pays the tab for MARTA is questioned. Only Fulton and DeKalb County residents pay a one-cent MARTA sales tax. Many urban neighborhoods have waited decades for the economic benefits associated with transit-oriented development. It is becoming increasingly difficult to find a parking space in some MARTA lots. At least a third of the cars parked in the lots are from counties outside Fulton and DeKalb. It appears that Fulton and DeKalb County tax payers may be subsidizing people who live in outlying counties (non-MARTA taxpayers) who park their cars at the park/ride lots and ride on MARTA trains into the city. Citizens continue to raise these issues, which are now being hotly debated in county commission meetings.

Public transit is nonexistent in many parts of North Fulton, Cobb, and Gwinnett Counties — all suburban areas experiencing rapid growth in service jobs. An abundance of "help wanted," "job vacancy," and "now hiring" signs can be found displayed in shop windows. Most of these jobs are in service, retail, restaurants, and fast food outlets. Few suburban teens and young adults want or need these jobs.

Cobb County created its own transit system, Cobb Community Transit, in 1989. With an annual operating budget of $6.56 million, the transit system operates fifty-eight buses and is suburban Atlanta's only independent transit system. The system carries 10,000 daily passengers. Recently, several Cobb County elected officials complained about bus patrons, many of them retail or fast food workers, littering their communities. The officials also charged Cobb Community Transit with bringing Atlanta youth and crime to the suburban malls.

Washington, D.C. Washington, D.C., the nation's capitol, is the seat of government power. Washington has no major industry. It is an administrative city made up of the district government, Congress, the White House, numerous government agencies, and monuments dedicated to former presidents, wars, and human struggle — all packed in a sixty-one-square mile area.

The district is also home to over 607,000 residents — mostly African Americans. The Washington metropolitan area, which includes parts of Maryland and Virginia, is the nation's eighth largest with over 3.9 million people. Washington has a clean, modern, efficient, and relatively new subway system called METRO. The METRO system began operation in 1967.

METRO's 1995 operating budget was over $6.3 million. More riders use METRO's subway than the buses. Over 552,000 riders use METRO subway each day compared to 441,000 bus riders. METRO operates 50.7 miles of rail on five major subway lines. The Red, Yellow, Blue, Orange, and Green lines run through the district and into Maryland and Virginia.

All of the major construction on the METRO has been completed, except for the mid-city stretch of the Green Line — a section located in the heart of the district's Petworth neighborhood, an old, established African American community. The original METRO Green Line mid-city plan called for the demolition of over 125 homes and businesses in an area that could ill afford to lose any housing or businesses. Local residents vehemently opposed this plan.

Both the course and design of the plan were altered after the community mobilized and brought their concerns to the attention of METRO officials. Kim McDaniel, one of the founders of Neighbors United to Save the Community and a resident of D.C.'s Petworth neighborhood, organized residents to influence METRO's plan for the mid-city leg of the Green Line.

Once the community mobilized and spoke with one voice, METRO officials began to listen. The work of Neighbors United to Save the Community effort paid off. Not only did the group alter the route of the mid-city segment of the Green Line, they did it without any residents losing their homes.

Community leaders also saved a portion of a historic fire station that will be used as a facade for one of the METRO buildings. The city was able to get a new fire station. This new station houses a community center. The city began to coordinate its other housing and business development work with the Green Line construction work. New businesses, shops, and affordable housing are now springing up along Georgia Avenue, a street long-associated with Howard University.

Chicago, IL Chicago is the nation's third largest city with over 2.8 million people. Chicago has been tagged the "City of Broad Shoulders," and the "Windy City." Chicago is a major transportation hub. As a the nation's leading distribution center, numerous freeways, highways, rail, and air traffic converge in Chicago, home to O'Hare Airport, the nation's busiest airport. Chicago has one of the oldest public transportation systems in the country. The Chicago Transit Authority has over 1.1 million daily bus riders. The system operates over 236 miles of rail. The "El," as Chicagoans refer to the elevated train system, carries over 400,000 riders each day.

Some of the older lines have been threatened for closure. When the Green Line, over 100 years old, was slated for closure, a coalition of residents and business people organized to save it. Cecelia Butler, an organizer with the Washington Park Community Coalition, and other residents spearheaded the grassroots struggle around the Green Line. Jacky Grimshaw, a staffer with the Chicago-based Center for Neighborhood Technology, was one of the technical advisors to the coalition. Center Neighborhood Technology worked with the community coalition to plan an alternative to closure.

The community plan linked transportation with neighborhood revitalization, business development, home ownership, and reversing flight from the central city. Recognizing that Chicago is a non-attainment city as far as meeting federal air quality standards, the community plan called for bringing other governmental units into the planning process. The community-driven coalition of residents, commercial, and industrial stakeholders made a difference in the transit authority's final decision about the Green Line.

The coalition and its advisors used existing requirements under ISTEA to make their voices heard. Not only did the coalition members achieve success in stopping the closure of the Green Line, but they also demonstrated that transit-oriented development can have positive spillover effects and serve as a catalyst in rebuilding the central city.

As an enterprise zone city, Chicago stands to gain over $100 million alone in new development funds. The infusion of needed dollars into Chicago's poorer neighborhoods has the potential of increasing the mobility through public transit and improving the overall quality of life in Chicago's low-income neighborhoods.

New York, NY New York is the nation's largest city, with over 7.3 million people densely packed in a 309-square mile area. New York has one of the oldest and largest public transit systems in the country. The New York City Transit Authority has an annual operating budget of about $3.5 billion. Over 3.5 million passengers ride New York subways each day, and an additional 1.5 million passengers ride city buses.

Manhattan, a borough of New York City, is renowned world-wide for its teeming skyscrapers. Harlem is one of Manhattan's oldest African-American neighborhoods; it gave birth to the Harlem Renaissance of the 1930s. Lennox Avenue, 125th Street, the Apollo Theater, are all symbols of Harlem, which is more than a neighborhood. Peggy Shepard, a co-founder of West Harlem Environmental Action, describes Harlem as "a snapshot of the African-American experience." Today, Harlem is a mix of upper, middle, and lower-income residents, mostly African Americans and Latinos.

All of the mass transportation systems and bus lines in the city pass through Harlem. Harlem is surrounded on three sides by freeways, and seven of the eight Manhattan municipal bus depots are located there. Bus depots and their fumes have significant environmental and health impacts on the community. Not surprisingly, Harlem has more than its fair share of environmental, health, and transportation problems.

Transportation concerns for local community organizers revolve around the issues of access, fairness, and equity. West Harlem Environmental Action and the New York City Environmental Justice Alliance are organizing local residents to link environmental, development, and transportation concerns in communities of color. Grassroots activists have made sure that their concerns are registered in the city's Empowerment Zone initiatives. Citizen working groups were formed around transportation and environment. Some of the recommendations of the working groups include highway cleanup, urban design improvements, bus depot clear air retrofit, improved access to the Harlem River waterfront, and Bronx and Harlem greenway.

West Harlem Environmental Action and its coalition members have taken on several city departments. For example, they have concentrated part of their energies on making the North River Sewer Treatment Plant safe, especially since the

$130-million state-of-the-art Riverbank State Bank Park is built on top of the treatment plant. Grassroots organizers are also collaborating with other environmental groups on the "dirty diesel" campaign — a drive to rid the Metropolitan Transit Authority (MTA) of polluting vehicles.

Recent city budget cuts appear to fall heaviest on the poor and people-of-color communities, like Harlem. These cuts are occurring at the same time studies point to links between rising childhood asthma and air pollution. Community organizers are demanding that more attention be given to the cumulative health impact of living near so many polluting facilities (including bus barns), highways, garbage transfer stations, and a massive sewer treatment plant. Their work is paying off. Local grassroots groups are now mobilizing and educating residents on the importance of getting involved in transportation decision-making.

Los Angeles, CA Los Angeles is the nation's second largest city, home to nearly 3.5 million people spread over 469 square miles. The Los Angeles-Anaheim-Riverside metropolitan area is home to over 14.5 million people, the second most populous metropolitan area in the country. Los Angeles is a city built around Hollywood, fantasy, dreams, sun, fun, freeways, and the automobile.

Southern California grew up with the automobile, turned its back on mass transit, and invented urban sprawl. Some 12.8 million people and 8 million automobiles are packed in the South Coast Air Basin. The Los Angeles basin is the smog capital of the nation, with air quality that is three times worse than any other area in the country. While Los Angeles traffic jams are notorious, and the area's smog problem has provided fertile material for jokes, freeway gridlock and unhealthy air are no laughing matter.

Watts, South Central, Compton, and East Los Angeles are probably more well known because of media coverage associated riots and street gangs than for problems associated with air pollution. African-Americans and Latinos live in these Los Angeles communities with the dirtiest air; the South Coast Air Quality Management District estimates 71 percent of African-Americans and 50 percent of Latinos live in areas with the most polluted air, compared to 34 percent of white people.[10]

Los Angeles' elaborate freeway system is built for the automobile. Urban sprawl is a direct response to a conscious effort to keep people in their cars, usually one passenger per car. Over two decades ago, a bitter fight erupted over the construction of the Century Freeway (105),planned to run through the heart of the African-American community. The NAACP filed suit to minimize the freeway displacement of African-American residents and businesses, but the freeway finally opened in 1992.

Freeways isolate, segregate, separate, and trap the poorest of residents in polluted "poverty pockets." Nowhere is this scenario more apparent than East Los Angeles. East Los Angeles is home to more freeways than any place in the country. For years, local residents have complained about their neighborhood being targeted for freeways. A class-action lawsuit was filed by residents of El Sereno (a Latino neighborhood) challenging the construction of a 4.5-mile stretch of the Long Beach Freeway (710) through their community.

The plaintiffs argued that the state-proposed mitigation measures to address noise, air and visual pollution discriminate against the mostly Latino El Sereno community. For example, all of the freeways in Pasadena and 80 percent in South Pasadena will be below ground level. On the other hand, most of the freeways in El Sereno will be above ground. White areas were favored over the mostly Latino El Sereno in allocation of covered freeways, historic preservation measures, and accommodation to local schools.[11]

Los Angeles transportation problems do not end with freeways. Its public transit system is mired in controversy. Los Angeles has basically a two-tiered public transit system: an older bus system and a new light-rail system. In 1993, it formed the MTA by merging the Los Angeles County Transit Commission and the Southern California Rapid Transit District. This new MTA has an annual operating budget of $3.1 billion. The bulk of the system is made up of buses: an average of 1.2 million passengers ride the MTA buses each day, while only 56,000 riders use the Red and Blue Line trains each day.

A class action lawsuit was filed on behalf of 350,000 low-income, people-of-color bus riders represented by the Labor/Community Labor Center, the Bus Riders Union, Southern Christian Leadership Conference, Korean Immigrant Workers Advocates, and individuals bus riders. The lawsuit is a direct challenge to the subsidies given to the new MTA rail lines. Labor Community Strategy organizers and their lawyers contend that these rail subsidies are made at the expense of bus riders. The lawsuit was settled out of court in October, 1996 in favor of the Bus Riders Union.[12]

In the summer of 1995, MTA opened a third rail line, the Green Line. The Green Line runs along Century Freeway and stops before it gets to the airport. Bill Lee, an NAACP Legal Defense Fund lawyer, tagged the Green Line, "a train to nowhere; it doesn't go to the airport, and it doesn't even go all the way to Norwalk." Grassroots groups are demanding efficient, affordable, and equitable transportation services and fair use of their tax dollars.

Bay Area, CA San Francisco is a major west coast seaport city with a population of 724,000 within 47 square miles. Tourists travel from all parts of the globe to ride on San Francisco's famed cable cars — one of the few remaining urban trolley lines. The San Francisco Bay Area is served by the Bay Area Rapid Transit system (BART). BART began operation in 1972 and has an annual budget of $244 million. Over 250,000 passengers ride BART trains each day. With the collapse of the Bay Bridge during the 1989 San Francisco earthquake, BART was the only means of transportation for many Bay Area residents.

Some neighborhoods are still waiting for the economic benefits that accrue from being near a BART line. One of these neighborhoods is the Bayview/Hunters Point neighborhood. Plans are now underway to extend the BART line into the Bayview/Hunters Point. The new line is slated to be built along the traffic-rich Third Street. Community leaders are cautious that local residents and businesses are not displaced by BART.

Henry Holmes, who directs the Urban Habitat Transportation Program, has been actively involved in BART's Third Street extension. Transportation is an integral part of its environmental justice and policy work. Some residents view the transportation along the Third Street Corridor as a means of neighborhood revitalization and economic development for current residents.

Just across the Bay lies San Francisco's sister city, Oakland. For years, Oakland residents have lived in the shadow of San Francisco, but the 1989 earthquake drew the national spotlight on both cities. During this disaster, a section of the Oakland Bay Bridge collapsed, along with the Cypress Freeway, killing dozens of motorists. West Oakland residents resisted plans to rebuild the freeway along the same route that split their West Oakland neighborhood in half. They organized themselves into the Clean Air Alternative Coalition, a group of residents, churches, and the NAACP Legal Defense and Education Fund, to locate the freeway further away from residential areas.

The West Oakland neighborhood already gets a large share of traffic from nearby industries, trains, an Army base, and a port. Its opposition also centered around the fact that people-of-color neighborhoods in Oakland have been overburdened with freeways that carry hazardous materials. These same neighborhoods also have more than their share of industrial facilities that release toxic emissions.

The Clean Air Alternative Coalition devised a freeway plan, which was rejected. But Community organizers were successful in getting the freeway rerouted. However, this was only a partial victory because the black community will still bear the brunt of the Cypress Freeway when it is rebuilt. The freeway will pass within a few hundred feet of a mostly black church.

Conclusion

The environmental justice movement has set out clear goals of eliminating unequal enforcement of the nation's environmental, public health, housing, employment, land use, civil rights, and transportation laws. The movement has expanded beyond a single focus on toxins to embrace just, healthy, livable, and sustainable communities. Transportation is a key ingredient in any organization's plan to build economically viable and sustainable communities.

Grassroots leaders are working on strategies to eliminate discriminatory and exclusionary practices that limit low-income and people-of-color communities' participation in decision-making. People must be at the table to speak for themselves. However, it not enough to have a place at the table; community leaders' voices must be heard and their views respected, even when these views may conflict with the dominant viewpoint.

The solution to environmental injustice, whether in transportation, housing, land use or any other area, lies in the realm of equal protection of all individuals, groups, and communities. Many of the economic problems in urban areas involving lack of mobility could be eliminated if existing transportation laws and regulations were vigorously enforced in a non-discriminatory way.

State DOTs and MPOs have a major responsibility to ensure that their programs, policies, and practices do not discriminate against or adversely and disproportionately impact people of color and the poor. Just transportation is not an unfunded mandate. It is the law.

Some groups have taken legal action and used the law as a tool to accomplish their goals, while other have chosen other routes. There is no cookie-cutter formula for dismantling discrimination and unjust policies and practices.

Litigation is only one tool in an assorted arsenal of weapons available to citizens, groups, communities working on social justice and transportation issues. One common ingredient in successful initiatives appears to be organization. Legal action is no substitute for having a well-organized, disciplined, and informed populace. Grassroots organizing is the foundation of movement building. This is true of all social movements.

Just and Sustainable Communities

Henry Holmes

A critical examination of our transportation system reveals much about historical and contemporary American society, and about racism, economic injustice and environmental degradation. The economic, social, cultural, political, and environmental patterns of our complex historical development as a nation are embedded in a transportation system many people take for granted. Today, near the end of the twentieth century, we are further away than ever from achieving true freedom, justice and equality for all people in this country. And our transportation system is no small part of this fact; it is also a major contributor to our obscene waste of natural resources and deteriorating environmental quality of life. All these conditions most adversely affect people of color, women, working, poor, young, elderly and disabled people.

Transportation is critical to healthy, livable and sustainable urban and rural communities. The transportation system influences, and in turn is influenced by, economic development decisions, land-use patterns, real estate investment decisions, and energy consumption patterns of the public and private sectors. The interests of those making transportation decisions (European-American middle and upper class, educated professionals primarily) are served, while the interests, perspectives and needs of people left out of the decision-making process (people of color, poor, working and transit-dependent people) are not. The values of social justice and ecological sustainability are not major priorities in the existing transportation system.

Poor people and people of color are subsidizing our addiction to the automobile. They pay the highest social, economic and environmental costs and receive the fewest benefits from an automobile-dominated transportation system. Highways cut through inner cities, creating environmental hazards and fracturing communities physically, socially and economically. Measurably higher levels of immediate and long-term toxic effects from air, water and noise pollution and debris degrade local land values and further destabilize urban areas. These same areas are challenged by low employment and economic opportunity, poor services, crumbling infrastructure and loss of tax revenues to the suburbs, which are now called "edge cities" or "exurbs."

Urban core communities become isolated. Their infrastructure decays and land becomes under-utilized as development goes elsewhere, duplicating infrastructure to support new urban sprawl and consuming ever more land, energy and other natural resources. The crumbling public transportation system is underfunded and neglected, directly contributing to the social, economic and environmental deterioration of our cities where nearly 75 percent of all Americans live. Of these, nearly 30 percent to 50 percent are transit-dependent — those too poor, young, old, disabled or unwilling to drive.

Many rural communities are not well served by the current transportation system. The residents of rural America are 43 percent of the disabled, 39 percent of the elderly, 32 percent of the unemployed, and 39 percent of people living below the poverty level. However, only 4 percent of federal spending for public transportation goes to rural communities, which have high numbers of people who are transit-dependent.[1] Even for those with access to motor vehicles, roads are often not maintained in areas of most need, and the costs of maintaining a vehicle compete with resources needed to provide for other basic human needs, causing financial hardship.

Social justice, ecological sustainability, and principles of environmental justice must be at the heart of creating healthy, livable, sustainable communities, cities and regions. A socially just and ecologically sustainable transportation system has the potential to increase job and income opportunities, promote efficient and healthy land use patterns, create environmentally safe communities, decrease fossil fuel energy consumption and improve the overall social, economic and environmental quality of life. But to improve public transit and other transportation alternatives, including bicycling and walking, and to protect public health and environmental resources, we must broaden and democratize the debate and policy-making process.

This chapter provides a conceptual framework for understanding the environmental justice dimensions of transportation policy, the transportation system, and its effects on urban communities of color, poor and working people. The interrelationships between transportation, community economic development, urban revitalization, land use, energy efficiency and environmental protection will be examined from the perspectives and experiences of urban communities of color and the Urban Habitat Program in the San Francisco Bay Area.[2] While much has been written on the transportation, energy, environmental and urban design linkages, very little has directly addressed the racial, class, cultural and environmental justice dimensions of transportation policy and our existing transportation system.

Transportation and Communities After World War II

The end of World War II brought about a housing boom previously unknown in the United States. Increasingly, those with financial means pursued living space away from the urban core, which was the center of commercial and industrial activity. As the Industrial Revolution reached its apex, and with the mass production of automobiles and enormous public expenditure on roads, many sought to escape the hustle and bustle of city life for a more pastoral existence away from the work center. This pattern of an expanding urban complex had been taking place for the last century, particularly in the northern urban areas, due to industrial expansion and European immigrants seeking economic opportunity in the New World. However, this pattern accelerated the economic boom period of the 1950s and 1960s during the height of the "cold war" in which the United States claimed its status as the leading military/industrial superpower. Federal mortgage subsidies made "white flight" to the suburbs possible for growing numbers of middle-class European Americans.

Suburbia, as we know it today, became the preferred middle-class lifestyle. With it came patterns of economic development, land use, real estate investment, transportation and infrastructure development that reflected race, class and cultural wounds deeply embedded in the psyche and history of the United States. Jim Crow — institutionalized segregation and apartheid against African-Americans and other nonwhites — was reflected in urban and suburban zoning codes, restrictive racial covenants in real estate investment and lending practices, redlining by financial institutions, discriminatory private business practices, and the distribution of public investments. All these served the interests of the policy-makers, usually the corporate elite who were typically European-American and middle class or wealthy.

Public and private investments were made to build and maintain the infrastructure necessary to support suburban development, from water and sewer systems to schools, energy delivery and transportation systems. Agricultural areas, greenbelts and open space surrounding cities were converted from rural land use to single family, low-density housing tracts, complete with local shopping areas and strip malls. This changing use of space, driven by newfound American affluence, federal highway subsidies and corporate interests, and influenced by social attitudes, including racism and class stratification, solidified the personal motor vehicle as the dominant transport mode. Nineteen fifty-six saw the birth of the interstate highway system, an ever increasing network of local road construction to support suburban development and public subsidization of private automobile transport. As the pace of inner city disinvestment and decay accelerated, those left behind — mostly people of color, poor and working European-Americans — were blamed for urban ills and left to cope with shrinking public and private investments.

Suburban development has created a transportation system in which priority is given to suburban lifestyles and travel patterns. Increased reliance on private automobiles has fueled the demand for more roadways and auto-centered infrastructure for travel to and from increasingly further outlying suburban housing, industrial and executive office parks. Disproportionate amounts of public money are spent supporting roads and automobiles to the neglect of those unable to drive and to the detriment of urban communities of color that suffer a heavy social, economic and environmental burden from the current transportation system. This pattern continues even in areas experiencing population decline. The current systematic disinvestment in public transportation through cuts and elimination of transit operating assistance and transit capital expansion, fare increases and service reductions exacerbates the inequities of the transportation system. Such disinvestment directly contributes to the social, economic and environmental deterioration of our cities. U.S. transportation policy continues to perpetuate an unjust and ecologically unsustainable transportation system.

Transportation Policy Destabilizes Inner City Communities: Big Burdens, Few Benefits

Environmental Destabilization

Suburban sprawl and uncontrolled growth increasingly displace people from where they live and work, thereby increasing travel distances, reliance on motor vehicles, traffic congestion, freeway gridlock, air pollution, ozone depletion, acid rain, global warming, and many related problems. Inadequate or non-existent public transit has created most of the transportation and air pollution problems in our cities.

A visit to any urban metropolitan area in the United States reveals the same pattern: freeway interchanges are most often placed in inner cities, creating a physical and psychological intrusion upon the economic and environmental health and psyche of these communities. Inner cities are literally choking to death on tailpipe emissions, air pollutants, and smog, experiencing high rates of respiratory disease and other adverse health effects. Previously stable and sustainable communities are ruptured and destroyed by massive highway projects designed to transport more people in automobiles to and from suburbs and out of the urban core.

Poor communities and communities of color also experience the pollution and physical displacement of locally unwanted land uses associated with the transportation system, such as oil refineries, gasoline manufacturing, leaking underground petroleum storage tanks, diesel bus barns, vehicle maintenance facilities, auto junk yards, and other high-impact and toxic uses.

Economic Destabilization

Job decentralization, the relocation of many jobs once located in central cities, and the movement of new retail, service, and information-sector jobs to suburbs further outside the urban core has a direct effect on employment levels, opportunities and income of inner city residents. There are strong relationships between job location, transportation access, employment opportunities and other factors such as race, class, education, skill level, and residence. This spatial mismatch has profound economic and environmental justice implications for people living in central cities.[3]

In our society, if one is unable to afford a car (including purchase, gasoline, maintenance, insurance, license, registration, smog, parking and other fees), one may not be able to afford a job. Low-income people tend to have older, fuel-inefficient cars and spend proportionately higher percentages of household income for basic transportation needs than do middle class and wealthy households. Reliance on public transit is often a disincentive in the eyes of prospective employers when evaluating job applicants, because deteriorating transit systems across the country are increasingly unreliable in meeting schedules, and serve fewer areas where job growth is actually occurring.

As manufacturing, service, retail, and information industries decentralize and jobs shift to suburbs and exurbs — a process aided by more freeways and other automobile-oriented infrastructure — inner-city areas are faced with declining employment and a narrowing range of job and income opportunities. Suburban job flight further exacerbates the economic deterioration of the central city by shrinking the tax base upon which it depends to maintain its current level of goods and services. Ironically, much of this suburban infrastructure was paid for by urban residents through regressive taxes to provide regional transit, roads and parking facilities for suburban commuters.

Social Destabilization

Economic and environmental decay in central cities also contributes to social decay and stress. Lack of effective, coordinated planning encourages suburban sprawl and disinvestment in central cities. Insufficient revenues and misplaced public policy priorities mean basic human needs and social services that contribute to the overall well-being of everyone in society go unmet, are neglected, or eliminated altogether. Homelessness increases due to lack of affordable urban housing. Crime, drugs and violence thrive because no value is given to human life and potential in communities viewed as disposable. Transportation programs that continue to support suburban commuter needs and development at the expense of the urban core will only serve to increase urban social stress and contribute to patterns of institutional racism, class bias, and systematic disinvestment in urban poor, working poor, and people-of-color communities.

Transportation and Reinvestment in Cities are Critical Links to Sustainable Communities, Cities and Metropolitan Regions

Principles Of Sustainability

Reorienting urban design and public policy to put people and the environment first is key to creating healthy, livable, sustainable communities, cities, and regions. An integrated approach to transportation and land-use policy is a critical element in the effort to achieve socially just and ecologically sustainable urban communities. A social justice approach to transportation planning can be guided by the following principles:[4]

- Transportation is a social investment affecting the social, economic and environmental quality of life in urban communities.
- Transportation projects should be used to reshape rather than reinforce inefficient urban land use, and reduce rather than increase adverse environmental impacts and waste of resources.
- Transportation planning should be conducted in full partnership with communities using a bottom-up instead of top-down approach to decision-making.

• Transportation investment decisions must result from an integrated land use, community economic development,and environmental planning process.

Along with the Principles of Environmental Justice adopted by the First National People of Color Environmental Leadership Summit in 1991, the basic concepts of social justice and ecological sustainability are helpful to describe the goals and principles of sustainable communities. Mere notions of social equity and environmental protection are not sufficient to address the complex real world experiences that inform the content and process of creating sustainable communities. Equity speaks to the distribution of benefits and burdens (narrowly defined from the perspective of middle class, educated policy-makers), but not to how and by whom policy decisions are made and the interests they serve. Environmental protection is too often addressed from a narrow conservationist perspective that ignores the ecological integrity of the whole and the human, social, cultural, spiritual, political, and economic dimensions of environmental issues and resources. The concepts of social justice and ecological sustainability suggest a holistic integration of these considerations.

Social justice is about meeting people's basic needs equitably, that is, fairly and justly. Social justice demands that societal institutions be accessible, responsible and accountable to all people in society, regardless of social or economic standing or other demographic characteristics.

Ecological sustainability is based on principles of ecology, which recognize the connectedness and interrelationship of all living things. Ecosystems are living systems; they are complex webs of relationships involving the natural world and human beings. Long-term survival (sustainability) of any species in an ecosystem depends on a limited resource base. A sustainable society is one that is able to satisfy its needs while maintaining its natural resources and life support systems. The more diverse the system, the more alternative relationships are available when other parts of the system break down. This applies to the long-term survival of future generations of human beings and the natural world of which we are a part.

Socially just and ecologically sustainable communities are those that assure a just, healthy and sustainable social, economic, and environmental quality of life as a minimum standard for all people.

A final, linear definition of sustainability or sustainable community is not possible or even desirable. Rather, these concepts can be viewed as the foundation of a larger context that incorporates many similar principles expressed from a variety of cultural and experiential perspectives. For example, in addition to the Principles of Environmental Justice, there are The Ahwahnee Principles of community planning,[5] emerging Fundamental Principles of Sustainable Communities from the 1994 Defining Sustainable Communities Conference,[6] and working principles and models of sustainability and justice from Sustainability and Justice: A Message to the President's Council on Sustainable Development.[7]

What does sustainability mean in the context of transportation, social justice, and the environment? If we meet the transportation needs of the most vulnerable people in our society — people of color, women, working, poor, young, elderly and disabled people and those who have the fewest transportation options — we meet the basic needs of everyone. By making public mass transit, bicycling, and walking the primary modes of urban transportation, and designing urban spaces to accommodate people, and not automobiles, we can reduce suburban sprawl and inner-city abandonment, while protecting public health and environmental resources.

The Transportation Link to Revitalizing Urban Communities

In communities like the Bayview Hunters Point District in San Francisco, a predominantly African-American and Asian community of 30,000 people, it is impossible to talk about transportation without also talking about community economic development. Like many urban communities of color, the need for economic opportunity and strong local economies that provide much needed jobs, income, ownership and investment opportunities are high priorities. Lack of economic justice and economic sustainability directly affects community well-being in the form of crime, underground drug economies, violence, and the neglect of youth with few prospects for a better life. Economic instability makes such communities vulnerable to becoming the dumping ground for everything nobody else wants in their backyards.Consequently, communities of color experience a lot of land use conflicts where heavy industrial activities and other polluting facilities are in close proximity to residences, schools, and churches. Much land is vacant and under-utilized and often contaminated from prior uses, land known as urban "brownfields" that could become potential community assets.

Transportation infrastructure, including public transit, is poor or non-existent and does not foster healthy land uses in a conscious integration of transportation and land use choices. Rather, it tends to be haphazard and actually exacerbates inefficient, conflicting land uses that bear little relationship to the overall economic and environmental needs of the community. Yet, focusing on the relationship between transportation and land use can uncover ways to address community economic development as a means to community revitalization and the building of healthy, livable, sustainable urban communities.

Transportation investments can be a vital link in revitalizing urban core communities. There is a compelling need for examples of urban revitalization strategies that work, where transportation policy plays a key role in achieving social justice and environmental protection by optimizing community economic development, promoting more efficient and healthy land-use patterns, increasing energy efficiency in transportation, reducing fossil-fuel consumption and motor-vehicle miles traveled, and providing clean air, land and water. Urban core communities, where many people of color, working and poor people live, can provide leadership to all of society in this regard. The experience of the inner city is the fundamental building block for reshaping the metropolitan complex, for it is here we find the intersection of all elements that result in social, economic, and environmental injustice. It is where we can find solutions not only for inner-city communities, but for the larger metropolitan region, as well.

Transportation must relate to the whole of community and support the basic needs of mobility and access so that housing, jobs, health care, education, social services, cultural facilities and commercial services are in close proximity to where people live, work, and play. Transportation investments are an important leverage point for focusing public policy on the interrelationships inherent in healthy, sustainable communities, and not just on isolated fragments of problems, which is too often the case. Transportation does not exist in a vacuum. Rather, transportation objectives are intertwined with social, economic, and environmental objectives.

San Francisco's Bayview Hunters Point District

Community activists in Bayview Hunters Point see their community as a prime example of an urban community left isolated by the freeway system and underserved by public transit. The San Francisco Municipal Railway (MUNI) has no light rail surface or subway service to the district or the southeastern part of the city. Yet, other parts of the city are well-served by the light rail system for the vibrant commercial and residential areas. Bus service in Bayview Hunters Point is sporadic and unreliable, particularly at night and early morning, because this area of the city is seen as unsafe.

Third Street, the main arterial into and through Bayview Hunters Point, currently experiences heavy motor vehicle and truck (including semi-tractor trailer) traffic, often at high speeds. This arterial serves as an alternative route to U.S. Highway 101 for many drivers traveling through the city or to and from the stadium at Candlestick Park. Congestion is high, especially during peak travel periods, with heavy concentrations of motor vehicle emissions, dust, and noise. These conditions have a debilitating effect on the social, economic, and environmental quality of life for residents.

Historically, Bayview Hunters Point has played an integral part in the development of San Francisco because of its prime location on the edge of San Francisco Bay. It was strategically important to the city and the region while the Naval Shipyard was operating and when San Francisco's Port was fully competitive with surrounding facilities. Today, Bayview Hunters Point has no thriving port operation, the shipyard (a federal Superfund hazardous waste site) has long been closed, and the area is destabilized by social, economic, and environmental blight.

In November 1992, MUNI initiated a transportation systems study of the Bayshore Corridor, which includes Third Street, the main commercial and residential arterial in Bayview Hunters Point. The city issued a final report including four light rail transit alternatives in January 1994. Though economic development was one of the important issues identified by the city's transit study, MUNI as a transit agency could do little on its own to address the larger community economic development, land use and environmental quality of life issues facing the community.

An independent community review was conducted to assess MUNI's planning process and light rail alternatives. As a result, a community-based light rail transit plan was developed by community residents, community-based organizations (the New Bayview Committee and Health Research Consultants), transportation planning consultants (Pittman and Hames Associates, a women-owned firm, one of whose principal owners grew up in Bayview Hunters Point) and the Urban Habitat Program, a nonprofit social justice and environmental organization that facilitated the community-based transportation planning process. This independent community partnership created the Bayview Hunters Point Social and Ecological Justice Transportation Plan.

The community transportation plan was based on an integrated approach to transportation and land-use planning, which seeks to optimize community economic development; promote more efficient and healthy land-use patterns; increase energy efficiency; reduce energy consumption; and improve the social, economic and environmental quality of life in Bayview Hunters Point and the South Bayshore Area of San Francisco. It provides a more holistic framework for addressing the many ways in which transportation affects communities, and for understanding how local community transportation needs relate to the larger metropolitan region.

A social justice approach was used to define, evaluate and recommend a transportation plan guided by the four transportation planning principles outlined in the preceding section. A social justice needs assessment was conducted, focusing on population, housing, employment/income, transportation, and environmental/energy characteristics of Bayview Hunters Point. Additionally, the plan developed specific social justice and environmental criteria to determine if a proposed transit alternative most efficiently and effectively:

- maximizes job/income opportunities for neighborhood residents;
- provides an improved level of transportation service to community residents;
- facilitates economic development that promotes environmental quality;
- facilitates economic development that promotes energy efficiency; and
- provides an implementation strategy to maximize job/income opportunities for the community.

Additional sub-criteria were tailored to specific concerns, goals and objectives identified and prioritized by the community. While some of these are unique to the particular demographics and circumstances of Bayview Hunters Point, others are more general and universally applicable in other communities, as well.

Key to community revitalization efforts in Bayview Hunters Point is developing Third Street as a transit corridor for light rail, and improving land use on the street by creating more compact and integrated commercial and residential areas; establishing centers for the sustainable development of complementary uses; restricting unhealthy uses; and making people, not automobiles, a priority. This development model is known as "transit-oriented development," and combines the goals of improving transportation access and mobility with affordable housing, community-based economic development (which incorporates commercial, residential, education, medical, social service, cultural facilities, and opportunities) and improved public and environmental health.[8] These objectives are consistent with many of the policy goals and objectives of the South Bayshore Plan, an area plan amendment to San Francisco's Master Plan; the latter was recently adopted by San Francisco's Planning Commission after extensive community consultation, community challenges and revisions over a four-year period.

Central to development of the community transportation plan was the process of the plan's development. Working with existing community-based organizations, the Urban Habitat Program organized a series of community planning meetings and a town meeting hosted by a local supervisor and attended by several city officials. These meetings were attended by 30 -100 residents, community activists, city officials, small business owners, and housing and community development leaders. Additionally, smaller working-group meetings and responses to a community survey were used to gather concerns, ideas, and resolve issues that led to the community's preferred light rail alternative and supporting recommendations.

Because of early intervention and strong community advocacy presence throughout the plan development phase, San Francisco city officials have taken the community's plan and recommendations seriously. In February 1994, the San Francisco Public Utilities Commission (predecessor of the voter-established Public Transportation Commission) formally adopted a resolution to include the community transportation plan with those proposed by city transit planners in a federal major transportation investment study. This analysis will result in one locally preferred alternative, expected to become eligible for federal transportation funding. City officials have conducted supplemental studies on two key recommendations from the community plan regarding the location of a light rail vehicle-maintenance and storage facility, and the use of "low floor" light rail transit vehicles in MUNI's transit system.[9]

The Bayview Hunters Point Social and Ecological Justice Transportation Plan is an example of building proactive leadership by taking the initiative to involve the community in the ongoing needs assessment, planning, project development, implementation, evaluation and decision-making process. Too often, communities are forced to react to outside agendas of the private sector or government agencies, in which "experts" decide what is best for the community. Participatory democracy demands more than just community "input." Communities must be true partners in the definition of issues, establishment of priorities and in shaping the outcomes of public policy decisions. This is a fundamental principle of building sustainable communities. In order to do this effectively and consistently, communities need the institutional capacity, information, technical assistance and resources to engage the long-term process of transportation and land-use planning, implementation and decision-making linked to all the elements involved in community revitalization.

The community's role has been important in forcing the city to look more holistically at community planning and to move towards interagency cooperation and collaboration. Ongoing community involvement is essential for making sure this happens and for holding public officials accountable to long-term commitment and follow-through. The underlying principles for developing a transit-oriented economic development strategy in Bayview Hunters Point are the principles of social justice, ecological sustainability and sustainable communities. Key to the long-term success of this effort is having the capacity at the community level to work with city agencies to deliver the transit project and transit-oriented economic development opportunities for community residents based on these principles, and to prevent gentrification and displacement of existing residents.

Political Reform Through the Convergence of Social Justice, Transportation Reform and Environmental Protection

Politically, there is enormous potential for new alliances and coalitions that share mutual interests in addressing multiple social, economic, and environmental justice goals and objectives. The quality of life in urban and suburban communities are mutually intertwined. Political struggles between local municipalities about land use development, suburban sprawl, transportation systems, shrinking public resources, servicing the debt on municipal borrowing and subsequent strain on inter-jurisdictional cooperation are ultimately regional in scope. The regional affects the local and the local affects the regional; there is no escaping this reality. Yet, the political constituency and tools necessary to address this state of affairs are sorely lacking. The long-term interests of the inner city cannot be served without addressing the patterns of public investment and policy-making that continue to support unsustainable suburban development and abandon the inner city. This wholesale human disinvestment, along with economic disinvestment, will have increasing disastrous results for all of society if it is not abated effectively and quickly. How can this be done?

The mutual interests and political support of social justice, transportation reform and environmental protection advocates must come together to build a strong power base that can reform the current public policy-making inertia. The linkages between these interests must be made explicit and immediately understandable to inner-city and suburban dwellers alike.

For example, from a social justice perspective, improving public transit is important for providing access to jobs, goods and services, and can be a catalyst for reorienting local land uses around transit hubs that can stimulate community-based economic development opportunities. From an environmental perspective, improving public transit can reduce reliance on automobile travel and its associated pollution, environmental degradation, congestion and suburban sprawl. In reality, the social justice and environmental interests in improving public transit are really the same, because both speak to the larger issue of public and private investments that impact development choices and patterns. These choices and patterns have very definite social, economic and environmental consequences.

Transportation reform is a natural nexus of social justice and environmental interests. Transforming this nexus into a proactive effort to save our nation's cities and protect our precious natural resources by creating healthy, livable, sustainable communities, cities, and regions has far-reaching political organizing and advocacy potential. It can address some of the fundamental dis-ease that underlies so much of contemporary life in United States society. Social justice and ecological sustainability, embodied in the Principles of Environmental Justice, must be at the heart of this political struggle and transformation. And struggle and transform we must, if we are to create a truly sustainable transportation system that is so critical to the future sustainability of our cities where the majority of people now live.

Linking Social Equity with Livable Communities

Don Chen

Introduction

Transportation is about making connections. This means meeting basic needs like getting to a doctor, making our streets safe for our children, and commuting to work. For decades, these social issues have been prominent in discussions about public transportation policy. Lately, however, decision-makers have grown to recognize a second set of connections: those that link transportation with broader societal issues, such as the environment. Both sets of connections have suffered from the U.S. transportation profession's singular focus on building highways and providing services for drivers. While there have been few efforts to establish common goals between social equity and environmental proponents, this is now changing because of worsening transportation conditions, new policies, and a growing awareness that a quality transportation system must address environmental, social, and economic factors.

The reasons behind the urgency to acknowledge these linkages are vast. Many have to do with the nature of transportation: it is an economic, social and environmental cost of doing business and of getting from here to there. These costs are manifested in the out-of-pocket costs to consumers and taxpayers, and the social and environmental costs of pollution. And typically, low-income and people-of-color communities bear the brunt of these costs while enjoying the fewest benefits because of racism, classism, exclusion from the policy-making process, and other forms of discrimination.

This imbalance is exacerbated by land-use patterns in the United States, where low-density suburban development has long been the dominant trend. Longer distances between jobs, services, shopping, and communities makes traveling more expensive for everyone, but for the disadvantaged, more expensive often means unaffordable, which puts many jobs, services, goods, and people out of reach. Increasingly, people are realizing that some transportation solutions involve locating desirable and important destinations closer to the groups that need access to them. In response, many grassroots neighborhood groups, community economic development advocates, and urban policy experts have promoted the development of jobs, services, businesses, and housing in low-income communities and communities of color.

Many environmentalists have arrived at the same conclusions — that to be a proponent of the environment, one must be a proponent of vital cities and communities. After all, sprawl development has a tendency to make environmental quality more difficult to attain because of the additional pollution and resource needs characteristic of low-density communities. Development also consumes open space, changes or eliminates habitats, and interferes with valuable natural processes such as flood control, run-off absorption, and erosion prevention. For them, the message is increasingly clear: make existing communities more livable so we don't have to keep building new, less efficiently designed ones.

Policy Levers

Transportation policy has traditionally avoided a holistic assessment of societal impacts. Issues involving low-income communities and communities of color in particular have been overlooked. There are only a few recent examples of federal laws that begin to acknowledge the relationships between civil rights and transportation, one being ISTEA (1991). ISTEA explicitly requires planners to examine the impacts of transportation on civil rights, although it does not explicitly call for assessments of how environmental justice is affected by transportation policies. The 1994 Clinton administration's executive order on environmental justice does — it requires all federal agencies to develop strategies that consider the impacts of their policies on racial justice and social equity. Still, a strategy that considers impacts is still in the realm of government rhetoric - it is not action. And it is not enough; other promising policy ideas that link the issues mentioned above have yet to be implemented or adopted.

The following sections discuss examples of areas where an understanding of the links among issues has led or could lead to positive solutions.

Adding Value to Communities

Community economic development is not a new idea. For decades, it has been widely touted as a win-win strategy by advocates of equity, the environment, housing, and civil rights because it strengthens communities from within. It is not an easy strategy to implement, however. It requires long-term commitment, hard work, persistence, resources, organization, and most important, funding and faith. In part spurred by the Los Angeles riots of 1993, many federal officials have called for new investment in central city infrastructure, services, employment opportunities, and amenities. This recent spurt of interest in community economic development has already dropped from the public debate, but the need for action is as urgent as ever.

Funding for urban redevelopment has been scarce over the last decade, diverted instead into projects for new suburbs. Fortunately, there are some creative ways to leverage other federal funding sources for use in developing disadvantaged communities. The potential applications of promising funding sources to transportation issues has not yet been thoroughly explored, but doing so may prove to be a useful step towards the goal of revitalizing urban centers.

Some are listed below:

- Money in the form of Community Block Grants administered through the Department of Housing and Urban Development has occasionally enabled communities to rebuild local economies.
- Housing and Urban Development administers the Community Viability Fund, which is designed to enhance the organizational capacity of community-based groups and institutions.
- Another lever may be found in the Community Reinvestment Act, which requires banks to demonstrate that they are investing in com mercial, residential and nonprofit projects in their own neighborhoods.
- As authorized in ISTEA, the U.S. Department of Transportation has funds that may be used for community economic development, includ ing: the Congestion Mitigation and Air Quality Improvement Program; the Enhancements Program; the Surface Transportation Program; and Transit Section Three funds that cover transit-related pedestrian facilities and street, shuttle, and station operations.
- The Clinton administration has established empowerment zones which provide funding for redevelopment and tax incentives for invest ment in a number of major American cities.
- There are funds for a variety of community development projects avail able from the Department of Health and Human Services.

Securing funding by no means guarantees success. Many urban reformers contend that current urban revenue streams and investment practices are part of the problem, perhaps because they are not part of a sound, unifying vision. Such a vision for urban rebuilding is critical to fostering sustainable, growing economies. This has proven to be challenging because providing a sound vision for a community requires community organizing, which is difficult to do when resources are scarce.

Jobs: Aiming at a Moving Target

Part of the challenge that community economic development advocates must face is migration of jobs to the suburbs. In the Greater Baltimore metropolitan area, for example, overall employment rose by 7 percent between 1980 and 1985, while central city jobs decreased by 8 percent. This discrepancy is largely the result of low unemployment rates in suburban areas. For example, while Philadelphia central city unemployment rate is over 10 percent, Philadelphia's suburban unemployment rate hovers around 3 percent. Other suburban boom areas include Norfolk-Virginia Beach, Memphis, and Tulsa, where employment rose by 126 percent, 154 percent, and 166 percent, respectively, between 1970 and 1980.[1] This is alarming from a number of perspectives. First, urban unemployment is rising in many central cities, diminishing opportunities for sustaining businesses in central-city communities. Second, the economic repercussions of unemployment adversely impact numerous other areas such as health care, education, crime, and housing, to name a few. Third, with intersuburban travel a national trend, metropolitan regions will have increasingly difficult tasks of addressing air quality and other environmental issues. Fourth, to make everything worse, the boom in the suburbs is encouraging more growth and land-use sprawl, reinforcing this cycle of relationships.

Some have sought to deal with issues of employment by focusing on the physical connections between home and work. Reverse commute programs, which have been tried since the 1950s, are becoming popular again. The Clinton administration, for example, has initiated a new Mobility for Work program, which is designed to link inner-city neighborhoods with suburban business districts through bus and van services. Without such reverse commute programs, many people wouldn't have jobs at all.[2] However, critics have noted that such arrangements forgive social segregation and thus resemble apartheid.

Others dealing with transportation and jobs point to the job opportunities that the transportation industry itself offers. Many recognize that jobs associated with major building projects tend to be short-term, and are therefore wary of viewing such projects as community development tools. More important, they note, is what's being built. Too often, transportation officials have entered communities with plans for major projects and the promise of jobs, and too often, those projects eventually had detrimental impacts on those communities. And even when appropriate, community-reinforcing projects are being built or managed while low-income people are left out. For example, minority-owned businesses have frequently faced an uphill battle in securing contracts for work. The primary beneficiaries of construction projects are large prime contractors. Expenditures by federal, state, and local entities are required by U.S. DOT Regulation 49 CFR, which states that certified companies owned by people of color, women, disabled, and other disadvantaged groups should receive strong consideration in the contract-selection process to maximize their abilities to participate in available procurement and contracting opportunities.[3]

Getting on Board: Public Transit

Even the most successful low-income community economic develop program won't be successful without the provision of transportation services that are affordable, efficient, convenient, and that provide sufficient geographical coverage. For many economically disadvantaged individuals, transportation options are often limited to mass transit. Indeed, low-income people constitute the largest share of total public transit ridership.[4] Despite this demand, urban and rural transit needs are frequently overlooked because wealthier communities tend to attract disproportionately large pots of transportation project funding. As transit service funding dries up, growing numbers of low-income people are choosing driving over mass transit, walking, and bicycling as their primary means of mobility. Mass transit use by poor commuters dropped by 26 percent between 1985 and 1989, while the use of single-occupancy vehicles rose by about 5 percent. Still, single-occupancy vehicles accounted for over 60 percent of total commute trips.[5] Part of the decrease in public transit ridership was caused by a 7-percent decline in the overall number of low-wage workers during that same period. However, according to the Nationwide Personal Transportation Survey, government budget constraints, the decrease in driving expenses, and the suburbanization and decentralization of jobs have also contributed to the overall decline in alternatives to the private vehicle.[6]

Although U.S. public transit services have been deteriorating over the last two decades, there is renewed interest in them as means to alleviate congestion and air pollution, and to improve access and mobility. The passage of ISTEA, which grants municipalities the latitude to shift highway funds to transit projects, was a clear signal that communities are beginning to recognize the limits and costs of car depedency.

Getting a Boost from Technologies

ISTEA also provides funding for the development of Intelligent Transportation Systems (formerly known as Intelligent Vehicle-Highway Systems). Such technologies, which greatly enhance the flow of information between public transit operators, managers, vehicles, and passengers, could in turn boost the performance of transit systems. The Federal Transit Administration recently created a Program to study Advanced Public Transportation Systems and their potential to improve transit service,operability, and ridership levels. As of yet, it is too early to tell whether or not transit systems will benefit from such technologies.

Locating People Near Transit

Land-use experts have also recognized these connections and many are proposing the development of land-use policies that are amenable to walking, bicycling, and public transit use. For example, transit-oriented development involves promoting densification, mixed land uses, and design for human scale.[7] Critics have charged that many of these designs lead to gentrification. Indeed, many neo-traditional neighborhoods are not affordable for low-income individuals. Zoning reform and other mechanisms, however, could address some of these concerns. A more promising effort isthe location-efficient mortgages. This project seeks to persuade mortgage lenders that households located efficiently (i.e., in dense, transit-rich neighborhoods) will incur lower transportation costs because they rely less on expensive automobile travel than the average household. The extra disposable income that can be used to finance a greater mortgage provides incentives for increased homeownership within urban areas, and places mortgages within reach of greater numbers of low-income families. The decreased reliance on driving both reduces related costs such as air pollution, congestion, and oil consumption, while reducing demand for new sprawl development.[8]

Bicycling and Walking Toward a Better Solution

Encouraging more people to walk, ride bicycles, and find other non-motorized means of access is another measure that benefits both the environment and poor communities. The social benefits and avoided costs resulting from bicycling are numerous. If only judged on the basis of cost, for example, bicycle riding in New York City is half as expensive as mass transit and a fourth as expensive as driving, even considering the replacement costs of bikes that are damaged by potholes and stolen (on average every three years).[9] Few projects, however, have emphasized the equity benefits of walking and biking because most bicycle-friendly regions in the U.S. are middle to upper-middle class communities. A greater national effort to promote walking and biking access and facilities in low-income neighborhoods is needed to match equity and environmental goals

The Need to Drive

While many of these measures are excellent win-win solutions, most people will want to and need to drive. For those who have access to a car, increased mobility may confer greater economic and social opportunities, while for others, such benefits are slim.[10] Not having to drive can save an average household roughly $1,000 per month, so the marginal benefits of getting a job that requires driving are frequently not enough for some people, especially if they do not otherwise need a car.[11] Any rise in driving costs can therefore force large numbers of poor commuters off the road.[12]

Increasing low-income drivership has mobilized many social equity advocates to demand that the costs of driving be kept down. This has created great strife between the equity community and other groups, including environmentalists, energy conservation advocates, and traffic managers, who want to control runaway growth in driving and traffic effects.[13] Drivers, they contend, are so shielded from the total social and private costs of automobility that there is an enormous overconsumption of driving as a private good; this results in a transport system generating close to $1 trillion in social costs every year.[14] Raising the price of driving through fees, tolls, taxes, and other measures would allow other modes of transport to compete more fairly and would create more social benefit in the long run.[15] The resulting policy-making impasse has been very visible in several recent policy initiatives, including the Clinton administration's British thermal unit tax, Southern California's higher parking fees, and California's pay-as-you-go car insurance bill.

In these issue areas, this disagreement cannot easily be reconciled because equity advocates regard driving as not a luxury, but a necessity. There are, though, numerous ways to address the regressiveness of environmental pricing policies. One is the bundling of environmental taxes with urban community redevelopment, non-motorized access and transport, mass transit, and incentives for energy efficient (and therefore cost-effective) driving behavior. Examples of encouraging efficient driving behavior include rewarding carpoolers with cash, benefits, preferential parking spots and high occupancy vehicle lanes. In Southern Los Angeles, for example, the Labor/Community Strategies Center fought for the passage of the Social Equity Clause of Employee Trip Reduction legislation, which requires employers to offer transit riders, walkers, bikers, and carpoolers a cash benefit that is equivalent to the after-tax value of a parking space. Employers also benefit because they can still deduct the pretax value of the parking space from their incomes. It is particularly cost-effective when one considers that a year-long transit pass only costs between $350 and $1,000, whereas a parking space costs between $1,000 and $3,822 a year.[16] The social equity clause also encourages employers to provide other benefits, such as showers and lockers for bikers and mass transit passes, rather than simply making driving more expensive.[17]

Providing Context: Remembering Cynthia Wiggins

These policy measures frequently lack urgency or context without an appreciation of how the issues affect people's daily lives. During the past several years, few stories illustrated the critical nature of these issues more than Cynthia Wiggins'. During the last year of her life, the seventeen- year-old found out just how hard it is for many inner-city Buffalonians to get to work.[18] After a fruitless search for work in her own neighborhood, Cynthia finally landed a job at Arthur Treacher's Fish and Chips in the decidedly upscale Walden Galleria Mall in the suburb of Cheektowaga. But finding a job wasn't her only challenge. As a non-driver, Cynthia's commuting choices were limited. To get to work, she had to travel 45 minutes on the Number Six, an inner-city bus which stopped about 300 yards short of the mall. She then had to cross a seven-lane highway with no crosswalks to get to her shift.

The commute proved to be too much for Cynthia. After getting off the bus on December 14, 1995, she was crushed by a dumptruck and later died of her injuries. A brief investigation of the tragedy revealed an ugly truth: for years mall officials had refused requests to allow the Number Six onto their property, despite the fact that buses from affluent areas (charter buses from Canada and suburban transit buses) routinely were permitted to pull up right in front of the mall. Shortly thereafter, mall officials finally let the Number Six enter its parking lot, but only after a chorus of civic leaders accused them of discriminating against inner-city bus riders, most of them low-income people of color.

Cynthia's story tells us much about ways in which racism continues to manifest itself in America's metropolitan areas — through geographic separation and concealed discrimination by private institutions. But the national press missed one lesson that can be gleaned from this tragedy: mall officials excluded the Number Six bus because they were able to get away with it. With little public accountability or scrutiny, mall officials found it easy to shut out inner-city bus riders.

Lessons Learned: The Broader Context

This lesson goes beyond shopping malls. For decades, federal transportation policy lacked a system of public involvement and did not ensure accountability and responsiveness to community and regional needs. Instead, the stated goal of the transportation profession was to build a highway system to foster interstate commerce and strengthen national defense. Local needs were eclipsed by these national goals, as evidenced by a well-documented history of encroachments of highway projects on urban neighborhoods, from the Century Freeway in Los Angeles to the Cross-Bronx Expressway.

But in the 1990s, this dynamic is changing. Public involvement and government accountability were elevated to a higher status when Congress passed ISTEA in 1991. Prior to ISTEA's passage, transportation policy was characterized by a top-down, closed-door, engineering-driven process. Today, the law requires that the public be allowed to participate in transportation policy-making at several key stages of the decision-making process. Specifically, transportation officials must tell: how the public involvement process will be structured; what the long-range transportation plan is proposed to include; how the plan will be carried out on capital projects; and what technical studies of major metropolitan investments are underway. ISTEA also features provisions that strengthen the public's power to keep government officials accountable for their actions. For example, it requires regional governments to develop long-range transportation plans that lay out their intentions for the next twenty years.

ISTEA provides funding opportunities for communities that have long been disregarded in transportation policy, especially low-income urban communities, isolated rural communities, and other communities that did not greatly benefit from decades of massive highway investment. ISTEA also includes a number of measures that try to chip away at this traditional bias toward funding highway construction. For example, the law gives states the option to "flex" money from their highway program into projects that support other modes, such as transit, walking, and bicycling.

Despite these new opportunities, results from ISTEA's first few years are mixed. More funds were spent on bicycling projects in the first eighteen months after ISTEA's passage than were spent in the previous eighteen years. And public involvement has been working well in most states. But discouraging news is also plentiful: several states continue to resist public participation; few states are actually moving funds from roadways to other modes; the federal government has been loath to enforce the air quality requirements in ISTEA and the Clean Air Act; and thanks to congressional budget cuts, funding for public transit has fallen sharply. The fiscal 1996 federal budget cut transit operating assistance by 47 percent for large cities and by 25 percent for small cities. Meanwhile, funding for highways increased by about 5 percent.

Now, numerous forces are lining up to roll back ISTEA's progressive provisions on public involvement, air quality, intermodalism, and infrastructure maintenance when the law comes up for reauthorization in September 1997. Chief among them are the powerful road-building lobby and a number of state transportation officials. To prevent this from happening, the public needs to understand what is at stake in the ISTEA reauthorization battles, and communities must speak out about their transportation needs.

For example, Chicagoans need to explain how the Congestion Mitigation and Air Quality improvement program funding used to rehabilitate the Green Line elevated train has provided a boost to community development and to improving transportation access in the Lake Street area. The citizens of Santa Cruz need to tell the nation about the Surface Transportation Program and Congestion Mitigation and Air Quality
improvement program funding that they spent on bicycle improvements throughout their county. People in Minneapolis have to describe how ISTEA enabled citizens to have a voice in the city's transportation future through the Neighborhood Revitalization Program. And the residents of San Francisco must showcase their historic Ferry Building, which was refurbished in large part thanks to ISTEA

Enhancements funds.

There are ISTEA success stories to tell. But perhaps the most important ones are those that have yet to be told. Today we still face daunting transportation problems that are closely tied to environmental, land-use, community-development, social equity, and fiscal troubles. Since 1980, for example, the rate of death from asthma-related illnesses has more than doubled, underscoring the need to control ground-level ozone levels caused by vehicle emissions.

Conclusion

This chapter has discussed access — physical access to jobs, goods and services, schools, doctors, and baby sitters — and financial access to transportation services. However, the most important form of access, the one that creates the types of access listed above, is political access. Environmental justice and social equity begin where the traditional top-down approach to policy-making ends. Grassroots community members are in the best position to know what is best for their communities. The only way a community's definition of a community can become reality is for grassroots activists and transportation officials to be part of a collaborative process in which everyone's needs are adequately represented. We hope that the ideas explored in this chapter help give birth to a long-term dialogue and collaboration that fulfils the potential for change that such a process holds.

ISTEA is a toehold in the effort to gain control over some of these problems, and communities require time and assistance to make use of this legislation so that more successes can be achieved. Ultimately, ISTEA is about more than just providing better transit service, building sidewalks, or reducing air pollution. It's about making communities across the country more livable. And to help people like Cynthia Wiggins, our next steps should be about making daily trips more affordable, more efficient, and safer to undertake so that their next steps do not have to cover seven lanes of traffic, after a forty-five-minute commute, to get to a minimum-wage job.

A Tale of Two Cities

Fern L. Shepard and Paul K. Sonn

America's urban areas have become forgotten places. Too many of our cities and their inhabitants are at risk from poor housing, poverty, economic abandonment, and inadequate transportation.[1] The poor infrastructure conditions in urban areas are a result of a host of factors including the distribution of wealth, patterns of racial and economic discrimination, redlining, housing and real estate practices, location decisions of industry, and different enforcement of land use regulations.

Inhabitants who live in American cities continue to be racially segregated. Nowhere is this separate-society contrast more apparent than in the nation's large metropolitan areas. Even small towns have not escaped this phenomenon. Some people "live on the wrong side of the tracks, and as a result receive different treatment."[2] Historically, institutionalized racism has been and continues to be a conspicuous part of American life, and as a result, people of color find themselves at a disadvantage in contemporary society. Institutionalized racism is part of the national heritage. Racism created this nation's dark ghettos, barrios, and reservations.

The black ghetto, for example, is kept isolated and contained from the larger white society through well-defined institutional practices, private actions, and government policies, including our transportation policies. Some two and a half decades ago, the National Advisory Commission on Civil Disorders implicated white racism in creating and maintaining the black ghetto and the drift toward two "separate and unequal societies."[3] These same conditions exist today.

The development of racially differentiated metropolitan areas did not just happen by accident. Private companies and individual citizens had help. Decades of federal government policies have played a key role in the development of spatially differentiated metropolitan areas where blacks and other people of color are segregated from whites and the poor from the more affluent citizens.

Many freeway and road construction projects cut paths through people of color neighborhoods, physically isolating residents from their institutions. African-Americans and Latino-Americans are regularly displaced for highways, convention centers, sports arenas, and a host of other downtown development projects. They are often forced to move into other segregated neighborhoods. The end result has meant community urban displacement, gentrification, limited mobility, reduced housing options and residential packages, decreased environmental choices, and diminished job opportunities.

Land use, economic development, and transportation policies flow from forces of production and are often dominated and subsidized by state actors. Numerous examples abound where state actors have targeted cities and regions for infrastructure improvements and amenities such as water irrigation systems, ship channels, road and bridge projects, and mass transit systems. On the other hand, state actors have done a miserable job in ensuring that economic benefits and burdens associated with development are equitably distributed.

This chapter explores transportation-related disputes in two distinct communities, Washington, D.C. and James City, North Carolina. Although the two communities are worlds apart in terms of their political and economic structure, they have a lot in common. Both communities have taken on government highway construction projects that threaten the health and safety of the local residents.

The "Two Worlds"of Washington, D.C.

There are "two worlds of Washington," the Wall Street Journal writes. One is the Washington of "cherry blossoms, the sparkling white monuments, the magisterial buildings of government . . . , of politics and power." Just over a mile away, the other world is known as Anacostia. Living on the "wrong side of the tracks" in Washington, D.C. means living south and east of Capitol Hill. More precisely, it means living in the neighborhoods bordering the Anacostia River, the most endangered urban river in the country.[4] There, in the shadow of the symbol of our democracy, the population is overwhelmingly African-American and far poorer than its white counterpart on the other side of the city.

According to 1992 statistics from the District of Columbia government, in the three city wards bordering the Anacostia River (Wards Six, Seven and Eight), the percentage of black population is 72 percent, 97 percent, and 91 percent respectively, and the percentage of households living in poverty is 15 percent, 18 percent, and 26 percent respectively.[5] By contrast, Ward Three on the west side of the city is only 6 percent black and has only a 6-percent poverty rate. The median household income in Ward Eight is $21,312, less than half the median household income of $48,967 in Ward Three. There too, environmental benefits are few and environmental burdens are many.[6]

This case study discusses the latest assault on the already-beleaguered neighborhoods along the Anacostia River — the proposed Barney Circle Freeway. It also discusses the combined community and legal efforts to stop the freeway.

Environmental Justice in the Nation's Capital

Environmental justice focuses on policies or practices that differentially affect or disadvantage individuals, groups or communities based on race, ethnicity, color, or income.[7] Environmental discrimination and environmental racism, when combined with public and private policies and practices, provide environmental benefits to whites and the affluent while shifting environmental burdens to people of color and the poor. Environmental racism is "as real as the racism found in housing, education, employment, and the political arena."[8]

In Washington, D.C., one need only look at the remarkably different treatment of the city's two rivers — both of which were historically severely polluted - to see a glaring example of environmental injustice and racism. The Potomac River, which flows through affluent and predominantly white neighborhoods, has been the beneficiary of over $1 billion in restoration funds.[9] By contrast, less than 1 percent of that sum has been spent on restoration of the Anacostia River. Because the Anacostia River's plight largely has been ignored by federal, state, and local governments, President Clinton recently called the Anacostia "a forgotten river."

As a consequence, the Anacostia River remains heavily polluted. In the tributary portions of the watershed, sediment, streambank erosion, and high bacteria levels are the most severe problems.[10] In the tidal reaches, the river suffers not only from high sediment and bacteria loadings generated and delivered from upstream, but also from the effects of combined sewer overflows. These overflows generate massive loadings of oxygen-demanding materials during storms that deplete oxygen the tidal river needs to support life. River sediments also contain high levels of toxic organics and heavy metals. Finally, debris in the tidal Anacostia represents a substantial impediment to its restoration.

In addition to a heavily polluted river, the African-American communities along the Anacostia River have had to absorb many of the city's major facilities, or what is often termed "locally unwanted land uses" (LULUs). Along the banks of the Anacostia, these LULUs include the D.C. Jail, D.C. General Hospital, D.C. solid waste incinerator, the city's electric generator, Robert F. Kennedy stadium, the D.C. Armory, several open pit dumps, and several sites with buried hazardous wastes.

In the last two years, these communities have been inundated with several new proposed LULUs for the banks of the Anacostia - the proposed Jack Kent Cooke Stadium (now slated for another site), the Children's Island theme park, and the Barney Circle Freeway. All of these projects were slated for construction along the banks of the river, and together they would have taken over 100 acres ofpark lands, despoiled the river, and added hundreds of cars and trucks to residential neighborhoods.[11]

The most egregious of these proposed LULUs is the Barney Circle Freeway. This proposed federally-financed freeway will be constructed adjacent to residential communities and will cut through scarce park lands on both sides of the Anacostia River. Construction of this freeway will have many severe environmental impacts, including:

- paving over seventeen acres of scarce park land and adding the sixth interstate bridge over the Anacostia River;
- excavating over 70,000 tons of hazardous waste (soil contaminated with lead, asbestos, and other cancer-causing agents) adjacent to residential neighborhoods;
- adding over 100,000 cars and trucks a day driving at freeway speeds adjacent to residential neighborhoods, adding substantial air pollution (about 170 tons a day) and noise pollution, and lowering property values;
- shifting traffic from the more affluent Capitol Hill neighborhoods into

the lower-income, predominantly African-American neighborhoods in southeast D.C.

In addition to being an environmental disaster for these neighborhoods, this proposed freeway exacerbates fiscal and transportation inequities. The Barney Circle Freeway will cost the federal treasury more than $200 million to construct. At the same time, the district's fiscal crisis already has resulted in severe cutbacks in city bus service and increases in transit fares, and it has threatened proposed Metro subway construction.[12] These are the very transportation services that are so important for the district's low-income city residents.[13]

Worse still, the Federal Highway Administration and district government so far have refused to evaluate an alternative to the freeway that would cost a fraction of the $200 million slated for the project. This community-supported alternative would provide missing ramps without taking homes or businesses and would not bisect park lands or require excavation of hazardous wastes.

From this description, the environmental justice implications of this project are obvious. But there is more. A project similar to this one was proposed twenty years ago on the other, predominantly white side of town.[14] It was defeated by community opposition and a lawsuit and the Federal Highway Administration never proposed it again. The residents fighting the Barney Circle Freeway have been waging a war against this project for over a decade and the Federal Highway Administration continues to push for its construction.

Community and Legal Efforts to Stop the Proposed Freeway

A coalition of local civic associations, neighborhood groups, African-American environmental groups, and regional and national environmental groups have joined forces in opposing construction of the Barney Circle Freeway.[15] Together, these groups are pursuing a campaign against the project that involves aggressive grassroots organizing, community education, lobbying local and federal officials and members of Congress, local and national media work, and street theater. The coalition opposing the project also has chosen to use the courts to challenge the freeway.[16]

Environmental justice has had several profound effects on environmental litigation, many of which are evident in the Barney Circle Freeway litigation. First, the environmental justice movement has expanded the concept of what constitutes an "environmental" issue. Traditional environmental concerns have tended to focus on natural resource and wildlife protection and clean air and water. As a result of the environmental justice movement, these concerns have been supplemented with a clearer focus on the quality of people's lives. As a result, the environmental justice movement has extended the concept of the environment to include protecting the rights of all people to a clean and healthy environment not only where they play, but also where they live and work.[17]

By expanding the concept of what constitutes an environmental issue, the environmental justice movement has expanded the notion of what constitutes a violation of environmental law. For example, the National Environmental Policy Act (NEPA), 42 U.S.C. section 4321 et seq., requires all federal agencies to evaluate and report on the potential adverse impacts of major federal action significantly affecting the environment. Under the broader definition of environment

advanced by the environmental justice movement, the government's analysis must include an assessment of
the health and environmental consequences and risks of a project, as well as economic and sociological impacts.[18] Failing to examine the socio-economic impacts of a project thus constitutes a NEPA violation. Pursuant to NEPA regulations that are binding on all federal agencies, the environmental effects or impacts that must be analyzed in an environmental impact statement include ecological, aesthetic, historic, cultural, economic, social, and health effects.

In addition to expanding the definition of what constitutes a violation of environmental law, the environmental justice movement has affected the legal theories used by lawyers in environmental litigation. For example, the environmental justice movement has led to powerful combinations of environmental and civil rights theories in single cases. It has brought into focus legal theories aimed at assessing the cumulative effects of multiple threats facing communities of color. Further, because environmental justice cannot exist without procedural justice, such as fair and free access to information, litigation under the Freedom of Information Act and National Environmental Policy Act is increasingly important.

In the Barney Circle Freeway suit, the litigation was designed around reinforcing the affected communities' political efforts. As the district's "dumping grounds," the Anacostia communities' central political message is focused on the injustice of putting another polluting project in their backyards. Accordingly, the legal theories in their case focus in part on the cumulative impacts facing the Anacostia communities from the numerous environmental threats already in their midst.

The suit also alleges a failure to evaluate the health and safety implications of excavating hazardous waste adjacent to residential communities under the National Environmental Policy Act, in addition to violations of the Clean Air Act, Intermodal Surface Transportation Efficiency Act, and section 4(f) of the Department of Transportation Act. An administrative challenge to the project under Title VI of the Civil Rights Act that focuses on the discriminatory impact of the freeway siting decision is being considered.

The legal strategy in the Barney Circle Freeway case also was designed to reinforce and strengthen the communities' political efforts. For example, the coalition discovered internal agency documents showing that over 70,000 tons of hazardous waste would be excavated adjacent to residential neighborhoods to construct the freeway. These residents had not been told of the hazardous waste or of the plans to excavate it during freeway construction. Moreover, internal agency documents revealed that government officials intended to spend over twice the amount of federal funds ($15 million versus $6 million) to avoid a public permit process on treatment and disposal of the hazardous waste.

To further their case that residents were being shut out of the process and that the government was withholding critical information about the project's impacts, the coalition filed litigation under the Freedom of Information Act to obtain all of the agency's documents on the hazardous wastes. These documents then became central items in the coalitions' organizing, political, and education efforts. The legal strategy was designed to support and buttress the community coalition's organizing.

Assault on James City, North Carolina

James City, an African-American community located near New Bern in eastern North Carolina, boasts a rich history of community-based resistance to racial oppression. This tradition of activist self-defense has been necessitated by a century of attacks on the physical integrity and historical heritage of the community, and on the well-being of its residents. The most recent episode in this history is still unfolding. It concerns a plan by the North Carolina Department of Transportation (NC-DOT) to build a major bridge and highway interchange within this community, which has already borne an unfair share of harmful highway projects.

James City has organized itself to resist this latest threat. As part of this campaign, the NAACP Legal Defense Fund, on behalf of the residents, filed an administrative environmental justice complaint with the Federal Highway Administration, seeking to have federal aid for this project suspended until the state addresses environmental equity concerns in the planning and execution of the project.

In order to place the current highway project in context, this case study begins by tracing the history of this remarkable community and of the treatment it has received at the hands of state and local government in North Carolina. Our analysis describes the highway siting and planning process that has occurred in the James City case, using this case study to illustrate the environmental justice review procedures and substantive standards that must be applied by state highway agencies if the environmental justice mandates of President Clinton's Executive Order Number 12,898 and Title VI of the 1964 Civil Rights Act are to be more than empty promises.

Founding and Reconstruction Era

The history of discriminatory assaults and community-based resistance is as old as James City itself. The settlement that came to be James City was first established in 1862 as a refugee camp for African-Americans freed from slavery when the Union Army occupied New Bern during the Civil War. Known as the Trent River Settlement, the camp was located at the fork of the Trent and Neuse Rivers, just across the Trent from New Bern. During the Reconstruction period, residents of the Trent River Settlement put down roots, transforming the camp into a permanent village. Named James City for Horace James, a chaplain in the Union Army who oversaw the settlement and later the North Carolina Freedmen's Bureau, the community grew into a small but vital black commercial center.

No sooner had Reconstruction ended when whites conspired to take back the James City site. James City's African-American residents fought this effort unsuccessfully, ultimately losing a court battle that deprived them of their land in 1893. Following this displacement, the community migrated south down the peninsula, farther away from the Trent River, where its members resettled and formed the community that is the present-day James City.[19]

History of Inequitable Highway Sitings

Over the course of the late twentieth century, North Carolina successively built and expanded a series of roads through James City. On each occasion, residents were displaced and land was taken from the community, including land of major historical significance. This process began in the 1950s when the state built U.S. 70 directly through the center of James City, physically dividing the community, taking the homes of many residents, and rending the community's social fabric.

Later in the 1970s, the state built a new bridge and highway bypass spur off U.S. 70. Route 70 Bypass was built through the Bridge Pointe area — the site of the original nineteenth-century James City. Construction of the U.S. 70 Bypass did great violence to James City's historical patrimony, for the state built the Bypass directly across the Near Cemetery — the community's oldest burial ground and one of the only surviving elements of the original James City community. The state literally paved over this cemetery containing the graves of both the community's founders and the families of many of James City's current residents.[20]

Recent Attacks: The Airport

More recently, in 1991 the nearby Craven County Regional Airport announced plans to build a runway extension, which would require taking the homes and property of members of the James City community and, equally importantly, would render inaccessible and possibly destroy one of the community's two remaining historic cemeteries,[21] which is located on property owned by the airport. James City organized itself in opposition to the project, protesting this latest attack on the community and its historical heritage. As part of this campaign, the NAACP Legal Defense Fund filed a Title VI environmental justice administrative complaint with the Federal Aviation Administration — the federal agency providing aid for the runway extension.

This organizing paid off. Although James City was not able to block the condemnation of homes, the residents obtained an order from the Federal Aviation Administration mandating that the U.S. Department of Transportation Uniform Relocation Act procedures apply. Moreover, the community negotiated a settlement whereby not only was the cemetery saved, but also the airport agreed to lease the cemetery and surrounding land to the James City Historical Society at no charge. In exchange, the James City Historical Society will maintain the site as a museum. The Historical Society has since brought to the museum site one of the only surviving plantation slaves' quarters from the region.

The Neuse River Bridge Project

While James City's residents were fending off the threat posed by the runway, state transportation authorities announced plans for the Neuse River Bridge project —a massive new $122 million-highway bridge and interchange complex. The bridge would replace an older swing-style bridge across the Neuse River located farther upstream near New Bern and would link up several of the region's highways. However, when the NC-DOT began planning the project, it proposed several alternative routes including one that would site the highway interchange in the heart of James City.

This plan would necessitate seizure of the homes of a score of this tiny community's residents, and would further fragment this neighborhood already divided by the highways built through James City in preceding decades. The siting plan also posed substantial air, noise, and visual pollution hazards, further compounding the adverse health effects of the highway infrastructure already sited in James City.

Facing this threat, the community again mobilized to resist this latest attempt to foist on James City an unfair share of the region's disruptive highway infrastructure. Residents voiced their opposition at public meetings and filed letters of complaint with the state and with federal civil rights officials, since the project was to be funded by the Federal Highway Administration. As part of this concerted campaign of opposition, the NAACP Legal Defense Fund, representing the James City community under the auspices of the James City Historical Society, filed another Title VI environmental justice administrative complaint, this time with the Federal Highway Administration.

In part because of James City's opposition, but also because of separate problems with the proposed site, the state abandoned its plan to place the interchange at the very center of James City. However, the state chose an alternative site that was also within James City. Although this new route will not actually physically displace many residents from their homes, the project will still have numerous harmful effects on the surrounding James City neighborhoods.

The increased traffic, as well as the construction work, will cause greater air pollution and the concomitant health hazards it brings. Noise pollution will increase markedly. The massive highway interchange structure rising sixty five feet, together with its supporting earthen embankments, will create a visual blight. And when combined with the states's plan to convert Route 70 into a more limited access highway, the interchange project will further divide and isolate the community, both inhibiting
travel between the two halves of the town that are divided by Route 70, and impeding access into and out of the community via Route 70. The project will harm efforts to preserve James City's historical heritage because one of the interchange ramps will be located on land abutting the now-paved-over former cemetery, thereby consuming some of the only remaining undeveloped property from the original James City. Finally, the project will harm James City economically. The previously detailed adverse effects will depress property values, while the impeded access to James City will harm businesses that depend on sales to travelers on Route 70. James City continues to oppose the Neuse River Bridge Project as currently planned, charging that the project still violates the environmental justice mandates of Title VI and the environmental justice executive order. The NAACP Legal Defense Fund, on behalf of the residents, is continuing to prosecute James City's environmental justice complaint with the Federal Highway Administration and is considering a range of options including suing in federal court to block the project.

A Failure of Process

The Neuse River Bridge Project offers a case study in the sort of planning

consequences that result from the failure of state highway agencies to incorporate meaningful environmental justice review into their planning processes. North
Carolina DOT conducted a detailed investigation of the environmental and traf-
fic-flow pros and cons of each of the identified alternatives. Although racial
effects could easily have been examined at the same time, NC-DOT inexplicably
but steadfastly refused to accord them this same serious treatment.

This refusal occurred despite a series of letters from the James City residents
over the course of the planning process reminding the state of its duty to gather
data on and then to scrutinize seriously the racial effects of the project's various
no-build and build alternatives. The U.S. Department of Transportation (DOT)
requires its agencies, including the Federal Highway Administration, to demand
from applicants for federal financial assistance racial data concerning the populations immediately surrounding and affected by each of the site alternatives considered. Applicants must report:

> "The proposed location, and alternative locations, of any facilities to be
> constructed or used in connection with the project, together with data
> concerning their composition by race, color and national origin of the
> populations of the areas surrounding such facilities."[22]

Such consideration of environmental justice effects is mandated by Title VI
and President Clinton's environmental justice executive order, since this is a federally funded project.

The remainder of our analysis details the planning failures demonstrated by
the Neuse River Bridge project that must be remedied if the promise of environmental justice is to be made real in highway construction projects.

Route Selection

NC-DOT initially considered a total of twelve possible locations for the project. However, all four routes that it selected for further consideration were ones
that would site a substantial portion of the project in James City. Since James City
is approximately 100 percent African-American while the region as a whole
ranges between 25 percent and 28 percent, it is clear that siting the project in
James City will have a disproportionate adverse racial impact. Under several of
the routes initially considered, as well as another proposed by the community,
James City — and hence African-Americans in the region — would have been
spared the brunt of the project's impact. However, NC-DOT neither identified
which routes would avoid an inequitable racial impact nor investigated whether
any of those routes would be feasible.

Title VI and the environmental justice executive order require that, in federally funded programs, racially disparate allocation of either burdens or benefits
must be avoided wherever possible.[23] At the siting stage, this means that a state
highway agency must canvass the range of possible sites and seek out routing
options that can avoid racially unfair impacts. Such impacts are tolerated under
Title VI and the executive order only if they are necessary, and there do not exist
any feasible alternative
routes having a lesser racial impact.[24]

When it came down to choosing between the two routes that were the worst and second worst for James City, NC-DOT did compare the number of residents displaced under the two plans and noted their racial breakdown. However, this analysis was far too truncated, as it only compared the bad and worse alternatives. Moreover, it appears from the record that NC-DOT's ultimate decision not to choose the very worst alternative was motivated as much by certain unrelated problems with the route as it was by any desire to avoid unfair racial impacts.

Less Discriminatory Alternative Mitigation Measures

If environmental justice concerns are taken seriously, in most highway siting cases state highway planners should be able to identify routes that satisfy their legitimate transportation and environmental needs and priorities while avoiding inequitable racial impacts. Of course, in some relatively rare cases, after good-faith investigation of alternatives, it will be determined that the only feasible route is one having a disparate racial effect. However, the state highway agency's duty to avoid racially discriminatory effects does not end there.

Title VI and the environmental justice executive order require planners to adopt any available feasible, less discriminatory alternative measures that will mitigate the adverse effects of the highway.[25] This means that where mitigation measures are available that would cushion the project's identified racial effects, the state highway agency is obliged to incorporate such measures into the project plan.

Equitable Allocation of Mitigation Resources

In addition to the duty to adopt available measures to mitigate disparate racial impacts, the Title VI nondiscrimination requirement governs allocation of mitigation resources. In the context of a highway project that, out of necessity, is sited at a location that has a disparate racial effect, this duty demands that the share of mitigation resources afforded the adversely affected minority community must be at least as great as the share expended to protect other non-minority communities.

The Federal Highway Administration Region 6 Title VI Implementation Guide, which was included as an attachment to its 1994 Civil Rights Implementation Plan Update submitted to the Justice Department, expressly admonishes that under Title VI, "Mitigation measures should be provided so that the resulting benefits and services are equally provided to minority and nonminority areas."[26]

In the James City case, the state highway agency rejected certain cheaper route alternatives because they would have had harmful effects on certain white communities. In this circumstance, the cost differential between these rejected alternatives and the next cheapest available route must be regarded as an extra mitigation expense incurred for the benefit of the white community involved. In light of the Title VI duty not to discriminate in allocating mitigation resources, NC-DOT therefore may not refuse to adopt available alternative implementation measures that would cushion the project's effects on James City, and that do not exceed in cost the amount spent on the white community.

In James City, there exist a variety of available alternative implementation measures that would cushion the project's harmful effects on the city's aesthetics, on the residents' means of mobility into and within the community, and on James City's historical heritage. NC-DOT has nonetheless refused to adopt these available mitigation measures, even though their cost appears to be less than the expense that the state has already incurred in order to shield white communities from the project's impact.

Conclusion

The Washington, D.C. community coalition opposed to the construction of the Barney Circle Freeway is continuing its fight for environmental justice. To date, its community and legal efforts have succeeded in preventing freeway construction and in forcing the Federal Highway Administration and district government to prepare a new environmental study on the project. This additional time and new information about the freeway's impacts have assisted community organizers in their political battle to stop the freeway.

While the Barney Circle freeway's opponents have not won their fight yet, they are well organized and committed to preventing construction of this project in their backyard. They continue to hope that the Federal Highway Administration and district government will reconsider their past commitment to the Barney Circle Freeway, and instead promote the community-supported, fiscally responsible, and neighborhood-sensitive alternative.

The James City community continues to fight to break a century-long pattern of inequitable treatment by state and local government. The residents are pursuing their environmental justice complaint with the Federal Highway Administration, while they also consider suing in federal court to block the project. This community's experience illustrates how highway planning must be reformed to incorporate serious environmental justice review if we are to break the painful historical pattern of unfair highway siting.

Transportation Efficiency and Equity in Southern California: Are They Compatible?

Michael Cameron

Introduction

Southern California's ground transportation system is the model that, for better or worse, is spreading to other metropolitan regions in the United States and internationally. In spite of the enormous mobility it affords, the Southern California model is plagued by severe congestion and pollution and provides residents with only one viable means of mobility — the household automobile. Automobiles are used for more than 95 percent of all personal travel.[1] Public transit carries roughly 3 percent of all trips.

The Southern California model has arisen both from conscious policy choices, such as road investment policy, and as a result of technological advances and consumer preferences. As the modern metropolitan transportation system evolves, it will continue to be shaped by these same forces. Looking ahead, policy makers have a host of objectives they seek to promote through transportation reforms. The most prominent objectives in recent years, as expressed in opinion polls and laws that call for transportation improvements, have been to reduce congestion and air pollution. Generally speaking, the primary push of transportation policy has been to increase efficiency.

Only recently, after a long absence, have concerns for transportation equity surfaced. The Americans with Disabilities Act of 1990 elevated the mobility rights of the disabled. More recently, the NAACP Legal Defense Fund, on behalf of a local grassroots busriders group, filed a civil rights case against the Los Angeles County MTA. President Clinton's executive order on environmental justice requires that the Federal Highway Administration pay closer attention to the equity and justice of its programs and policies.

While the resurgence of interest in transportation equity is welcome and overdue, in practical political terms it is likely to remain a subordinate issue to overall concerns with efficiency. This chapter considers the degree to which efficiency and equity objectives can be pursued simultaneously. Specifically, it examines the distributional impacts of market-based efficiency reforms such as congestion pricing and other user fees.

The first section examines the degree to which Southern California's transportation system is both inefficient and inequitable. The second section considers the likely impacts of one sample market-based reform, a five-cent fee per vehicle mile travelled (VMT fee), on both the efficiency and equity of the current system. Finally, the third section considers means for mitigating any adverse equity impacts of market-based efficiency policies.

Southern California's Transportation System: Efficiency and Equity

Efficiency

Southern California is a growing region of 15 million people.[2] It is the youngest major metropolis on the globe and is an international wellspring of social change. One of the region's most distinguishing features is its transportation system. Los Angeles, the region's center, is the city of the automobile. To move its 15 million people, the region has a fleet of 9 million vehicles and a grid freeway system unlike any in the world.

The overall mobility advantages of the system are causing other regions in the United States and the world to pursue similar systems. In spite of its popularity, however, the Southern California system is infamous for its pollution and congestion problems. While efforts to revert to an older model of transportation, such as those that feature rail or bus transit systems, seem doomed to fail, it also appears that the current system cannot continue in its present form.

To help frame the issue, Table 1 presents an accounting of the measurable costs and benefits of the region's transportation system. The mobility and access benefits of personal travel are obvious but are hard to measure. As they use the transportation system to get to jobs, schools, medical care, basic services and recreation, residents of Southern California take 45 million automobile trips (three per person) and drive 290 million miles per day. The value of this travel can be measured by people's willingness to pay for it (which is more than they actually pay for it). Using information on people's travel choices and their sensitivity to the price of travel, it was possible to estimate that the aggregate benefits of auto travel in the region, in 1990, equaled $78.2 billion per year (Table 1).[3]

Although public transit ridership is relatively low compared to automobile ridership, in absolute terms it is a significant service, especially for those people who ride it regularly and have no other means of travel. Public transit carries roughly 1.3 million riders per day. Based on people's willingness to pay for transit, the benefits of transit travel in the region are estimated to be $1.5 billion per year. Combined with the value of auto trips, the total value of personal transportation benefits in the region is estimated to be $79.7 billion.

In exchange for these transportation benefits, residents of the region give uptime and money, and through air pollution, their health. In 1990, residents spent over $34 billion on automobile purchases, maintenance, fuel and insurance (Table 1). This huge amount represents roughly 9 percent of the region's $370 billion economy. Transit riders paid roughly $.3 billion in transit fares. Residents also paid $4.2 billion in fuel and vehicle taxes and fees, and in special retail salestaxes dedicated to funding transportation.

Table 1: Benefits and Costs of Surface Transportation Southern California, 1991 (in billions of dollars)	
Benefits	
automobile travel	$78.2
public transit	1.5
total benefits	$79.7
Costs	
automobile expenses	34.1
transit fares	0.3
taxes	4.2
air pollution	3.7
congestion	7.7
total costs	$50.1
Net Benefits	$29.6
Source: Efficiency and Fairness on the Road	

In addition to direct monetary payments for transportation, residents also paid for transportation through congestion and pollution costs. Recurring congestion was estimated to have cost motorists $7.7 billion in wasted time (not including extra vehicle costs or commercial delay). The adverse health effects caused by ozone and particulate pollution originating from cars is estimated to be $3.7 billion. The total cost of the region's transportation system, therefore, is estimated to be $50.1 billion. Given the gross benefits estimate of $79.7 billion, the net benefits of the region's transportation system are estimated to be $29.6 billion.

With regard to efficiency, Table 1 reveals that there is cause for concern. The external costs of congestion and pollution represent 23 percent of the total costs. Furthermore, although estimates of pollution and congestion costs are highly speculative by nature, these particular estimates are fairly conservative. The congestion costs do not include commercial delay or the extra automobile insurance and maintenance costs associated with bad traffic. The pollution cost includes the health damages associated with ozone and particulate matter only, excluding those related to carbon monoxide and the costs of other environmental damages, such as ground- and surface-water contamination, greenhouse gas emissions, etc.

Further evidence of the inefficiency of the system is the low occupancy rates of vehicles. At least eight out of ten cars on the road carry only one person. At this rate, each household that can afford it owns one vehicle for each licensed driver. The average family spends more than $8,000 per year on their two cars - more than they spend on health care or food. In light of these inefficiencies, the public objective of greater transportation efficiency has merit.

Table 2: Distribution by Income Quintile of the Benefits and Costs of Surface Transportation Southern California, 1991 (in annual per capita dollars)					
Income Quintile					
Benefits	**1**	**2**	**3**	**4**	**5**
automobile travel	$1,530	$3,510	$4,940	$7,410	$10,830
public transit	110	100	100	100	130
total benefits	$1,640	$3,610	$5,040	$7,510	$10,960
Costs					
automobile expenses	$ 490	$1,500	$2,180	$3,310	$4,830
transit fares	30	20	20	20	20
taxes	140	210	270	370	520
air pollution	270	270	270	270	270
congestion	60	180	320	660	1,570
total costs	$ 990	$2,180	$3,060	$4,630	$7,210
Net Benefits	$ 650	$1,430	$1,980	$2,880	$3,750
Source: Efficiency and Fairness on the Road					

Transportation Equity

Increasingly, transportation is becoming a necessity for human survival. Jobs, schools and other opportunities are, more often than not, farther from affordable housing than a person can walk. Without means for getting from one point to another in a fast, reliable and safe manner, a person is denied the opportunity to live a fully independent and prosperous life. Yet, despite its importance, there is little public attention paid to the question of whether people have the mobility services they need. In fact, there is surprisingly little known about exactly how much mobility or physical access is needed to meet the minimum daily needs of a person living in a sprawling metropolis like Southern California.

Although the U.S. Constitution protects a person's right to be free from inhibition to travel (commerce clause), it provides no protections for ensuring that each person has a minimum level of necessary transportation resources. Such provisions are included in many state constitutions for primary education services, but not for transportation services.[4] The Americans With Disabilities Act requires public agencies to provide the same transit services for the disabled as they do for others, but the law affects a very small amount of transportation resources and a relatively small number of people.

Given the sparse amount of legal, political and academic attention paid to the issue of transportation equity and transportation rights, it is very difficult to definitively evaluate the equity of Southern California's or any other regional transportation system. A step in that direction is an evaluation of the distribution of transportation resources among groups of people. Although there are many demographic groupings that are relevant to the issue of transportation equity, including age, race, gender and geography, perhaps none is more relevant than income, since cost is probably the single greatest inhibitor of personal mobility and access.

Table 2 indicates the distribution of Southern California's transportation benefits and costs across five income groups, each representing 20 percent of the population. The first income group represents the 20 percent who earn the least, the highest income group represents the 20 percent who earn the most and so on. Table 2 reveals how the total costs and benefits from Table 1 are distributed among income groups.

Not surprisingly, the bulk of gross mobility benefits go to the high income earners. The average person in the highest income group traveled roughly thirty-four miles per day, more than three times as far as the average person in the lowest income group, who traveled roughly ten miles per day.[5] The average middle-income person traveled twenty miles per day. Thus, the 20 percent of the population that earned the highest income accounts for 32 percent of travel; the middle 20 percent accounts for 19 percent of all travel; and the lowest 20 percent accounts for only 9 percent of all travel.

Measuring the benefits of these levels of travel using the willingness-to-pay methodology, whereby benefits are a function of how much a person travels and how much they are willing to pay for that travel, reveals that the benefits for the average person in the highest income group are estimated at $10,960, the benefits for the average middle-income person are $5,040 and for the average lowest-income earner $1,640, (Table 2).[6]

Almost all of the travel done by individuals in each income group is by car. Although individuals in the lowest income group are twice as likely to ride transit (6 percent mode share) as individuals in higher income groups (3 percent mode share), the relative mode share for transit is still small. This does not suggest, however, that transit is unimportant because the concept of the "average" person is, in the case of transit, misleading. It is unlikely that many people rely on transit for 6 percent of their travel. Especially in the low-income group, some individuals depend on transit for all of their travel, while others rarely use it. Presumably most high-income transit users also have access to cars.

The distribution of transportation costs is proportional to the distribution of mobility benefits. Generally, those who travel more, pay more, and suffer more congestion. The important exception to this rule is pollution exposure, which is not highly correlated with how much a person travels.

The single largest travel expense for most individuals is automobile ownership, maintenance, fuel and insurance. Table 2 indicates that the average person in the highest income group spends roughly $4,830 per year on automobile expenses, compared to $2,180 for individuals in the middle-income group and $490 per person in the lowest income group. This difference is a reflection not only of the relative amount of travel done by people in different income groups, but also of differences in automobile ownership. Poor people own fewer cars than the wealthy. In the Southern California region, there is roughly one vehicle for every person in the highest income group, one car for every two people in the middle-income group, and one car for every three people in the lowest income group.

The distribution of transit fares reveals that, on average, low-income individuals spend the most on transit fares. Table 2 indicates that the average low-income person spends $30 per year on transit compared to $20 per year for the average person in the other income groups. However, the notion of the average person's transit expenditures is misleading since some people, especially in the low-income group, are heavily reliant on transit and others use transit very little. Thus the average transit user, although they are relatively few in number, spend much more than $20 to $30 per year. In fact, a regular user using a discounted bus pass would spend $42 per month (in 1991) for the pass, or $504 per year on transit.

One important difference in the transit fares paid by individuals in different income groups is the amount paid per mile. Because low-income travelers tend to take shorter transit trips than wealthier riders taking express commute services from the suburbs, and because the fares are charged per trip, low-income transit riders pay more per mile than anyone else. The average transit fare was fourteen cents per mile for the lowest income patrons and ten cents per mile for the highest income patrons.

People also pay for transportation through taxes and fees. The distribution of transportation taxes and fees is especially important since they are costs that government can change. Table 2 indicates that the average person in the lowest income group spent $140 per year in transportation taxes and fees compared to $270 for middle-income individuals and $520 per year for high-income individuals. Although the absolute tax burden increases with income, in general, transportation taxes are regressive, meaning that low-income taxpayers pay a higher percentage of their income on taxes than individuals who earn more. Table 3 shows the mix of taxes and fees used to pay for investments in roads and transit in the region. Table 3 also shows that the share of income paid for these taxes and fees is 2.5 times greater for low-income individuals than for high-income individuals. Although the flat vehicle registration fee is the most regressive (3.5 ratio), the worst fee from an equity standpoint is the retail sales tax due to its magnitude (taking .8 percent of income from low-income earners). Fuel taxes are also very regressive. The least regressive fee, the vehicle license fee which assesses 2 percent of a vehicle's market value, is also the largest fee for high income individuals (since they generally own the most valuable cars).

The health costs of transportation-related air pollution are significant in Southern California, but the incidence of reduced health across different demographic groups is poorly understood, with the exception that inland (eastern) locales suffer much greater exposure to pollution than those in the west. Due to a lack of reliable data, this study assumes that the distribution of health costs is even across income groups.[7] Table 2 indicates that the average person experiences $270 in health costs due to pollution from the transportation system.

Traffic congestion is yet another significant transportation cost. Congestion costs are typically measured in proportion to people's wages. Because higher-income people earn more and tend to travel more, they bear the majority of congestion costs. Table 2 indicates that in 1991 the average individual in the highest income group lost time valued at $1,570 due to congestion, the average individual in the middle income group lost $320, and individuals in the lowest income group lost $60 to congestion.[8]

The bottom line with regard to these various costs and benefits is reflected in the distribution of net transportation benefits, or gross benefits minus costs. Table 2 shows annual net transportation benefits for income groups: the lowest income group received $650; individuals in the middle group received $1,980; and high-income individuals received $3,750. These estimates suggest the transportation system currently favors people in proportion to their income. The primary reason for this skewed distribution is the high cost of owning and operating automobiles. The direct costs of owning and operating a car absorb from 15 percent (for low income individuals) to 22 percent (for middle-income individuals) of people's disposable income. Most people spend more on their cars than they do on health care.

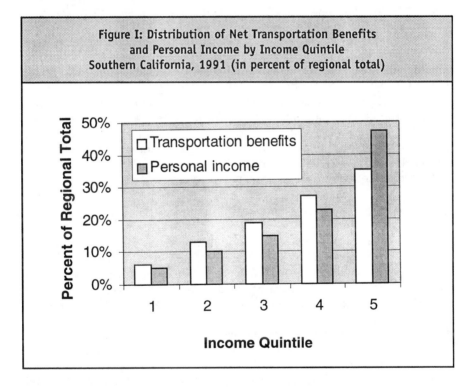

Figure I: Distribution of Net Transportation Benefits and Personal Income by Income Quintile Southern California, 1991 (in percent of regional total)

Figure 1 indicates that the 20 percent of the population in the lowest-income group receives 6 percent of the total regional transportation benefits compared to 5 percent of regional income. The middle group receives 19 percent of transportation benefits and 15 percent of income. The 20 percent of the population in the highest income group receives 35 percent of transportation benefits and 47 percent of income.

This evaluation does not reveal whether or not the existing system is fair, since there is no agreed upon standard for the level of transportation benefits that each individual needs to live independently. However, when this distribution is compared to that of Chicago, it appears that the auto-based system of Southern California imposes more hardship on low-income residents than the relatively dense and transit-rich Chicago area. Whereas in Southern California the median per capita income in the lowest income group is $4,100 and median transportation costs are $660 (16 percent of income), in Chicago the median income is higher ($5,600) and transportation costs are lower ($530, or 10 percent of income).[9] This data supports, but does not prove, the hypothesis that the cost of the car reinforces poverty.

Finally, comparing the distribution of income with the distribution of transportation benefits suggests there is reason for serious concern about transportation equity. The transportation system distributes its benefits somewhat more equally than income is distributed, but barely so for those with the lowest incomes. If anything, Figure 1 suggests the current transportation system is redistributing social wealth towards those in the middle.

This section provides some cursory estimates of both the efficiency and equity of Southern California's surface transportation system. It suggests policies are needed to increase efficiency and to promote a more equal distribution of transportation benefits. One set of policies being advocated for increasing efficiency is market-based policies that seek to charge motorists for both the pollution and the congestion they create. Although the efficiency case for these policies has been studied extensively, relatively little is known about how they would affect transportation equity. The next section of this paper examines the case for market-based transportation policies, and estimates their likely impacts on the existing distribution of transportation benefits and costs.

Market-Based Transportation Policies

Southern California's transportation problems can be thought of as resource allocation problems. From an efficiency standpoint, more resources are being used to provide mobility than is necessary. From an equity standpoint, the distribution of mobility benefits appears to leave some people with too little. The allocation of transportation resources is the result largely of market forces. Not surprisingly, therefore, policy-makers in search of efficiency solutions are considering ways of improving the efficiency of the transportation market.

In simplest terms, markets are expected to yield efficient outcomes when the price of goods reflect their full social costs. As Table 1 indicates, the price paid by motorists leaves out an estimated 23 percent of costs of automobile travel when pollution and congestion are considered. In response to low prices, individuals are consuming more transportation than is efficient. If the price people paid were higher, and if it reflected the costs of congestion and pollution, people would drive less, and pollution and congestion would diminish.

Based on this theory of market efficiency, many transportation analysts have been calling for implementation of transportation pricing policies such as congestion pricing, smog fees, VMT fees, and other variants of these policies.

Table 3: Distribution by Income Quintile of Transportation Taxes and Fees Southern California,1991 (percent of per capita median income)

	1	2	3	4	5	Ratio1:5
Federal Gas Tax	0.62%	0.56%	0.42%	0.35%	0.22%	2.9
State Gas Tax	0.73	0.65	0.49	0.42	0.25	2.9
State Sales Tax on Gasoline	0.35	0.31	0.24	0.20	0.12	2.9
State Motor Vehicle License Fees	0.52	0.40	0.41	0.49	0.40	1.3
State Registration & Other Fees	0.34	0.26	0.20	0.16	0.10	3.5
Retail Sales Tax	0.80	0.58	0.48	0.42	0.28	2.9
All Transportation Taxes	3.35%	2.75%	2.24%	2.03%	1.36%	2.5

Source: Efficiency and Fairness on the Road

Table 4: Comparison of Transportation Benefits and Costs With and Without a Five-cent VMT Fee Southern California, 1991(in billions of dollars)

	Current Transportation System	$.05 per Mile VMT Fee	Change
Benefits			
automobile travel	$78.2	$74.3	($4.0)
public transit	1.5	1.9	0.4
total benefits	$79.7	$76.2	($3.5)
Costs			
automobile expenses	$34.1	$30.9	($3.2)
transit fares	0.3	0.4	0.1
taxes	4.2	3.9	(0.3)
air pollution	3.7	2.2	(1.5)
congestion	7.7	5.7	(2.0)
VMT fee	-------		4.5
new revenues	-------	(4.1)	0.4
total costs	$50.1	$43.5	($6.6)
Net Benefits	$29.6	$32.7	$3.0

Source: Efficiency and Fairness on the Road

Congestion pricing seeks to assess time of day (and place) prices to road-use similar to the way the long-distance telephone service is charged (higher prices during the peak period and lower prices in the off-peak). Smog fees seek to charge people for their auto use according to the amount of pollution they emit — those who drive farthest and drive dirty cars would pay the most. A VMT fee is less precisely targeted than congestion pricing or smog fees but arguably would be easier to implement. For each of these fees it is imagined that they would be imposed and collected by some government agency, using advanced technologies that would eliminate the need for tollbooths.

Generally speaking, the efficiency aspects of these policies have been widely studied, while the equity aspects are poorly understood. This section briefly covers the likely efficiency and distributional impacts of one sample market-based policy, a five-cent per mile VMT fee. Such a fee would be roughly equivalent to a $1.25 per gallon gas tax.[10] This section analyzes the likely effects of the fee on the efficiency estimate in Table 1 and on the distributional estimates in Table 2.

Efficiency of a Five-Cent per Mile VMT Fee

Market-based efficiency fees will probably result in lower total vehicular travel. While a reduction in total vehicular travel may on balance be a desirable social goal, the loss of travel by itself does impose a loss of trips that provided people with some utility. Hence efficiency fees would result in a reduction of gross mobility benefits. Using an advanced travel forecasting model, TRIPS, it was estimated that a five-cent per mile VMT fee would reduce total vehicle miles traveled in Southern California by approximately 11 percent.[11] The value of these lost trips, using the same willingness-to-pay methodology described earlier, is roughly $4 billion (Table 4). The TRIPS model also estimated that roughly one out of ten of these forgone automobile trips would shift onto transit. The value of the additional transit trips is estimated to be $.4 billion. Thus the overall effect of the fee would be to reduce gross mobility benefits by $3.5 billion (rounded) from $79.7 to $76.2 billion per year.

Because people would travel less they would also spend less on their automobiles. Over the long run, such a fee would not only reduce the amount people use their cars but it would also induce some people to choose to not own a car (or a second or third car). According to the TRIPS model, the five-cent per mile fee would reduce total spending on cars by $3.2 billion, from $34.1 billion to $30.9 billion per year (Table 4). Because transit ridership would go up, roughly $.1 billion more would be spent on transit fares. The reduced use of automobiles would also reduce the amount people pay in existing transportation taxes such as the gas tax and vehicle license fees. Table 4 indicates that spending on taxes would decline by $.3 billion.

Since the primary purpose of implementing efficiency fees is to reduce pollution and congestion, it is important that the five-cent per mile fee have that effect. Table 4 indicates that health costs associated with transportation-related air pollution would decline from $3.7 billion to $2.2 billion for a reduction of $1.5 billion. This improvement stems from a 10-percent reduction in ozone precursors and an 11-percent reduction in particulate pollution.[12] Thus, the impact of the fee on pollution would be significant. The 11-percent reduction in VMT would lead to a 29-percent reduction in hours of congestion delay.[13] Total congestion costs would be reduced by $2 billion from $7.7 billion to $5.7 billion annually (Table 4).[14]

In addition to these changes in benefits and costs, the efficiency fee in and of itself represents a new cost. A five-cent per mile VMT fee would cost motorists roughly $4.5 billion per year (roughly the same amount generated by the existing system of transportation taxes and fees), all of which would end up in the public treasury. There is no single obvious purpose for which government should spend this money. Presumably it could be reinvested in transportation, spent on other general government programs, or returned to taxpayers through tax offsets. It is beyond the scope of this paper to evaluate those options. For purposes of this cost-benefit analysis, it is assumed that each dollar paid is subsequently returned to the taxpayers. Thus the net effect of the fee would be zero, except for the cost of administering the fee collection and paying for the transit expansions needed to accommodate the additional transit demand. Adjusting for these expenses, Table 4 indicates that the net effect of the fee would be a new cost to motorists of $.4 billion.

Therefore, the total impact of the five-cent per mile VMT fee would be to reduce gross mobility benefits by $3.5 billion, reduce gross transportation costs by $6.6 billion, leaving a net result of a $3-billion (rounded) increase in annual net benefits (Table 4). This analysis demonstrates why policy-makers are considering implementing efficiency fees. From a system-wide efficiency perspective, a five-cent per mile fee would improve the performance of Southern California's transportation system by 10 percent.

Equity of a Five-Cent per Mile VMT Fee

The analysis summarized in Table 4 persuades many that implementation of transportation efficiency fees is a good idea. As presented, however, it does not address who would benefit and who would not. Although not everyone need benefit for an efficiency policy to be desirable, it is critical that those who already struggle to make vital trips not face even more barriers to travel.

Table 5 presents the estimated impact of a five-cent per mile VMT fee across the five equally-sized income groups examined in the first section of this chapter. The fee would reduce travel in all income groups, but more so from the low-income groups. The average individual in the lowest income group would lose $250 worth of travel per year, compared to $340 for individuals in the middle group, and $150 for individuals in the highest income group. Although region-wide VMT fees would drop by 11 percent, automobile travel by those in the lowest income group would drop by 29 percent, middle-income individuals would reduce auto travel by 12 percent, and those in the highest income group would reduce their travel by only 3 percent. Individuals in all income groups would recover some of those trips on transit, but relatively little.

These results confirm what many people intuitively suspect — that efficiency fees would most likely fall hardest on those who can least afford them. In addition to reducing the travel of the poor the most, it is plausible that since the poor currently take relatively fewer leisure trips than the affluent, the trips given

Table 5 Distribution by Income Quintile Comparision of Transportation Benefits and Costs With and Without a Five-cent per Mile VMT Fee Southern California, 1991 (in annual per capita dollars)						
		Income Quintile				
		1	**2**	**3**	**4**	**5**
Current System:	**Net Benefits**	$ 650	$1,430	$1,980	$2,880	$3,750
Change in:	**Benefits**					
	automobile travel	($250)	($380)	($340)	($310)	($150)
	public transit	30	40	40	20	20
	total benefits	($220)	($340)	($300)	($290)	($130)
	Costs					
	automobile expenses	($160)	($310)	($280)	($270)	($150)
	transit fares*	10	10	0	0	0
	taxes	(30)	(30)	(30)	(20)	0
	air pollution	(110)	(110)	(110)	(110)	(110)
	congestion	(30)	(70)	(90)	(180)	(350)
	new efficiency fee	110	230	300	420	570
	new public revenue	(100)	(210)	(270)	(380)	(510)
	total costs	($310)	($490)	($480)	($540)	($550)
	Net Benefits	$90	$150	$180	$250	$420
With $.05 VMT Fee	**Net Benefits**	$740	$1,580	$2,160	$3,130	$4,170

Source: Efficiency and Fairness on the Road
* Per capita transit fare costs do not show an increase for some income groups in part because all figures are rounded off to the nearest $10.

up by the poor would be vital ones, such as to work, school or medical services. Clearly, if efficiency fees are going to be implemented fairly, some means must be found to either reduce their impact on the poor, to provide mobility alternatives for the poor, or both.

The impact of the five-cent per mile VMT fee on the costs paid by individuals, such as on cars, taxes and health costs, is also indicated in Table 5. With respect to expenditures on cars, the second and middle groups save the most

($310 and $280 per person per year respectively) in response to the fee based on both the amount of travel they forgo and the value they place on their travel. Individuals in the first and second groups consume enough transit that their transit-fare costs increase noticeably (Table 5). The incidence of transportation taxes would go down from $20 to $30 per person in all income groups except the highest income group (whose individuals do not reduce their travel by much, so they continue to pay roughly the same amount of transportation taxes).

The significant air pollution reduction expected from a five-cent per mile fee is estimated to benefit people in all income groups equally, saving individuals roughly $110 per year in health damages (Table 5). Reduced congestion costs are enjoyed primarily by high-income individuals, who would save $350 per year. This result reflects the fact that they travel the most and therefore would experience the time savings more than individuals in other income groups. The average person in the middle income group would save $90 per year in reduced congestion costs, and individuals in the lowest income group would save the least, an average of $30 per person per year. Finally, assuming that the efficiency fees are returned to drivers either through offsetting tax reductions or through valued public services, most individuals would experience a modest cost increase due to the fee (Table 5).

The bottom-line net impact of this evaluation indicates that the average person in each income group would be better off as a result of the five-cent per mile VMT fee. This result is plausible for the upper three, perhaps four, income groups, but it is highly questionable for the lowest income group. The time savings and reduced exposure to pollution probably offset the lost travel for individuals with middle to high incomes, since they don't lose much travel, and what they do lose are probably
discretionary trips. For low-income travelers, however, it is very difficult to imagine that the lost access — a 29 percent reduction in trips from an already very low level of travel — could justify the reduced air pollution and congestion costs.[15]

Furthermore, even if every income group did gain from the five-cent per mile fee, one still cannot conclusively prove that the fee is equitable. The resulting distribution of benefits still heavily favors the higher- income groups. Moreover, it remains unclear whether all people would have access to the transportation services they need to be self-sufficient. Clarity on these two points can come only after an equity standard of mobility and access is established and can be used to gauge the equity of each person's situation.

Alternative Market-Based Policy Designs

The prior section analyzed in detail one potential efficiency fee, a five-cent per mile VMT fee. There are a great number of variations between this and other fee types, and for any fee type there are a host of implementation options that would significantly affect how the policy would work and who it would impact. These alternatives are equally important for both efficiency and equity goals, but will be considered here only for their potential to reduce the adverse equity impacts identified in the prior section. The three variations considered in this section are the use to which fee revenues are put, the potential for using lifeline pricing, and the type of fee implemented.

Transportation efficiency fees have the potential to generate large amounts of public funds. Although the five-cent per mile fee considered above, which would generate as much public revenue as the existing system of transportation taxes does, would generate perhaps more than any other imaginable fee, other fees would still generate substantial amounts. The issue of what to do with these revenues is perhaps one of the most pressing questions regarding the desirability of using efficiency policies. Presuming the public will again trust public institutions to put money to good use, it is entirely unclear how the public would choose to have the funds spent. If they are used to reduce other taxes, especially regressive taxes such as the sales tax, low-income individuals could find pricing policies to their advantage. Alternatively, it is likely that efficiency policies will gain acceptance only if they are accompanied by some level of investment in alternatives to the car. Conceivably, revenues from efficiency fees could be invested in transit services designed especially to benefit low-income travelers.

While it is entirely possible that targeted investment of fee revenues could make the program acceptable or even desirable from a low-income standpoint, the politics of public budgets, especially recently, tend to reduce the chances of this outcome being realized. Nonetheless, the fairness of transportation efficiency fees cannot be judged without specific plans for how the resulting revenues would be used.

Another means of mitigating adverse impacts on the poor is the use of lifeline pricing. The potential for charging different amounts to different people is fairly easy to imagine given the high technology meters that are envisioned for implementation of market-based transportation fees. The most complete proposal to date, which is for peak-period pricing on the San Francisco-Oakland Bay Bridge, called for exempting motorists who earned 150 percent of the poverty level. The policy was based on the lifeline pricing systems used by the local phone and electric utilities, and would have required candidates for the bridge discount to be certified through the same process used by the utilities. If they are administratively feasible, as was the case with the Bay Bridge, lifeline pricing systems present one promising method for reducing the inequities of transportation efficiency fees.

Lastly, different types of fees affect different users. The flat VMT fee analyzed in the second section would have affected every motorist. Peak-period highway pricing would affect only those people who use the highways during rush hours. Smog fees would fall hardest on those who drive the most and those who drive the dirtiest cars.

The first test case of congestion pricing in the United States was expected to come on-line in late 1995 on a private toll road connecting Orange and Riverside counties in Southern California. The new road runs parallel to an existing freeway and will provide motorists the alternative of choosing the freeway with congestion or the tollway without congestion. This variation of efficiency fees will have no detrimental impact on low-income motorists, although some argue that the new road is damaging in that it sets a precedent for a two-tiered transportation system.

Conclusion

In conclusion, the equity impacts of efficiency fees are likely to be significant. If the fees are implemented without regard to equity, they could have significant adverse impacts on individuals who already struggle to make vital trips to work, school and services. On the other hand, if designed with explicit equity objectives in mind, efficiency fees could improve mobility for all people.

Given the relative lack of attention given to transportation equity compared to efficiency, a priority of equity advocates should be to clarify the mobility needs and goals for those individuals who are currently underserved. Although concerns for the transit-dependent have long been voiced before transit operating agencies, relatively little is heard about the effects of the automobile-based transportation system on people with limited economic means.

In the long run, any reforms that break down the monopoly that the automobile has on mobility, and that increase the diversity of mobility options available, is desirable from an equity and an efficiency standpoint. By eliminating implicit subsidies to the car, efficiency policies have the potential to level the playing field whereby higher-occupancy modes can compete. These modes should not only cost less than the single-occupant car, but they should also result in reduced environmental harm, reduced congestion, and reduced need for costly road expansions that devastate human and wild habitats alike.

The jury is out on whether market-based transportation policies will be implemented on a broad scale. If they are, they will, one way or another, affect the distribution of mobility and access benefits among different demographic groups. It is imperative that explicit distributional objectives be identified and advocated before the policy debate moves much further ahead.

Confronting Transit Racism in Los Angeles

Eric Mann

A dramatic increase in the cost of public transportation in Los Angeles County was challenged in 1994 by advocacy groups on behalf of the county's 500,000 minority poor. On September 1, the Labor/Community Strategy Center and its Bus Riders Union initiated a class action civil rights suit, and were joined by co-plaintiffs, the Korean Immigrant Workers' Advocates, the Southern Christian Leadership Conference, and represented by the NAACP Legal Defense and Educational Fund. We challenged the proposed imposition by the Los Angeles County MTA of policies that would: increase the one-way cash fare for a bus ride from $1.10 to $1.35; eliminate the existing monthly bus pass (which had been set at $42 per month for unlimited use) so that passengers would have to purchase each ride separately; and set up a zone system on the Blue Line rail system that would raise the fares more than 100 percent for more than 50 percent of the passengers.

Such increased costs would have had a disproportionate and irreparable impact on the county's minority communities and the bus-riding public, of whom more than 80 percent are Latino, African-American, Asian/Pacific Islander, and Native American. Moreover, by the MTA's own statistics, "MTA riders are profoundly poor . . . over 60 percent of MTA riders reside in households with total incomes under $15,000." A typical MTA rider is a person of color (Latino or African-American/black), in her twenties, with a household income under $15,000 and no car available to use in lieu of public transit. This results in substantially decreased mobility for the vast majority of MTA's 350,000 daily bus riders who take an average of 2.5 trips a day — for a total of 1.3 million rides.

Combined with very high subsidies for commuter rail lines to predominantly white suburban areas, the proposed MTA policies violated Title VI of the Civil Rights Act of 1964, which mandates that federally funded projects cannot "exclude from participation," "deny the benefits of" or "discriminate based on race, color, or national origin" against African-Americans and all people of color.

After two years of hearings and negotiations, the class-action suit was settled out of court. Weekly, biweekly, and monthly bus passes are now affordable for the transit-dependent in Los Angeles, and the MTA committed to increase buses and service. The following account details the struggles and challenges to win those hard-earned rights.

The Context

Los Angeles County is a multiracial political jurisdiction of 8.7 million residents, of whom 3.4 million are white or Anglo, 3.1 million are Latino, 1.1 million are African- American, and 1.1 million are Asian/Pacific Islander (according to 1990 census data). These racial demographics are heavily overlaid with a disproportionate percentage of urban poverty. For example, there are 500,000 workers in Los Angeles County who work an entire year for less than $10,000, of whom more than 75 percent are Latino, African-American, and Asian-American. Similarly, unemployment levels for black men in South Central Los Angeles between the ages of eighteen to thirty-five are more than 55 percent.

There is a causal relationship between mobility and a potential escape from poverty. The MTA bus system is a critical link in ameliorating or exacerbating that situation. The vast majority of Los Angeles County's low-income minority residents live in an inner-city core in the communities of South Central Los Angeles, Pico Union, East Los Angeles, Koreatown, the southeast corridor of Vernon, Commerce, and Downey, and the Harbor communities of Wilmington, Harbor City, and San Pedro.

For many years, the city's previous "two-tiered" transit system was divided between private transportation (cars) and public transportation (buses). While most Angelenos of all races drove cars, the public transportation system — run for many years by the Southern California Rapid Transit District (RTD) — was understood to be the avenue of last resort for the urban poor, the elderly, the disabled, and students; and as the city's urban poor became increasingly Latino, black, and Asian Pacific Islander, so did the composition of most of the bus ridership.

Even within the bus system, however, racial discrimination was reflected in policy. For many years, bus lines to predominantly white suburbs from Pasadena to the San Gabriel Valley to the San Fernando Valley had better service, more direct express routes, and newer buses. This was justified with the argument that mass transit in the suburbs had to compete with auto use, whereas for the urban poor, most of whom were minority group members, many of them were "transit-dependent" since they could not afford to purchase a car. For many years, the fight of the city's low-income minority communities for equal protection of the law and equal access to public services took place within the Rapid Transit District (RTD), the bus system that later became part of the MTA (the unified agency that handled most of Los Angeles' public transit, which was mostly a bus system).

Formation of the MTA and the Rail Project

With the passage of Proposition A and Proposition C in 1980, there was a move to supplement Los Angeles' bus system with high-speed rail projects through sales tax revenues. The advantage of the projects was to move a relatively small number of people in a straight line at a relatively high speed to and from areas of high concentration. But Los Angeles County, covering more than

4,000 square miles (the MTA covers an area of more than 1,400 square miles) has few areas of density to justify the high costs of rail construction. Even if the entire system was built (which would be unlikely, considering the huge costs and MTA's fiscal crisis), the projected rail system would only serve 11 percent of the population who would live within a half mile of a rail station. Given these structural constraints, most transportation planners are split between the view that rail is an outright misuse of public funds for a city like Los Angeles, and that rail is at best a supplementary component to the bus system.

In actuality, the MTA is attempting to construct a 400-mile rail system with fewer than 250 stops, while the bus system covers approximately 4,000 miles with more than 30,000 stops. Thus, any effort to make rail the centerpiece of a mass-transit system defies the mandate of the MTA to develop rational and cost-effective policies to serve the vast majority of mass-transit riders, regardless of race, color, or national origin.

These issues of race-blind transportation analysis are directly relevant to the issues of transportation equity and the "equal protection" provisions of the Fourteenth Amendment, and the "non-discriminatory" provisions of federally-funded programs under Title VI of the Civil Rights Act. Any decisions to "overbuild" rail projects in a way to not supplement but to actually defund, destabilize, and drive riders off mass transit with fare increases and service cuts is racially discriminatory in both intent and effect, considering that:

- the MTA was warned by many transit planners that rail projects had to supplement and enhance the bus system;
- the bus system was understood to serve the vast majority of mass transit riders, while the rail system presently serves less than 5 percent of the riders served by bus; and
- the vast majority of mass transit riders are minority group members.

With the formation of the Los Angeles County Transportation Commission (LACTC) in 1976, two complementary but essentially competitive public agencies were formed to handle Los Angeles' transit system — the MTA for the buses and the LACTC primarily for the rail lines. This institutionalization of a "bus" versus "rail" structure led to a growing polarization of the funding for predominantly low-income inner-city communities and predominantly higher-income and white suburban communities. Moreover, since the LACTC was given financial control over the RTD, the discriminatory policies that took the form of a "rail" versus "bus" debate were institutionalized from the beginning.

With the passage in 1980, of Proposition A a half-cent sales tax providing $340 million per year in transit funds, there was a temporary boost to the bus system. For the first three years after Proposition A passed, bus fares were reduced from eighty-five cents to fifty cents (using 20 percent of Proposition A funds). This decreased fare generated, to the surprise of some, dramatically increased bus ridership — showing that in a city of very low-income people (the vast majority of whom are people of color and 57 percent of whom are female), the relationship between fare structure and overall bus ridership is highly volatile: fare decreases lead to significant increases in ridership while fare increases lead to significant decreases in ridership.

Annual ridership rose from a low in 1982 of 354 million unlinked one-way trips a year, just before the additional fare subsidy was implemented, to a peak of 497 million in 1985, the last year of the subsidy. Since 1985, the funds previously dedicated to bus-fare subsidies were used for rail construction (as mandated by the proposition), but additional discretionary funds (abundantly available) were never sought to maintain the fifty-cent fare. Instead, the fare returned to eighty-five cents and then $1.10. Moreover, service cuts paralleled fare increases. In fiscal year 1988, bus service covered 93 million revenue vehicle miles. In 1993 that figure fell to 81.8 million. The 1997 projection is 78 million.

As expected, with increased fares and decreased service (less frequent buses, longer waits between transfers and greater security problems), bus ridership has plummeted more than 20 percent to below 376 million rides per year. The latest round of proposed fare increases and service cuts are projected, by the MTA itself, to reduce ridership another 6 percent.

Throughout this decline of service and ridership, the existence of the RTD at least provided an organized constituency that could fight for equity, or at least less discrimination, with the more powerful LACTC that held its purse strings. But fueled with Propositions A and C dollars, and having the fiscal authority to often determine what was discretionary, the LACTC became a powerful structure in which rail lines, rail contracts, and rail ridership — as small as it was — was the overwhelming priority.

The structuring of Propositions A and C attempted to create clear guidelines for the dispersal of funds between bus and rail. Proposition A mandated:

- 35 percent for rail construction and operations;
- 40 percent discretionary transit money for bus or rail; and
- 25 percent for transit flows to cities (essentially funds to individual cities to help create a mandate for the passage of the proposition).
  Proposition C mandated:
- 40 percent discretionary for transit, ridesharing, and bicycle programs;
- 25 percent for streets and highways (primarily for high occupancy vehicle lanes);
- 20 percent discretionary for local governments;
- 10 percent for commuter rail or high-speed buses on freeways; and
- 5% for transit security.

As can be seen, a great deal of these funds are not truly "locked in," but allow enormous flexibility and discretionary spending. Thus, for the MTA to exercise this "discretion" by spending the vast majority of funds on rail projects, while consistently defunding the bus system, claiming business hardship, involves both malfeasance (by undermining even the chance of a mass transit system to serve the vast majority of public transit riders) and racial discrimination against low-income minority bus riders. This is a classic Title VI violation, and reflects how government rewards primarily white and affluent constituencies, and punishes primarily low-income, people-of-color constituencies.

The Fight for Transportation Equity

Initiated in 1989, the Strategy Center began a transportation equity project in 1991, focusing its work on the needs of working people, low-income people, and bus riders. Our work was motivated by a philosophy of environmental justice, the primacy of the needs of the working class, and a challenge to the corporate domination of society — especially in what should be the "public arena." After a year of intense study, our vision of mass transportation involved the Four Pillars Strategy and we focused on a Billions for Buses Campaign. Soon after, the battle over discretionary funding and racial discrimination took center stage.

In the fall of 1992, RTD experienced a budget shortfall of $59 million. Turning to LACTC, RTD staff argued that they had already made all necessary efficiencies; moreover, bus fares constituted about 35 percent of the total costs of operation — a figure far higher than that of rail. RTD asked LACTC to allocate $59 million from Proposition C discretionary funds to cover the shortfall.

The Strategy Center and Bus Riders Union project argued as well that since Proposition A and C funds came from the sales taxes of all Los Angeles residents, and there were 1.3 million riders on the bus system and less than 65,000 riders on rail projects, the defunding of the RTD to create a "budget shortfall" was an illegal use of public funds; the defunding benefited a small rail ridership and punished bus riders. The theme of taking public funds specifically paid for by all Angelenos and using them to fund the suburbs and defund the inner city was raised explicitly by the Strategy Center.

Through our intervention, the vast majority of the shortfall was restored without the threatened alternatives of fare increases and service cuts, but rather than finding discretionary funds from possible rail projects, the LACTC took some of those funds from future bus purchases. Even though there was no fare increase at this time, the structure of the argument was framed: the LACTC wanted to use discretionary funds for rail projects and thereby create shortfalls in bus funding that would be solved through fare increases and service cuts.

In 1992, the California State legislature passed AB 152 that established the MTA. Partially as a result of this continued conflict between the two transit agencies, it proposed their merger into a new mega-agency, the Metropolitan Transportation Authority (MTA). There were two points of view as to whether the creation of the MTA would reduce or exacerbate the already two-tiered, unequal, and racially discriminatory transit policies. One argued that the existence of the RTD offered a chance for minority communities to have a smaller budget but at least some control over it; whereas with the formation of the MTA, the confiscation of bus funding for rail projects would be accelerated under one institutional framework, and discriminatory impacts would be increased. The other argued that with the creation of the MTA, the goal of a coordinated, coherent transit agency serving all Angelenos equally and fairly regardless of race would at least be possible, since the agency would have to coordinate rail and bus, white and minority, suburbs and inner cities, rich and poor. For the low-income minority bus riders, the vast majority served by the MTA system, this debate was moot — the legislature went on to establish the MTA, and the battle for transportation equity moved full force to the MTA.

The new agency conducted a national search, and hired Franklin White, formerly commissioner of the New York State Department of Transportation. Early in his tenure, the Strategy Center arranged a cordial meeting at which its representatives, and those of Concerned Citizens of South Central Los Angeles, the Southern Christian Leadership Conference, and other community groups urged Mr. White to protect and expand the bus system. Strategy Center representatives argued that there was an urgent need for a moratorium on rail spending because of cost overruns, structural problems in rail construction, and an impending deficit that would threaten the urgently needed expansion of bus service. It is important to emphasize that the first intervention on the issue of business necessity came from the Strategy Center.

In July,1993, we urged the MTA to:

- allocate $1 billion in addition to farebox revenue per year to the bus system, an attempt to increase service in the most overcrowded bus system in the United States;
- impose a moratorium on rail projects except for those the MTA is legally obligated to pay in fiscal year 1992-1993.
- make a comprehensive assessment of the financial resources required to renew old and create new infrastructure to support the bus system.

The Strategy Center asked the MTA to exercise fiscal restraint and responsibility; all projects must be comprehensively scrutinized so that if the agency promised to both expand bus service and rail service but did not have the funds, hard choices would be subject to democratic and non-discriminatory review.

Increasing Fares, Ending Bus Passes, and Cutting Services

Partially because of the Strategy Center's intervention, CEO White agreed to a proposal to expand bus service on forty of the most overcrowded bus lines, but did not agree to a moratorium on rail construction to find ways to pay for it. White told the *Los Angeles Times*:

"There is genuine concern about opening glossy new rail lines while the condition of the inner-city bus rider continues to deteriorate. This board is determined to not let bus conditions deteriorate as a consequence of the rail construction effort and they are showing it very clearly."

The Strategy Center agreed with the sentiment, but not the content. As director of the Strategy Center, I was quoted in the same newspaper: "In return for giving us forty buses they want to sign off on all rail construction."

In August, 1993, as the MTA approved a $3.7-billion budget, it allocated $97 million for a Pasadena Blue Line rail extension still on the drawing board; this followed the pattern of allocating the "first leg" of rail projects with an $871-million projected budget (not even counting the purchasing of rail cars or cost overruns), with no plan as to how to complete or even extend the project in the following years. The line would merely compete with existing bus routes while taking away funds for urgently needed bus service. Moreover, after originally allocating $40 million from rail funds that it did not have, the MTA agreed to a motion for an additional $57 million, after being instructed by Mayor Richard Riordan that they should "find ways" to find the money. Alternate board member Antonio Villaraigosa begged the board to not spend one of the last pots of discretionary funds, but was overridden by the entire board.

As the *Los Angeles Business Journal* reported (August 30, 1993):

> "Representatives from the Labor/Community Strategy Center issued a demand that the MTA spend $1.5 billion per year for five years on the buses, with a moratorium on rail contract awards until long-range funding is locked in for the bus system.
>
> 'MTA politics have been reduced to a race against time by several board members to get rail lines in their district before the money runs out,' said Lisa Hoyos of the Strategy Center. The demand was endorsed by several speakers including a variety of politicians.
>
> 'Clearly, buses are the stepchild in Los Angeles County,' said Congressman Xavier Becerra (D. Los-Angeles.) The MTA did not even discuss the center's demand."

This public discussion raises the following three points relevant to the need for the temporary restraining order:

1. There was a widespread public discussion about a deteriorating inner-city bus system and buses being the "stepchild" of the MTA. A separate and unequal, overwhelmingly minority, inner-city bus ridership receiving second class and deteriorating service was openly acknowledged by the CEO of the MTA, a U.S. congressman, and the media.

2. Aggressive efforts were made in 1993 to force the MTA within its normal functioning to place a moratorium on funding pending a full accounting; the agency was warned that its expenditures would cause future fare increases and service cuts.

3. The MTA pushed ahead with funding for rail projects despite this warning, and according to the business journal, refused to even discuss the motion we presented.

In December 1993, Assemblyman Richard Katz, who had brought the MTA into existence through state law, criticized the MTA for again sacrificing the needs of inner-city, overwhelmingly minority bus riders:

> "The MTA was pressured last week to fix up its bus fleet. . . . [Richard Katz], chairman of the Assembly Transportation Committee, said he opposes legislation to raise the cap on the MTA's bond-issuing capacity to build more rail lines.
>
> Katz called MTA Chief Executive Franklin White to task for pursuing legislation to increase the MTA's bonding capacity when the bonds would have to be paid back using sales tax revenue that could be better spent focusing on the deteriorating inner-city bus system. . . . Franklin White admitted that, 'there was no money available to transfer from rail construction to bus operations,' saying that all flexible funds were 'spoken for with political commitments.'

Katz challenged that premise, saying that the MTA clearly was continuing to commit money to rail projects at the expense of the ailing bus fleet: . . 'People in the inner city are not getting the service that they need.'"

Again, before the recent fare increases and service cuts, there was a publicly understood and repeated criticism of the agency, this time by the very state legislator who authored the bill that created it, linking bus deterioration; the inner city (understood to be overwhelmingly minority); the diversion of sales tax revenue from bus to rail; fiscal mismanagement; irresponsibility in abdicating even the attempt to provide equality and equity in the mass transit system; and acknowledgement by the board's CEO that board politics were responsible for the diversion of funds from under-represented, inner-city communities.

Public Outrage About the Proposed Fare Increases

Mandated by federal law, the MTA held a public hearing April 23, 1994 on its proposed fare increases and service cuts. What followed was an unprecedented outpouring of public concern from a wide variety of organizations representing many constituencies for whom the proposed fare increases would constitute irreparable harm. Many people testified about the unworkability of the existing MTA fares and services before any changes were proposed:

- Elderly groups testified that because the MTA buses are so slow in coming, and connections and transfers are so difficult, they cannot travel on the buses at night and feel imprisoned in their homes.
- Low-income workers explained that the existing bus schedules are so unreliable that they have to leave for work hours before they have to report, for fear of being late and losing their jobs.
- Representatives of low-income workers testified that for workers making $10,000 to $15,000, even the $42 monthly bus pass was a lot of money and that any increases in the bus pass (let alone its elimination) would cause significant hardship.
- Many blind groups talked about the difficulties and dangers of standing on street corners waiting for buses for almost an hour, and urged the MTA to increase bus service.
- Many night-shift workers, such as janitors and service workers, talked about waiting an hour for a bus; they described having to travel as much as two hours by bus to locations outside the inner city looking for better-paying work.
- Families talked about the expenses of buying bus passes for two children (students) and two adults on one income of less than $15,000; they urged the MTA to find other alternatives to raising fares and decreasing services.

Many of the MTA board members did not attend the hearing, or attended for only an hour or two, and talked to each other during most of the testimony. When many of the 800 people asked the MTA board members to respond to their concerns, they were told that since it was a "public hearing," the board was there to listen, not to respond.

The MTA Votes for Discriminatory Funding that Violates Equal Access to Transportation

Within the scope of one week, the discriminatory policies of the MTA came into full play. On July 14, 1994, the MTA board voted to:

- raise the bus fare from $1.10 to $1.35 — a 23-percent increase;
- eliminate the $42-per-month working people's pass;
- institute a ninety-cent bus token that can be purchased at selected outlets (not on the bus itself); and
- reduce bus service on several bus lines.

The MTA argued that those fare increases and service cuts would save the agency $32 million per year out of a total budget of $2.9 billion.

Los Angeles Times reporter Bill Boyarsky attended the meeting. He wrote a scathing critique of the MTA board, not primarily for its policies, but for the myriad violations of due process that characterized the meeting:

"The MTA board's conduct while pushing through a fare increase at a meeting Wednesday was so outrageous that it's hard to single out its most offensive act. . . .

The MTA board was rude to those testifying against the fare increase. Members and aides walked around the rostrum, chatting as if it were a cocktail party. . . . I've seen such inattention at other legislative meetings, but never to this degree. One speaker made a futile attempt to attract the attention of the board members. Pointing to some of the protesters, she said, 'This is their first experience at a public meeting. Is this the way you want to treat them?' She was ignored.

One legal-minded MTA critic told me he was particularly irked by the way the board ignored the Brown Act, which requires government agencies to conduct their business openly. No copies of the final fare increase proposal, devised by Los Angeles County Supervisor Gloria Molina, were made available to the audience, a step required by the Brown Act. . . . Finally, there was the board's refusal to grant opponents of the increase another ten minutes to speak. . . .

The MTA's actions hurt the poor in ways that have longterm effects. You could see this at Wednesday's hearing. Some of the speakers said they used adult student passes to attend night school to learn English, and the increase would make the trip to class more expensive. 'We want to have a better life,' one of them said. 'We want to speak with the teachers and help [our children] with their homework.'"[1]

The following week, the MTA approved a $2.9-million 1994/95 budget that included an expenditure of $123 million for the Pasadena Blue Line light-rail system. The $123-million expenditure was virtually identical to the MTA's stated $126-million operating deficit.

Besides the expenditure of $62 million directly for the Pasadena line, the MTA diverted:

- $32.8 million from reserves created from high occupancy vehicle projects expected to be completed under budget (anticipated reserves on projects not yet initiated);
- $18 million from a fund used for message signs, sensors, and other traffic operations; and
- $10 million in capital operating funds.

This budget validated our charges that budget shortfalls for bus operations are always presented as written in stone, whereas budget shortfalls for rail projects are always overcome by "discretionary" maneuvering of funds that a week before did not seem to exist.

The board voted these expenditures over the warnings of CEO White. As the *Los Angeles Times* reported, White warned the board:

"This organization is broke and has been broke for the last three years. This is not a cash management issue. If money from the high occupancy vehicle fund is taken, from where will it be replaced? Last year should have taught us that we have to get back to a sensible policy, which is don't spend money we don't have."

White's statements verified many of our charges:

- When we asked the MTA not to spend $57 million in discretionary funds for the Pasadena line and other rail projects, there was already a structural crisis of overspending on rail projects that demanded a moratorium to protect the bus system.
- The MTA is spending money they don't have for rail projects, while imposing fare increases upon a ridership of whom more than 60 percent have a family income under $15,000, and more than 80 percent are in the minority.
- Thus, the two-tiered, separate but unequal policies of the MTA are using a $2.9-billion annual budget to undermine the functioning of the mass transit system, and to subject a low-income minority ridership to undue hardship and discriminatory impact.

On September 1, 1994, we challenged the MTA's policies by launching a class action civil rights suit. Judge Terry Hatter issued a temporary restraining order and stopped the MTA from increasing bus fares, which held for six months.[2] Then, in a pre-trial compromise between the Strategy Center and the MTA, the MTA agreed to drop the price of the monthly bus pass from $60 to $49, but to raise the one-way bus fare to $1.35 — protecting most those who used the bus most, the transit-dependent.

Reaching a Settlement

Before an out-of-court settlement was finally reached in 1996, terms of the agreement were negotiated and disputed at length. Throughout the mediation process, the Strategy Center, Bus Riders Union and our attorneys, the NAACP Legal Defense and Educational Fund, had reasonably similar assessments warranting an out-of-court settlement. However, at the eleventh hour, we disagreed with our attorneys about the final terms of the class-action settlement. Specifically, new language was introduced into a draft settlement stating that, if the MTA was able to find ways to restrict the $42 monthly general bus pass to low-income people, it would be able to raise the price of the general pass as high as it wanted for everyone else.

Moreover, while every other component of the proposed settlement would be subject to a four-step process (discussion and debate in a joint working group, efforts to resolve disagreements among the attorneys, submission to a special master to resolve the dispute, and ultimate resolution by the court), the language about a possible low-income pass seemed to indicate that the MTA, after merely "consulting" with the proposed joint working group, could essentially impose new fares.

We were adamant that the final terms of the settlement had to be changed. Moreover, we had brought this suit on behalf of all 350,000 bus riders as a class, and had never advocated any remedy that pitted one group of bus riders against another. The Legal Defence Fund attorneys assessed that, even with the unclear provision, the agreement was in the best interests of the class and filed the agreement with the court.

However, if we did not immediately challenge the efforts to turn a $42 bus pass for all bus riders into one restricted to low-income people who would show documentation, and if we did not directly challenge the MTA's implied right to both create a two-tiered pass system and do so outside the procedural constraints of a consent decree, we would be in danger of signing away our rights to challenge it later. We feared that if we did not file an objection, we would be saddled with language that could unravel significant parts of the agreement even before it began, and weaken our power to protect the pass prices for all bus riders.

The Strategy Center, Bus Riders Union, and Legal Defense Fund decided to handle this problem through a "limited substitution of counsel." As such, for the limited duration of a fairness hearing, and the limited objective of challenging one key component of the agreement, we would be represented by attorney Amos Dyson, a Strategy Center and Bus Riders Union member. We would ask the judge to indicate to the MTA that no provision of the agreement could be changed without submission to the special master and eventually the court, and to record specific and vigorous objections to a two-tiered bus-pass system.

We consulted broadly throughout the United States before our challenge. We received significant support from several constitutional and civil rights scholars; they agreed with us that signing a legally-binding, ten-year consent decree containing such a provision could, if the MTA implemented it, place us on the wrong side of history. While tenured constitutional scholars did not face our own organizing dilemma, the combination of strong leadership and a belief in our own principles brought us to Judge Terry Hatter's Court with great firmness and trepidation.

Consent Decree

Finally, on October 28, 1996, the class action lawsuit against the Los Angeles MTA was settled out of court. While the court did not rule on the validity or constitutionality of a future low-income pass, it clearly ruled that any future moves by the MTA to amend the agreement would have to go through the far more rigorous and fair ground rules that cover all other components of the consent decree.

The courthouse victory celebration of more than 100 Bus Rider Union members who had packed the courtroom was a profound experience of elation and jubilation. We had stuck to our principles, stayed loyal to our membership's wishes, won the legal battle to strengthen our hand in the joint working group, and had established a civil rights precedent to make class-action settlements more democratic and subject to modification by key participants. Moreover, we maintained a positive relationship with the Legal Defense Fund during this difficult period and are once again represented by them as part of the consent decree.

Immediately after Judge Terry Hatter signed the consent decree, we met with four officials of the MTA to convene the first meeting of the joint working group, a central provision of the consent decree. The joint working group implicitly acknowledges the differing interests between the bus riders and the MTA and the many unresolved issues in the consent decree itself. Thus, it establishes a new, court-ordered deliberative body composed solely of the MTA and the Bus Riders Union to resolve issues of fares, service, new bus-stop construction, budget, and virtually every other issue affecting the bus system for the next decade. If issues cannot be resolved, then the special master, and if necessary, the federal judge, become involved.

Terms of Settlement

The main achievements of the settlement include improvements in mass transportation for all bus riders, and public policy precedents for grassroots organizers in every city in the United States. Specific elements of the settlement include the following:[3]

1. The monthly general unlimited-use bus pass was reduced from $49 to $42. As we advocated, this sets the precedent that bus-pass prices can go down as well as up, and that "needs based" rather than "market based" pricing of public services paid for with public funds must drive transportation fare policy. In a nation in which a $5.25-an-hour minimum wage is a public policy debate, and many workers in Los Angeles are forced to work for less in sweatshops, reducing the price and protecting the unlimited use bus pass is the single greatest achievement of this agreement. Before we went to court, the MTA had just voted to eliminate the general bus pass altogether.

2. The bi-weekly general bus pass was reduced from $26.50 to $21. This is very important because it establishes the precedent that if we want to encourage public transportation use, government, not the consumer, must absorb the costs of administrative fees that otherwise would make purchasing two biweekly passes more expensive than a monthly pass. We argued that one obstacle to greater mass transit use was the prohibitive price of the bus pass and the burden on families of accumulating $49, or even $42, on the first of the month, the same time that the rent is due. Under the past system, a person who could not afford $49 a month had to pay $53 a month for a bus pass, in two $26.50 bi-weekly installments. One of the court settlement victories for public policy is that gov-

ernment takes the responsibility to help make public transportation affordable by creating a $42 monthly and $21 bi-weekly pass so that people are not punished financially and can continue to use the bus all month.

3. The agreement creates a new, unlimited-use $11 weekly pass. In urban centers throughout the United States, when a growing percentage of working people labor at minimum wages or slightly higher, even a $21 bi-weekly pass creates obstacles to public transportation use. Painfully, the result is not that people don't use public transportation, but as the "poor get poorer," they pay for each fare at $1.35 plus a twenty-five-cent transfer because they can't accumulate $23.50 or $49 at any given time (or even in the new fare structure, $21 and $42 at any given time.) In the past, when low-income people ran out of money, they just didn't go places. As such, their life was reduced to "home to work," and they were denied the right to go to church, to visit family, to attend cultural and educational programs, or even to look for better jobs.

The $11 weekly pass is the single most tangible breakthrough in public transportation policy, and one that will cause shock waves in San Francisco, New Orleans, Chicago, and New York if groups there are capable of building on our victory. For many low-wage workers who drive gas-guzzling cars with no insurance, the $11 weekly pass will get a growing number of low-income people out of their cars and back on public transportation.

Moreover, this establishes the principle that governmental policy (too often subsidizing the rich and penalizing the poor) must approach the important environmental goal of reducing auto and fossil fuel use by providing incentives for voluntary reduction in auto use. This is a great victory for our work, because we have vehemently opposed pricing theories advocated by many mainstream environmental groups to discourage auto use. We have argued that such theories are class-biased: charging more for gasoline or congestion pricing on highways would not deter those who are wealthy or even comfortable. In the absence of a first-class public transportation system, the affluent would simply pay the tariff to continue to use their cars or purchase gas; those who are transit-dependent would pay more for poor public transportation, while those who are not low-wage workers would simply pay more for gas before waiting two hours for bus service to work.

4. Overcrowding is reduced. We had wanted the MTA to simply agree to purchase 1,000 or more new buses over five years to reduce overcrowding and to increase rider demand. In the settlement process they resisted this proposal. Instead, we reached the following compromise:

- The MTA agreed to purchase 102 buses over the next two years to decrease overcrowding and increase service on the most overcrowded lines.
- The MTA agreed to reduce standees from a present level of twenty or more on a bus with forty-three seats, to an average of eight standees during peak hours by 2002. In 1997, 2000, and 2002 there are substantial, verifiable goals which if not met, will involve "re-allocation" (the MTA's dreaded word) of funds from "other sources" (meaning rail) to bus to increase bus service. New buses will be purchased "as needed" to reduce load factors to the agreed-upon levels.

5. Bus service is expanded to new areas. Another major victory in the realm

of policy was convincing the court-appointed mediator that we did not want a "ghetto and barrio bus improvement plan," but rather a comprehensive regional transportation plan for all races and classes. We needed service both within and out of East Los Angeles, Koreatown, Pico Union, San Fernando, South Central, and to diverse locations from Disneyland to the San Gabriel and San Fernando Valleys and Orange County. We did not want express buses and trains for suburban riders into the central business district (where only 8 percent of the jobs are presently located) but a bus-centered, multi-modal transportation system to employment, cultural, recreational, medical, and family centers throughout Los Angeles County and beyond. The consent decree provided the following:

- The MTA agrees to purchase fifty new buses emanating from inner-city areas to be used over the next two years as a pilot project to medical, job, and recreational centers.
- During those two years, the joint working group will develop a plan for a five-year expansion of bus service that will require the MTA to purchase a significant (but unspecified) number of new buses. Our own study indicates at least 500 new buses will be needed for that objective alone (but of course we do not expect the MTA to agree with that figure). Nonetheless, it could involve several hundred new buses to "expand the horizons" and the service of inner-city bus riders to areas of the county from which they have been segregated for decades.

Plans for the Future

At first, many of our members were against the agreement, because in truth so much of the agreement is vague, ambiguous, subject to interpretation, and resolution in the court of public opinion and public affairs. But it is clear to us now that ambiguity is its strength.

The uncharted waters of the joint working group move us into the realm of policy and governance, in which the Strategy Center and Bus Riders Union have the chance to wage the struggle for the future of transportation policy in a far bigger arena. The ten-year federal court jurisdiction provides some protection against some of the most egregious violations of the agreement, but does not substitute for "good old grassroots" democracy and advocacy.

For example, Los Angeles County is currently reducing the services of its medical facilities, which is creating massive transportation problems; many of the facilities that are the least expensive to operate are not in the most convenient arenas for transit-dependent people. But now the agreement creates an opportunity for the Bus Riders Union to work with doctors, nurses, hospital administrators, and patients to develop transportation profiles of entire communities and their medical needs for the joint working group.

Throughout the United States today, the only "democratic" choices offered are which reductions in services people prefer — bus fare or hospital care, chronic or acute medical care, lower wages or no jobs at all. But now a court-ordered agreement has raised people's expectations and created a structure to set policy for mass transportation in the most auto-dependent and air-polluted city in the United States. This so exciting that our main concern is whether we can rise to the challenge. The key to a longterm victory in this arena involves many interrelated components:

Financial strength and independence is needed to protect a core staff and expand it to shape the policies of a $3-billion-a-year transit agency. However, funds that would in any way restrict our initiative and autonomy will not be accepted.

A media budget is needed to expand a powerful multi-racial, multi-class constituency of bus riders, middle-class professionals, environmentalists, transportation advocates, religious, intellectual, and governmental leaders.

An expanded staff budget is needed to cope with joint working group meetings from which the public is excluded. Other staff members must fulfil our role as organizer/policy advocate within the arena of public discourse.

A continued increase in core constituencies is needed to reach the 9 million people in our county. For example, on October 5, 1996 we organized the largest march for civil rights and mass transportation in the city's history. More than seventy-five organizations helped in that event to support the Billions for Buses Campaign and to pressure the MTA to remove the low-income pass language from the agreement before the October 28th court hearing.

Strategic action must be taken against the MTA's efforts to undermine the agreement. For example, the only African-American member of the MTA board told the media that the bus riders "should not get their hopes too high about this settlement because there is very little money to implement it." And there is talk of a statewide reorganization of the MTA; we will propose an elected MTA board to avoid an even less accountable structure.

The "Make History" public art project must continue. For two years, the Strategy Center and Bus Riders Union worked to create a synthesis of public art and public advocacy. Many successful cultural and public-education collaborations include: organizer Kikanza Ramsey's "Make History — Fight Transit Racism — Join the Bus Riders Union" bilingual full-color poster; a citywide bus shelter ad campaign; an ongoing visuals committee composed of professional and community-based artists; the upcoming Bus Riders Union Dance-a-Thon; and comprehensive multimedia documentation, including the crucial work of Strategy Center Publications. The cultural component of the struggle is not considered simply a good way to raise the visibility of the Billions for Buses campaign, but rather a conscious and considered expression of the multiracial, multilingual community of low-income bus riders.

We must play a greater role in national and international movement-building. Many grassroots groups throughout the United States have asked us to organize regional and national conferences and meetings to explore how the Strategy Center and Bus Riders Union "organizing model" can be debated, dissected, and applied. Other groups have shared their ideas for "sister city" projects, dilemmas about movement building, and problems with monitoring and enforcing agreements with government and corporate entities. We need to find the resources and capacity to play a greater role nationally and internationally so that our fledgling experiment can find new allies.

Our historic victory has become a springboard to a broader social movement. The key to success in Los Angeles will not be to complain to the special master or judge for every violation of our hard-earned agreement. Rather, the key is to maintain and act on our vision of a bus system in which affordable, clean, efficient, and comfortable transportation becomes the norm and the expectation.

Race and the Politics of Transportation in Atlanta

Sidney Davis

Race, politics and transportation have had a long and intimately connected history in the Atlanta area. Major transportation facilities, such as Interstate 20, for example, while conceived as important and valuable links in the metropolitan freeway system, also isolated and separated Atlanta's black and white residential communities. Former Mayor Ivan Allen tried to block off Peyton Road as a means of reducing neighborhood accessibility and of implementing racially-motivated policies.[1]

Political gains made by black citizens in state and local governments and their progress in reducing housing and labor-market discrimination make such uses of transportation facilities and expenditures to disadvantaged black Atlantans much more difficult to accomplish. The link between race, politics and transportation continues nevertheless and finds voice through the action of suburban voters who continue to reject the extension of Metropolitan Atlanta Rapid Transit Authority (MARTA) service into their counties. For example, attempts to bring Cobb and Gwinnett Counties into the MARTA system have failed, with Cobb County opting to develop its own bus system.

The MARTA Referendum

About twenty years ago, the U.S. Department of Transportation funded research at Clark Atlanta University (then Atlanta University), which produced a remarkable series of documents dealing with transportation issues in Atlanta. The research included analyses of the MARTA referendum, passed in November 1971; a review of the decision-making processes of the MARTA board of directors as they related to the passage of the MARTA referendum; and examination of the transportation needs of Atlanta's black community.[2]

That research clearly linked the passage of the 1971 MARTA referendum to the agency's accommodation of major demands made by the black community for improved service, equitable representation on the MARTA Board of Directors and affordable fares. While the initial heavily subsidized, low fare of fifteen cents is now a dim memory, rejection by black voters of an earlier (1968) rapid transit plan stimulated several major changes in the 1971 plan, which have had profound impact over the long run: the new plan proposed a dramatic expansion and coordination of a bus system with the rail system to provide vastly improved transit service throughout the city. The 1971 plan also shifted financing for the local share of transit-system costs from the relatively slow-growing property tax base to a sales tax that could produce higher revenues. And lastly, the highly visible and effective role of black citizens in reshaping the MARTA plan significantly enhanced the community's decision-making power and influence. The black community became a force to be reckoned with, especially in matters related to public transportation expenditures.

The Atlanta University research also documented the special difficulties facing black female heads of households. These were linked with problems of low incomes, lack of convenient transportation access to jobs and services, and housing market discrimination.

While MARTA has improved transit service significantly in the community, those benefits have not come cheaply, particularly in terms of the household dislocations brought about by the system's construction. The vast majority of residential displacements, for example, occurred in black neighborhoods. Initial estimates indicated that almost 1400 households would be displaced by construction. Almost 85 percent of the individuals making up those households were blacks whose incomes were considerably below the average household income in the city.[3]

These initial estimates of residential displacements have been reasonably close to the actual number; as of March 1994, a total of 1647 households have been displaced as a consequence of MARTA's construction activities.[4]

Big Budgets and Big Impact

The MARTA budget and planned transportation expenditures by state and local governments provide convincing evidence of transportation's importance: no other capital expenditure by local and state governments, except perhaps utility infrastructure, even comes close to that of transportation. It is estimated that MARTA's construction costs to date are approximately $1.8 billion. MARTA, for example, has a 1994 fiscal year operating budget of almost $211 million; it anticipates additional spending of about $164 million for capital improvements, which includes rail extensions toward Dunwoody; and payment of almost $81 million to service loans obtained to finance system construction.[5] Expenditures by state and local governments to facilitate vehicular movement are equally impressive. The Atlanta Regional Commission's latest publication, Atlanta Regional Transportation Improvement Program FY 1994 to FY 1999, which summarizes all transportation projects to be built over the next six years, provides an indication of their size: over $1 billion in transportation "improvements" have been programmed.[6] The overwhelming share of these expenditures is for road projects. The size of these outlays provides a frame of reference with which to judge their impact on the lives of black Atlantans. Such transportation expenditures influence how households go about choosing where to live. They help determine how expensive it is to get to work, both in terms of travel time and cost. And because travel fills other important human needs, such as education, social interaction and shopping, the availability of transportation services is also an important determinant of the quality of life.

Several other dimensions of transportation expenditures are important.

Because of their size, they have substantial business and employment impacts. The hundreds of millions of dollars spent to develop the transportation systems in the Atlanta area represent significant potential business opportunities for black entrepreneurs. The operation of these systems also provides access to relatively well-paying jobs. The 1996 Olympics, for example, not only accelerated planned capital investment in transportation facilities, but also opened up new opportunities for business people and individuals seeking jobs.

A good starting point for developing additional insight into the status of black Atlanta with respect to transportation is by examining 1980 and 1990 data developed by the U.S. Department of Commerce's Bureau of the Census. This information, while limited to the journey to work, does provide valuable information as to where black Atlantans are working, how they are getting to their jobs and how long it is taking them to get to their places of work.

How Black Atlantans Get To Work

Black and white Atlantans overwhelmingly prefer using an auto for getting to work. While the transit system is of great importance in furnishing mobility, the decentralization of jobs throughout the city and the greater metropolitan area makes many journey-to-work trips by transit arduous. Table 1 provides quantitative insight into the journey-to-work mode choice for 1980, followed by discussion of comparable data for 1990.

In 1980, almost 73 percent of all black males and about 58 percent of all black females used a private vehicle for their journey to work. In spite of this clear preference for auto usage, a significant share of black workers rely on public transportation services. Black workers, in fact, were at least twice as dependent on public transportation services as their white counterparts. It is therefore clear why the vote on the 1971 MARTA referendum was of such vital concern to black Atlantans.

Table 1: Mode Choice By Workers Age 16 and Over Living in Atlanta By Race and Sex, 1990				
	Black		White	
	Males	Females	Males	Females
Car, Van or Truck	72.7%	57.5%	78.8%	76.7%
Public Transit	22.6	38.8	11.5	15.6
Other	4.7	3.7	9.7	7.7
Total	100.0%	100.0%	100.0%	100.0%

Source: U.S. Bureau of the Census, 1980 Census of Population and Housing.
U.S. Department of Commerce.

The choice of whether a person makes the journey to work by a private vehicle or by transit is largely influenced by economic circumstances. This is confirmed by transit system research. The most recent MARTA survey, Final Report On-Board Bus and Rail Survey, which captures the demographics of transit system ridership, indicates that almost 52 percent of weekday riders have incomes of less than $25,000 per year and that almost 34 percent had no available auto with which to make their weekday trips.[7] Of course, the significant benefit of transit availability should be realized. That study indicated that 42 percent of transit system passengers could not make their weekday trip without MARTA. That a substantial number of black Atlantans use transit is a reflection of income constraints, rather than preference for public transportation, or that transit necessarily provides them with more convenient or efficient access.

The 1980s saw major expansion and improvement of the road and transit systems in the Atlanta region. These improvements, in turn, are reflected in mode choice, particularly for a repetitive trip such as the journey to work. It appears that using a private vehicle is declining for almost everyone except black males. In 1980, an estimated 38.8 percent of black females used public transit for getting to work (Table 1). By 1990 (Table 2) this had dropped to slightly less than 35 percent. Black males, on the other hand, used public transportation slightly more in 1990: 24.3 percent in 1990 compared to 22.3 percent in 1980.

Table 2: Mode Choice By Workers Age 16 and Over Living in Atlanta By Race and Sex, 1980				
	Black		**White**	
	Males	**Females**	**Males**	**Females**
Car, Van or Truck	70.9%	60.2%	87.5%	84.6%
Public Transit	24.3	34.9	4.2	5.2
Other	4.8	4.9	8.3	10.2
Total	100.0%	100.0%	100.0%	100.0%

Source: U.S. Bureau of the Census, 1990 Census of Population and Housing, Public Use Microdata Sample "B". Special data extract prepared by the University of Georgia.

While transit access clearly has improved during the last decade, the dispersal of jobs throughout the Atlanta metropolitan region, rising incomes, and improvements in the road network have resulted in the private vehicle being the mode of choice for most Atlantans regardless, of race. However, the greater affluence of white Atlantans compared to black residents clearly is reflected in mode of choice: in 1990, about 5 percent of Atlanta's white workers relied on public transportation compared to about 30 percent for black Atlantans. Within the black community, women are far more likely than black men to rely on public transportation services.

Travel Time for Black Atlantans

Most people regard a thirty-minute commute as reasonable. This observation, at least for private vehicular modes, is reinforced by travel-time-to-work data gathered by the U.S. Bureau of the Census. About 87 percent of these trips taken by black males and females are thirty minutes or less in duration. Transit trips, on the other hand, take much more time. For black males, only 54.4 percent of the trips by public transportation for the journey to work take thirty minutes or less. It is significantly less for black females: only 44 percent of the journey to work trips taken by public transportation take thirty minutes or less to complete. A more complete picture of these travel times is presented in Table 3.

Journey-to-work trips lasting more than one hour are unusual, although about 7 percent of black females and 10 percent of black males (based on 1990 census data) using transit make such lengthy trips. The difference in transit-travel times by race suggests that white males and females are traveling to more transit-accessible locations, e.g., the central business district, than black males or females. As a consequence, their transit times are significantly less.

Direct comparison to journey-to-work travel times for 1980 is not possible with the published material available. Table 4, however, does provide insight into the average travel time to work by race and mode for 1980.

Clearly, the average travel time to work, regardless of mode, was and still is significantly longer for black males and females than for white males and females. Such differences would not be expected in the absence of housing and labor market discriminatory practices. The legacy of those practices continue to make the cost of mobility excessive for African-Americans living in Atlanta.

Where Black Atlantans Work and How They Get There

It would not be surprising to learn that most black Atlantans work within the city itself and that relatively few travel to suburban counties. It is surprising, however, to see how few black Atlantans make such out-of-the-city work commutes, given the rapid suburbanization of jobs. It is just as surprising to see that white Atlantans follow a similar pattern. In 1990, for example, 3.7 percent of black males living in Atlanta went to work in Cobb County; 5.1 percent of white males made a similar commute (Table 5). The pattern is similar for females: about 5 percent of all black female workers commute to Cobb County while 6 percent of white females make that specific journey to work. Atlantans exhibit a strong affinity to live in relatively close proximity to place of work, regardless of race or gender. More than 64 percent of black males and 67 percent of black females, (along with 61.6 percent of white males and 67.5 percent of white females) who reside in Atlanta also work in the city. Approximately 14 percent in each category also commute to Dekalb County, while 11 percent of black males and 7.9 percent of black females (compared to 7.4 percent of white males and 5.4 percent of white females) commute to Fulton County.

Table 3: Travel Time To Work For Persons 16 Years and Over Living In City Of Atlanta By Race And Sex, 1990

Travel Time by Mode	Black		White	
	Males	Females	Males	Females
By Car, Van or Truck				
< 30 Minutes	87.0%	87.7%	93.1%	92.0%
31-60 Minutes	12.1	11.7	6.5	8.0
> 60 Minutes	0.9	0.6	0.5	0.0
By Public Transport				
< 30 Minutes	54.4	44.0	77.7	50.8
31-60 Minutes	35.5	48.8	17.4	43.2
> 60 Minutes	10.1	7.2	5.0	5.9

Source: U.S. Bureau of the Census, 1990 Census of Population and Housing, Public Use Microdata Sample "B".

Table 4: Mean Travel Time to Work for Persons 16 Years and Over Living in City of Atlanta By Race And Sex, 1980

Average Travel Time to Work (in minutes)	Black		White	
	Males	Females	Males	Females
Car, Van or Truck	26.6	25.1	19.7	19.0
Public Transport	44.0	45.6	31.3	31.7

Source: U.S. Bureau of the Census, 1980 Census of Population and Housing. U.S. Department of Commerce.

Table 5: Work Place Destination for Workers Age 16 and Over Living in City of Atlanta By Race And Sex, 1990

Workplace Destination	Black		White	
	Males	Females	Males	Females
Atlanta	64.3%	67.0%	61.6%	67.5%
Fulton City (Not Atl)	11.0	7.9	7.4	5.4
Dekalb City (Not Atl)	14.4	14.9	14.9	13.7
Cobb City	3.7	5.1	5.1	6.0
Gwinnett City	2.6	1.9	3.8	2.8
Clayton City	3.3	2.9	2.4	1.8

Source: U.S. Bureau of the Census, 1990 Census of Population and Housing, Public Use Microdata Sample "B".

The lengthy travel times reported in Table 3 for black males and females using public transportation can be explained, in part, by their work-trip distribution pattern. A small but significant portion of them are traveling outside of the city for jobs on trips that are long, probably requiring several transfers (Table 6). For example, while only an estimated 1.9 percent of black female workers travel to Gwinnett County for jobs (Table 5), 53.9 percent of them make that trip by public transportation (Table 6). Such trips require a great deal of time. White women, on the other hand, do not make such an onerous journey: none reported taking transit to Gwinnett County (or to Cobb and Clayton Counties, for that matter).

Additional Evidence of the Importance of Transit Services

In 1989, MARTA commissioned a survey to determine the socio-economic and demographic characteristics of its passengers, as well as to gain insight into their trip-making behavior.[8] The results of this work provide a useful supplement to the information provided by the Census of Population whose transportation data is restricted to a fairly narrow focus. The MARTA-sponsored study reinforces the importance of the work trip as pre-eminent among all trip purposes, and provides explicit data with which to compare alternative trip-making purposes (Table 7).

Table 6: Workplace Destination by Mode for Workers Age 16 and Over Living in City of Atlanta By Race And Sex, 1990				
Workplace Destination by Mode	Black Males	Females	White Males	Females
Car, Van, Truck				
Atlanta	65.2%	58.0%	83.4%	80.3%
Fulton City (Not Atl)	81.0	76.0	93.8	92.7
Dekalb City (Not Atl)	73.9	57.1	94.8	93.2
Cobb City	84.1	69.7	100.0	100.0
Gwinnett City	93.3	46.1	100.0	100.0
Clayton City	100.0	73.5	81.2	82.9
By Public Transportation				
Atlanta	28.2%	35.0%	4.4%	6.7%
Fulton City (Not Atl)	16.9	24.0	6.2	7.3
Dekalb City (Not Atl)	24.4	42.9	5.2	2.3
Cobb City	15.9	26.9	0.0	0.0
Gwinnett City	.7	53.9	0.0	0.0
Clayton City	0.0	26.6	11.6	0.0

Source: U.S. Bureau of the Census, 1990 Census of Population and Housing, Public Use Microdata Sample "B"

It is interesting to note that even on weekends, the transit system provides substantial service for persons making the journey-to-work trip. One additional table provides important insight into the value of public transportation to system users. Riders were asked what transportation alternatives they would use if MARTA service were not available. Their response to that question is recorded in Table 8.

While it is comforting to note that most people could have continued to make trips without MARTA, a great many could not. The relevance of this information to Atlanta's African-American community is profound: since almost two-thirds of MARTA's riders are black, a great many of them would simply not have a viable alternative and could not travel.

The Consumer Significance of Transportation Costs

Consumer outlays for transportation rank as the third largest component of the household budget, behind housing and food. Based on data from the 1991 Consumer Expenditure Survey, black households spent over 15 percent of their total average annual consumption budgets on transportation, compared to about 33 percent for housing and 17 percent for food.[9] The results of the national consumer expenditure survey are shown in Table 9. The survey also provides consumption data on the Atlanta metropolitan area. These consumption patterns do not differ appreciably from national averages: about 16 percent of household expenditures in Atlanta were for transportation, 33 percent for housing, and a little over 12 percent for food.

Income-related differences exist in the share of annual consumer-unit expenditures devoted to transportation, although they are not as large as one might expect. Data reported in the Consumer Expenditure Survey for the nation as a whole show that consumers in the lowest 20 percent in terms of income

Table 7: Trip Purpose by Day of Week			
Trip Purpose	**Weekday**	**Saturday**	**Sunday**
Work	63.7%	46.9%	38.6%
Shopping	5.4	22.7	9.1
Meal	0.8	1.1	5.6
Medical	1.5	0.5	0.9
College	10.8	2.8	2.7
Personal	13.4	25.1	42.0
Other School	4.5	0.9	1.1

Source: Hoyt, George & Associates, Final Report On-Board Bus and Rail Survey RFP#135 (Metropolitan Atlanta Rapid Transit Authority, October 1990). pp. 1-28.

Table 8: Mode Choice Alternatives Without MARTA			
Alternative Mode	Weekday	Saturday	Sunday
Would not Go	42.0%	38.0%	45.5%
Would Drive	36.8	34.2	33.3
Ride with Someone	17.9	21.5	16.7
Source: Hoyt, George & Associates, Final Report On-Board Bus and RailSurvey RFP#135 (Metropolitan Atlanta Rapid Transit Authority, October 1990). pp.1-32.			

allocate about 14.1 percent of total annual expenditures (about $1,898) to transportation compared to 16.3 percent (about $9,388) for the highest income group. While more disaggregated data that reflect expenditures by race and specific urban location might show a higher share of income devoted to transportation, the published data available suggest that the allocation of income by low-income households for transportation services ranks behind their need for food and shelter. The tremendous disparity between the absolute amounts spent by low-income consumer units ($1,898) compared to those in the highest income group ($9,388) for transportation services also reflects the significant constraints on mobility which affect individuals with low incomes.

While the differences in relative shares of income devoted to transportation differ only slightly between income groups and between races, the actual size of those expenditures obviously is larger, the greater the income. With respect to black households, because they on average have significantly lower incomes, they are constrained to purchasing less transportation service.

Table 9: National Average Annual Consumer Unit Expenditures by Race, 1991			
Total Black White			
Average Annual Expenditures	$29,614	$20,091	$30,794
Food	14.1%	16.7%	14.2%
Housing	31.2	33.3	31.1
Transportation	17.4	15.1	17.6
Source: Bureau of Labor Statistics, Consumer Expenditure Survey 1990-1991 (U.S. Department of Labor, September 1993) Table 7, pp. 38-41. Note: The category of white includes all races except black.			

Black households improve their mobility not through the allocation of more income for this purpose, but by substituting the use of their own time for their lesser purchasing power. Thus they experience longer trip lengths and/or more elapsed time in reaching their destinations by taking fewer trips and using public transportation.

Employment and Minority Business Enterprise

The hundreds of millions of dollars spent annually on transportation by MARTA and state and local governments represent significant employment and business opportunities for black Atlantans. Sharing in these opportunities has been a key goal of the black community leadership. Minority Business Enterprise Data from MARTA for its Minority Business Enterprise Program (MBE) indicate that since 1988, it has awarded an aggregated average of about 17.3 percent of its contract awards to firms that it classifies as minority business enterprises; about 3.5 percent of those contracts go to women's business enterprises.[10]

MARTA maintains a goal of 25 percent Disadvantaged Business Enterprise (DBE) participation in contracts that are federally assisted.[11] However, if this goal were also applied to all MARTA contracts, then they have fallen short of target. As Table 10 indicates, the amount of contracting activity undertaken by MARTA is considerable: well over three-quarters of a billion dollars within a five-year

Table 10: Contract Awards by MARTA FY 1989 - FY 1993					
Year	Total Award (Millions)	MBE Awards	%	WBE* Awards	%
FY 1989	$34.97	$7.55	21.6%	1.01	2.9%
FY 1990	162.88	31.10	19.1	5.92	3.6
FY 1991	45.16	9.42	20.9	1.95	4.3
FY 1992	571.51	91.98	16.1	19.87	3.5
FY 1993	23.42	4.57	19.5	.39	1.7
Total	$837.94	$144.62	$17.3	$29.14	$3.5

Source: Metropolitan Atlanta Rapid Transit Authority, Award of Contracts: FY 1989 -1993 (Office of the General Manager). Unpublished internal report. *WBE is Women's Business Enterprise

Table 11: Contract Awards by Georgia Department of Transportation FY1990 - FY1993					
Year	Total Award (Millions)	MBE Awards	%	WBE Awards	%
FY 1990	$279.65	$14.75	5.3%	$15.17	5.4%
FY 1991	396.44	18.25	4.5	30.13	7.6
FY 1992	381.03	20.58	5.4	26.06	6.8
FY 1993	330.46	16.97	5.1	18.89	5.7

Source: Georgia Department of Transportation, DBE/WBE Participation in Contracts (Office of Equal Opportunity). Data represent DBE/WBE share of the federal portion of contracts.

period of time. If MARTA had achieved a 25 percent goal for these contracts, total awards to disadvantaged business enterprises would have amounted to about $209.5 million. However, only $173.8 million was actually awarded to MBE and WBE contractors. Thus, almost $36 million in additional contracts would have gone to support minority entrepreneurship had the MARTA goal been reached. Clearly that is not a small amount of business.

The Georgia Department of Transportation also maintains a DBE/WBE target for projects financed with federal funds.[12] Their combined federally-established target for DBE including WBE is 10 percent, which they are currently exceeding (Table 11). The state's transportation commissioner and the Board of Transportation also recently established a more ambitious target of 14 percent of federal contracts, 4 percent of state contracts, and 12 percent of consulting contracts for DBE/WBE firms.[13] Virtually all of these DBE/WBE contract awards were as subcontractors, rather than prime contractors. The expenditure levels for the Georgia Department of Transportation, similar to MARTA, are considerable and the share going to DBE/WBE firms amounts to tens of millions of dollars each year. However, at present, the state agency has achieved only one-third of its goal for DBEs.

Employment in Transportation Agencies

In 1993, approximately 70 percent of MARTA's full-time work force of 3,710 persons were identified as black, with the largest share being black males. African- Americans are found in virtually every major employment category and pay grouping (Table 12).

Table 12: MARTA Employment by Major Employment Class			
Employment Class	Total Employed	Black Males % of Total	Black Females % of Total
Officials/Admin.	116	50%	6%
Professionals	235	45	31
Technicians	57	16	72
Protective Service	327	20	59
Para-Professional	401	48	1
Admin. Support	1,767	60	23
Skilled Craft	430	39	12
Service/Maintenance	327	20	19
Total	3,710	48%	23%

Source: Metropolitan Atlanta Rapid Transit Authority, State and Local Government Information (EEO-4) (Office of the General Manager Assistant for Equal Opportunity). Data for employment as of June 1993.

Table 13: Georgia Department of Transportation Employment by Major Employment Class			
Employment Class	Total Employed	Black Males % of Total	Black Females % of Total
Officials/Admin.	38	3%	0%
Professionals	1,449	6	3
Technicians	1,101	14	4
Protective Service	274	11	4
Para-Professional	174	16	10
Admin. Support	429	4	27
Skilled Craft	498	27	1
Service/Maintenance	2,444	40	4
Total	6,407	22 %	5%

Source: Georgia Department of Transportation, State and Local Government Information (EEO-4) (Office of the General Manager Assistant for Equal Opportunity). Data for employment as of June 1993.

Black women are significantly under-represented in the officials/ administrators and para-professional employment classifications, and over-represented in the protective service class. Black males, on the other hand, appear to be well represented within most employment classes within MARTA, especially as officials and administrators.

The employment patterns at the Georgia Department of Transportation are significantly different from MARTA.[14] Most of the jobs are in the Atlanta labor market area and thus important for black Atlantans as employment potential. At the transit agency, the distribution of total black workers (except for the under-representation of black women previously noted) by employment class generally reflects the expected distribution based on total number of workers employed. At the Georgia Department of Transportation, however, African-Americans are clearly under-represented in the better jobs, particularly those job categories identified as officials/administrators and professionals (Table 13). These positions normally would be regarded as representing the leadership of the department. They would also tend to be the highest paying. On the other hand, black men and women are significantly over-represented in jobs classified as service/maintenance.

While state transportation agencies historically have been white male-dominated, the successful operation of MARTA indicates that it is possible to attract and keep black managers and professionals. The Georgia Department of Transportation's performance with respect to addressing this residual consequence of labor-market discrimination needs to be improved greatly.

Conclusions

The exercise of political power in the public arena has had a significant beneficial impact on the benefits accruing to black Atlantans from both the investments made in transportation facilities and the services they provide. MARTA is a notable example. Both jobs and entrepreneurial opportunities have flowed into the black community as a consequence of its construction and operation. Having said that, there is much more to be done. Because building transportation facilities is capital-intensive involving hundreds of millions of dollars of construction costs, a small shift in percentage share of those outlays going to black businesspersons could amount to huge sums. If MARTA sets a goal such as the 25% share and then achieves less, this is unsatisfactory. This is true not only for MARTA, but for other transportation agencies as well, particularly the Georgia Department of Transportation, which has annual expenditures in the hundreds of millions of dollars. Transportation agencies also need to begin to seek out minority prime contractors, rather than subcontractors.

Examination of data on employment at the state transportation agency also reveals the significant negative consequences of historic labor-market discriminatory practices that prevent African-Americans from being a major part of the management and leadership of the organization.

The issue of mobility for individuals is also more than just having available physical facilities. Low incomes constrain the array of choices of where people live and work. A superior road network that encourages the dispersal of activity is a disadvantage to those whose travel mode choices are limited to transit. This is especially true for black women, whose incomes typically are lower than those of their male counterparts and who are, to a significant degree, transit-dependent. Twenty-two years ago, Goldberg and Williams highlighted this issue in their research, Transportation Needs of the Atlanta Black Community.

While improvements in the MARTA system have been extraordinarily beneficial to black Atlantans, male and female, much of their current mobility difficulties are income-related. Finding ways of improving the income status of black Atlantans will go a long way toward addressing the many issues related to mobility confronting them daily.

The Legacy of Jim Crow in Macon, Georgia

David G. Oedel

On the Bus in Montgomery, Alabama

On her way home from work in the early evening of December 1, 1955, forty-two-year-old Rosa Parks, a tailor's assistant in the men's department of Montgomery Fair, boarded a crowded bus.[1] About halfway back, in the empty, last row marked for whites, Rosa Parks sat down because all the rows for African-Americans in the rear were already full. As the ride continued, three other African- Americans joined her. However, when several white riders later boarded and sought seats in Ms. Parks' row, the three African-Americans who had been sitting with her relinquished theirs — a customary indignity. But Rosa Parks, weary of indignity, laid silent claim to the seat she held.

Minutes later, the white driver employed by the National City Bus Company, James Blake, exercised his lawful prerogative by having Rosa Parks arrested for her arrogance. The next month, in the midst of a bus boycott organized by Rosa Parks' pastor, Rev. Martin Luther King, Jr., Rosa Parks lost her job. The bitter boycott extended until late in 1956. In 1957, Rosa Parks left Montgomery to live in Detroit, where she still lives in 1995.

Rosa Parks' quiet plea for respect was publicly noted as an early landmark in the civil rights struggle, which over the next decade led down a tortured path[2] to the Civil Rights Act of 1964. Title VI of that act purported to guarantee race-blind access to public accommodations, including buses and lunch counters, supposedly to address problems like those suffered by Rosa Parks.

As this chapter details, however, the promise of Title VI, insofar as it was to make public transportation accommodations evenhandedly available to all Americans, has been quietly but effectively evaded by local officials, transit authorities, departments of transportation, city planners, voters, and federal and state bureaucrats around the country. Through a steady stream of seemingly innocuous funding and operational decisions, these officials and citizens have, since 1964, quietly but effectively restricted the mobility of poor African-Americans and other disfavored minorities who do not own cars. Meanwhile, those same officials and citizens have simultaneously lavished public funds on transportation accommodations favored by the car-owning majority, who have used the new and improved roads, streets and highways in effect to live free from close contact with poor African-Americans and others similarly situated.

Today, public transit remains vital to the lives of people like Rosa Parks, too poor or otherwise unable to own cars, who struggle to survive in the neighborhoods that lie rotting near our urban centers. Public transit, however, has lost much of its ability to help rescue them from their plight, because a ticket today on the city bus in many communities like Montgomery, Alabama, is a ticket to nowhere.

Since 1964, downtown Montgomery, Alabama, has gradually given way to the malls and conveniences of suburban Montgomery, while the bus routes operated by the Montgomery Transit System have remained relatively static. A few years after Rosa Parks was discharged from her job at the downtown department store, for instance, the owners of that store relocated to a shopping center in the periphery. Decades later, however, the city's buses haven't yet tried to trace the flight of such stores. Montgomery's old bus routes still link poor African-American neighborhoods with a depressed and increasingly vacant downtown, but few, if any, routes establish a firm lifeline to the new, geographically dispersed locus of power in Montgomery's periphery.

Even if Montgomery's buses were geographically rerouted to provide occasional access to key areas of opportunity in the Montgomery periphery, they would still prove essentially useless to most carless job seekers because the system's days and times of operation are severely restricted. Buses in Montgomery operate only until 6:30 in the evening, Monday through Friday; Saturday service is limited, and there is no service on Sundays and holidays. Meanwhile, entry-level employers in the malls and other thriving businesses in the periphery typically require their newest employees to work evening, weekend and holiday shifts. In part because one cannot rely on the bus system for transportation at such times, it is increasingly difficult for a modern-day Rosa Parks to use Montgomery's city bus to go to work.

Not surprisingly, over 90 percent of the people who pay fares on the Montgomery city buses are African-American. They are treated in accordance with their station. Regardless of blistering sun or torrential rain, the city bus system maintains just three bus shelters. For their bus privileges, moreover, such as they are, the riders pay dearly. Montgomery's transit system sports a "farebox recovery ratio" of more than 50 percent, meaning that about half the system's cost is derived from fares paid by its poor riders, though they are ill-prepared to bear such expense. The individual fare is $1. By contrast, of course, the roads in Montgomery have no tolls, and are freely accessible to all who own cars.

In short, elaborate road systems have extended suburbia's sprawl around Montgomery, while the stagnant, deteriorating transit system has grown useless as a vehicle for poor African-Americans to escape poverty. The promise of Title VI in Montgomery - to make public transportation equally accessible — has been evaded and broken by providing carless African-American residents with inferior transportation services on the pretext that both the buses and the roads accommodate all equally. In fact, however, a longstanding pattern of planning and funding assures that the Montgomery buses accommodate car-less African-Americans relatively poorly, while the roads accommodate the predominantly white class of car owners relatively well.

Montgomery was not the only community in America during the 1950s with a transportation problem involving race, nor is it the only community with a kindred problem in the 1990s. This chapter details a similar pattern of discriminatory transportation service in another southern community, Macon, Georgia. But such discrimination is not peculiar to the South.

Just as racism and classism were not isolated to the South in the 1950s, racism and classism are not uniquely southern problems in the 1990s. Far from it. Discrimination in the economics of public transit has recently become the focus of lawsuits in both Los Angeles[3] and New York.[4] A lawsuit challenging the allocation of funding within Philadelphia's public transit system was filed in 1989.[5] Apparently the earliest transit-funding challenge was raised in Dallas in the 1970s in the form of a administrative action filed with the U.S. Department of Transportation, which resulted in a finding of discrimination by the federal authorities and voluntary remediation.

Those actions rely on many of the same legal theories that gave rise to an administrative complaint filed in 1994 with the U.S. Department of Transportation on behalf of transit-dependent residents of Macon, Georgia. However, all the other cases to date have only challenged the allocation of funding within public transportation modes. The Macon case is unique in one key respect, as it is the first modern challenge to the discriminatory nature of transportation planning and funding in a much broader context — in the context of both highway funding and transit funding. The Macon complaint points out that the technical bureaucratic segregation of transit subsidies from other transportation subsidies inherently serves to discriminate against people without cars, who are disproportionately poor and African-American. The Macon complaint is the most comprehensive challenge yet to business-as-usual in transportation planning and funding at the primary level of transportation planning — the MPO.

A brief overview of the legal issues involved in all these cases is provided later in this chapter. Title VI of the Civil Rights Act, constitutional law, the Americans with Disabilities Act, and federal transportation law are discussed in terms of how they may be affected by patterns of discrimination.

On the Bus in Macon, Georgia

The Macon/Bibb County Transit Authority operates a faltering local public transit system in Macon, Georgia. Together with its owners - Bibb County and the City of Macon - and its private-sector predecessors, the Transit Authority has limped along for decades without evolving in accord with the shifting demographics, economics and needs of the community. With only minor adjustment, the Transit Authority's routes have remained essentially unchanged for over thirty years, petrified in the transit patterns that existed at the commencement of integration.

It is well known in Macon that poor people without cars, most of whom are African-American, cannot navigate meaningfully in the modern, decentralized environment of Bibb County and Macon. It is also well known that the Transit Authority provides very limited services that make it effectively impossible for thousands of poor people in Macon without cars, most of whom are African-

American, to integrate commercially in the community.

Macon is a small city in Middle Georgia with a relatively static population for about thirty years. However, a substantial part of Macon's population moved to the periphery during that same period, similar to population migrations to the periphery of Montgomery and other cities.

The City of Macon and Bibb County, with the help of the Georgia Department of Transportation and the U.S. Department of Transportation, oversee the planning, funding, construction or purchase, operation and maintenance of the area's roads, streets, highways, traffic signals, public buses, paratransit vans, and municipal airport. The city and county deliver their transportation programs through such agencies and authorities as the Macon/Bibb County Planning and Zoning Commission (P&Z); the Macon Area Transportation Study (the MPO responsible for transportation planning pursuant to the requirements of federal transportation law); the Macon Area Planning Study (for overall development planning); and the Macon/Bibb County Transit Authority.

The Transit Authority, which physically operates the city bus system on behalf of the city and county, is wholly owned and controlled by them. Its board of directors is composed solely of three city appointees and two county appointees. Although the Transit Authority does not directly receive federal funding, it does indirectly receive federal funding for planning and related transportation services provided by P&Z and other agencies. The City, County, Planning and Zoning, and Georgia Department of Transportation (GDOT) regularly seek to avoid their own culpability for the state of public transit in Macon by emphasizing the formal separateness of the Transit Authority; but in fact, the authority remains firmly under their guidance and ultimate control.

The Transit Authority's service has two legs: the fixed-route bus system, using thirty-nine buses to provide traditional bus services on eleven fixed routes; and the paratransit system, discussed later, serving persons with disabilities. The vast majority of the Transit Authority's fixed-route riders, at least 89 percent in 1993, are African- American. It is well known locally that while the white population generally travels in private vehicles, fixed-route buses are generally reserved for African-American residents.[6]

Funding of Transportation Services in Macon

In 1993, the Macon and Bibb County planned to devote approximately $33.65 million of federal, state and local funds for roads, streets and highways, over $10 million of which was to come from federal funds. Meanwhile, in stark contrast, the city and county budgeted less than $1.4 million for public bus transportation during the same period, none of which was to come from federal funds. The federal funds earmarked for Macon were split up by GDOT among the other small cities in Georgia, specifically, Savannah, Augusta, Rome, Albany and Athens.

In theory, Macon's extensive road network may be used (or at least indirectly enjoyed) by the entire population. In fact, however, the roads operate as instruments of isolation for many residents without cars, facilitating white flight to the periphery while restricting access by lower-income African-Americans to training opportunities, jobs, schools, colleges, churches, community activities, housing and stores.

Only a tiny portion of the population regularly utilizes the municipal airport. Nevertheless, both the Transit Authority and the municipal airport receive approximately the same amount in public funds, though the Transit Authority in its weakened state still serves approximately thirty times more people than does the airport.

The road network already operates well by national standards, and yet, under the guidance of the city, county, P&Z and GDOT, roads continue to receive the vast majority of public expenditures on transportation. Meanwhile, no significant effort is made to enhance the funding of public transit, and in particular, discourage the Transit Authority from accepting federal funds. In contrast, all other comparable cities in Georgia apply for and receive federal funds for their transit systems. Moreover, the City of Macon, Bibb County, P&Z and GDOT regularly solicit massive infusions of federal funds to enhance the road network.

Plans for the future are even more discouraging. In November, 1994, the voters of Bibb County narrowly passed a 1-percent sales tax on food and other items that is expected to raise over $120 million in revenue over five years. Although all of the money must be spent on transportation, no more than $2 million of the proceeds may be devoted to public transit, according to the wording of the referendum.[7] With matching grants, the sales tax is expected to result in over $314 million in new transportation projects, less than 1 percent of which would be devoted to the transportation needs of the carless citizens of Macon.

In short, although economic development of white-dominated business and residential areas regularly succeeds as a rationale for extending or improving roads, streets and highways in Macon at the public expense, economic development of low-income African-American residents regularly fails as a rationale for publicly supporting the kinds of transportation services that low-income African-Americans need to develop economically.

Meanwhile, the Georgia Department of Transportation goes out of its way to foster the perception that transit, unlike the roads, should be evaluated solely on the basis of how little public funding is needed to support it. In its annual Transit Fact Book, for instance, GDOT lists as performance indicators only such factors as cost efficiency (operating expense/revenue vehicle mile and operating expense/revenue vehicle hour), cost effectiveness (operating expense/unlinked trip, operating expense/passenger mile, and farebox recovery ratio), and service effectiveness (unlinked trips/revenue vehicle mile and unlinked trips/revenue vehicle hour). Nowhere does GDOT give any indication of how the service might perform in meeting the needs of those without private means of transportation. The implication is that service is not an important measure of transit performance. The Transit Authority regularly touts itself as among the most "efficient" in the country.

In sum, officials in Macon and Bibb County, in coordination with the majority of voters and the state and federal bureaucracies, facilitate the disproportionate allocation of state, federal, and local funds among the public service transportation systems, relatively underfunding those services of most value to African-Americans.

Discriminatory Effects on African-Americans

The underfunding of public transit effectively restrains the freedom of movement, employment, education, training, housing, living conditions and community life of the Transit Authority's riders and potential riders, most of whom are African-American. Meanwhile, the relative overfunding of streets, roads, and highways greatly facilitates the freedom of movement, employment, education, training, housing, living conditions, and community life of the car-owning class, which is predominantly white.

According to the 1990 census, Bibb County has a population of 149,967, 42 percent of whom are African-American. The City of Macon has a population of 106,640, 52 percent of whom are African-American. African-American citizens in the community have a yearly aggregate income per household of just over half of that of the white population.

The relative poverty of the African-American population in Macon and Bibb County restricts African-American access to private transportation. Of the 14 percent of all households in Bibb County that have no cars, 74 percent are inhabited by African-Americans. Twenty-eight percent of all African-American households lack cars, in contrast to only 6 percent of white households.

The percentage of residents in Bibb County who lack private transportation substantially exceeds the 14 percent of households that reported having no car. In a sprawling, increasingly decentralized community like Macon where each household has over 2.5 members on average, one car may not be enough to meet the transportation needs of all household members. In Macon's African-American households, furthermore, the cars are more likely to be old, of poor quality and unreliable. In other words, of the 65 percent of all African-American households in Bibb County that have no car or one car, it seems reasonable to infer that a substantial proportion — perhaps half of the African-American population in Bibb County — may lack effective private means of transportation. Indeed, according to a recent unscientific study of the City of Unionville, an African-American neighborhood in Macon, over 40 percent of the residents indicated that transportation to work is a problem.

In short, it is not surprising that relatively poor public transit service tends to have a greatly disproportionate effect on African-American residents of Macon and Bibb County because they have disproportionately high rates of poverty and low rates of car ownership. Bus services in Macon, such as they are, are largely used by lower-income African-Americans, who made up 89 percent of the Transit Authority's ridership on its eleven fixed bus routes in 1983, and who probably make up an even greater proportion today. Meanwhile, the Transit Authority's para-transit system, which gives door-to-door service on twenty-four-hour notice, is devoted solely to persons with disabilities.

The Human Effects of Isolation and Transit Underfunding

In Macon, Georgia, the hours and days of the Transit Authority's operations are tightly constrained: on weekdays, service stops at 6:45 P.M; the schedule is limited on Saturdays; and there is no service on Sundays and holidays. In contrast, before mandatory integration and a sharp decline in white ridership, Macon's bus system ran late at night every day.

The Transit Authority's routes are also severely constrained in geographic reach. Its eleven fixed routes have remained largely unchanged since the 1970s when the city and county bought out what had been a partly private bus system. Little attempt has subsequently been made to modify the routes, despite a shift of Macon's socioeconomic center to the periphery. Year after year, Macon's traditional downtown center has been steadily abandoned by whites in favor of developments in the northern and western peripheries. Although most of the new development has occurred away from existing bus lines, the bus lines have never been changed to facilitate access by bus riders to the new centers of economic, social, educational and political power. The bus system is still tethered by a hub-and-spoke design to a dying inner city.

In a wide variety of ways, restrictions on the Transit Authority's operating hours and geographic reach have in turn curtailed the freedom and opportunities of those who rely on the system or who would rely on a better system. Perhaps the most glaring effect of the Transit Authority's limited service is on the ability of African-Americans to gain access to good jobs.

For example, many young African-Americans still in high school are often willing to work, but can do so only after school, during the evenings, and on weekends and holidays. If their families lack reliable cars, as they commonly do, many of these young people are discouraged from seeking work; the bus system cannot help them.

Even if a low-skill, carless jobseeker is not hindered by a school schedule, the bus system still cannot be relied upon for transportation to most entry-level positions. Such jobs typically require evening, weekend and holiday shifts. At those critical times, Macon's bus system is silent.

Meanwhile, Macon's largest employers are located on the periphery away from any bus line: Brown & Williamson (cigarettes), Riverwood (paper mill), Cagle's (chicken processing), Cigna (insurance data processing), and the hotel operators and fast food establishments along Riverside Drive and Tom Hill Sr. Boulevard.

One result is that the first and most important question on the lips of Macon's employers of unskilled labor is, "Do you have a car or some other reliable (private) way to get to work?" The absence of a car means the absence of a job, because the bus system is typically useless for a worker. A vicious circle thereby begins to turn, funneling a disproportionate number of unskilled, carless African-Americans to the bottom.

After leaving school, many young African-Americans faced with substantial transportation obstacles in addition to the normal difficulties associated with beginning work become discouraged about their chances to make it in a traditional occupation. The consequences in some cases — crime, drug abuse, sexually transmitted disease, and teenage pregnancy — are disastrous. Although better transportation alone can solve no pervasive social problems, it remains a critical common link in the efforts of many in Macon's African-American community to escape generations of poverty.

The bus system's limitations not only reduce the employment opportunities available to African-Americans. Negative effects are also felt by African-Americans as they go about a wide range of daily activities. For example, the biggest supermarket chain in the area, Kroger, is not efficiently served by the system. While two of the fixed routes pass near two Kroger stores, the routes do not swing down access roads and into the store parking lots to permit most potential riders to ride. The two largest Kroger stores in the county lie in white neighborhoods, and not on bus lines, as does a large discount supermarket, FoodMax, a variety of discount drug stores, a new Publix supermarket, and a wide assortment of growing enterprises. Conversely, a largely abandoned shopping center where anchor tenant K-Mart closed about 1991, is still served by the system. The new K-Mart, located in an area of vigorous commercial activity, remains unserved by the Transit Authority. In short, riders of the bus system are often forced to accept higher prices and poorer selection, despite being economically ill-equipped to bear such costs.

Churches, which constitute some of the liveliest, most fertile and supportive gathering places for the African-American community in Macon, are not served by the system at the critical times, on Sundays or during weekday evenings.

Young people cannot use the system to facilitate their attendance at after-school functions, or to attend church and social gatherings when they are usually held, on weekends, evenings and holidays. Their parents, likewise, cannot use the bus system to attend parent-teacher conferences, school board meetings, school events, school sports activities, and other school-related occasions during the evening hours or on weekends.

Even on the Authority's limited routes, the frequency of operation can be so minimal as to discourage use. For instance, students who use public transportation to attend Macon College, even for a single 11:00 A.M. class, must devote the entire day to the ordeal. After rising before 6:00 A.M. to catch the first bus from their homes to the downtown transfer station, the students must wait to catch the single morning bus from the transfer station to the college at 7:30 A.M. Late in the day, they have only one opportunity to retrace their routes.

Limitations on the bus routes also restrict the housing options available to its African-American riders, making it effectively impossible for them to live in much of the more desirable lower-income housing stock, like some of the housing available in the Bloomfield Road area and in some North Macon apartment complexes not served by the system. Thus the service provided by the Transit Authority has confined many African-Americans to housing projects, older neighborhoods and poorer housing stock, perpetuating segregated housing patterns. The segregated housing leads in turn to segregated social activities like shopping, movie-going, dining, etc., that many members of the African-American community would choose to conduct in integrated settings if transportation did not pose a barrier.

Because most of the Transit Authority's riders and potential riders are African-American, the relative underfunding of the Transit Authority is partly, perhaps largely, responsible for the unlawfully discriminatory effects listed here. Of course, underfunding alone may not be the sole cause of inferior transportation service. Poor transportation service to African-Americans may also have resulted from the Transit Authority's operational actions and omissions over the years, as planned, facilitated and ratified by the city, county, P&Z and GDOT.[8]

Whatever the particular mechanism, however, the bottom line is that the transportation services provided to African- Americans in Macon are patently inferior to those provided to whites.

Incidental Effects in Macon on People With Disabilities

Bibb County has 4,306 citizens with mobility limitations that qualify them for paratransit services under the Americans with Disabilities Act, according to a 1993 study prepared by P&Z for the Transit Authority.[9] Because of the poverty of the transit system in Macon, the Transit Authority underserves the population of persons with disabilities. Only one bus was handicapped-accessible as of 1994, and only one of the eleven fixed routes offered even occasional service to persons with disabilities. The Transit Authority operates only three vans to service the needs of thousands of potential riders, and presently intends to offer only one more such van in 1997.

In short, persons in Macon with disabilities are unable to participate in the benefits of the Transit Authority's service to the same extent as regular passengers. The fact that the City of Macon and Bibb County are not taking seriously their obligations to people with disabilities is apparent when one considers the steps taken by other cities in Georgia. While Macon intends to have made only 15 percent of its fixed-route buses accessible to handicapped persons by 1997, 39 percent of Albany's fixed-route buses and 84 percent of Augusta's fixed-route buses were already accessible to handicapped persons by 1993. Further, while Macon had one paratransit van per 2,153 eligible persons during 1993, Columbus' ratio was 1:1,025, and Albany's, 1:499.

In sum, the government of Macon and Bibb County is in blatant violation of the Americans with Disabilities Act, and oversees the worst transit system in the state (and perhaps one of the worst in the country) from the standpoint of persons with disabilities — not counting, of course, those communities offering no transitservice at all.

What has been Done in Macon?

Grass roots activism has percolated for years in Macon on the issue of public transportation, but with little visible effect. The local chapter of the NAACP has long complained about the system, for instance, as have a host of private citizens. A public forum on the problems, attended by hundreds of people, was held in 1994 and attended by some of the city's leaders. However, change has been slow in coming. Transit riders and their representatives are regularly given short shrift at public hearings on transportation matters. Indeed, their political power seems too weak to ensure deference to their concerns in the democratic processes of local government.

In 1994, an administrative complaint was filed on behalf of a group of transit riders in Macon with the U.S. Department of Transportation by Georgia Legal Services, the Legal Defense Fund, and the author. The U.S. Department of Transportation announced about a year later in June, 1995 that it would accept jurisdiction of the case despite Macon's refusal to accept federal transit funds.

However, as of December, 1996, no investigation had apparently been started.

Does the Law Prohibit the Underfunding of Public Transit?

Several laws may be invoked to challenge the relative disregard for and underfunding of public transit in places like Macon, Montgomery, Los Angeles, New York, Philadelphia and Dallas, where transit finance claims have already been raised. But it is important first to realize what these legal claims are not about. In general, carless transit users (or would-be users) have never claimed that they assert constitutional rights to governmental provision of transportation (which have never been held to exist). Rather, such persons have only asserted the right for their distinct interests in transportation to be fairly and duly accommodated in the overall public planning and funding of transportation-related services.

In short, the argument on behalf of transit riders and would-be transit riders is that the government may not lawfully plan for and subsidize the transportation interests of some citizens while largely ignoring the transportation interests of other disfavored classes of citizens. Depending on the particular circumstances of the case at hand, this proposition can be understood in several alternative ways:

1. As a claim that potential beneficiaries of public subsidies are excluded, consistent with status as members of disfavored categories of race and class (may be the case where no transit services are provided at all despite the existence of great need by significant numbers of carless residents);

2. As a claim that beneficiaries of public subsidies are selected, consistent with their status as members of favored categories of race and class (may be the case where elaborate and expensive road projects are offered primarily to facilitate comfortable and convenient car transit by majority groups, leaving poor carless minorities trapped in decaying centers);

3. As a claim that persons with disfavored status are provided with benefits in relation to their numbers that are disproportionately inferior to the benefits provided to those with favored status in relation to their numbers (may be the case where the expenditures on transit are grossly disproportionate to the expenditures on roads, streets and highways, while differences in the respective sizes of the groups are less disproportionate, e.g., the Macon case);

4. As a claim that particular policies and procedures for the distribution of transportation subsidies unfairly impede access to the benefits by those most in need of assistance (may be the case where users are charged relatively little for road use in comparison with the charges borne by transit users);

5. As a claim that a benefit to a favored category of persons is harmful to a disfavored category of persons (may be the case where a road opening up a peripheral area for the favored operates as an instrument of isolation for disfavored minorities who are left behind without cars, or where such a road destroys the physical integrity of a low-income minority neighborhood);

6. As a claim that a particular project or allocation has been proposed or finalized without proper planning, community input, or consideration of environmental impacts, the latter defined broadly to include effects to people as well

as nature (may be the case where an MPO fails to follow procedures required by law).

Persons and organizations challenging the underfunding of public transit may make claims under the Equal Protection Clause of the U.S. Constitution and the equal protection guarantees in state constitutions. However, to prevail under those theories, plaintiffs must generally show a that purposeful discrimination was a motivating factor, a showing that has proven difficult for some plaintiffs in other contexts.[10] The Supreme Court has suggested that the inquiry into discriminatory purpose is a "sensitive" one that may rely on circumstantial, as well as direct, evidence into such considerations as the overall discriminatory impact of the decision, the historical setting of the issue, the specific sequence of events leading to the challenged decision, any abnormal procedures in the challenged decision-making, and the particular legislative or administrative history of the challenged decision.[11]

Plaintiffs may also challenge discriminatory transportation planning and funding under Title VI of the Civil Rights Act of 1964,[12] generally without a showing of intentional discrimination to the extent that the effects of discrimination are unjustifiably disproportionate.[13] Though Title VI lay in a state of relative dormancy during the 1980s,[14] it is now being revived. The Civil Rights Restoration Act of 1991,[15] combined with the Clinton administration's more recent directives for the administrative agencies to revive enforcement of Title VI under the rubric of environmental justice,[16] means that transportation must be provided in an evenhanded way across the whole spectrum of transportation services.

Carless citizens may also assert a fundamental federal constitutional right to travel freely across state lines, to migrate without impediment from one state to another, and to reside in whichever state one chooses, pursuant to the Privileges and Immunities Clause of the U.S. Constitution.[17] Professor Lawrence Tribe has further suggested that a constitutional right to travel may be understood to arise in connection with equal protection, or as an aspect of one's fundamental rights of privacy and personhood.[18] The Court has given the right to travel more deference than one's right to be free from state-imposed tax burdens under the Commerce Clause.[19] A constitutional foundation may also arise from the Due Process Clause to the extent that withdrawals of benefits target members of minority populations. To the extent one's fundamental rights have been infringed, one need not demonstrate that the infringement resulted from a discriminatory purpose.

One of the traditional legal wellsprings of the environmental justice movement is the National Environmental Policy Act (NEPA).[20] NEPA creates various restraints on the ability of federal agencies to engage in any actions significantly affecting the quality of the human environment; the act broadly covers social and economic impacts as well as impacts on natural resources. When proposing actions, federal agencies are obliged under NEPA to assess potential environmental impacts, to conduct cost-benefit analyses, to engage in systematic study of the basic problems implicated, to ensure public participation in evaluation, and to foster decision-making that is sensitive to the possible extrinsic effects of the action.[21]

Classes of poor persons may also challenge discriminatory subsidization of transportation under some of the same laws that protect the rights of racial minorities to equal treatment by governmental authorities.[22] Discrimination on the basis of poverty is not presently given the same degree of scrutiny that the courts give to discrimination on the basis of race, but the courts remain at least somewhat skeptical about discrimination against the poor.

For instance, in the case of San Antonio Independent School District v. Rodriguez, the Supreme Court refused to recognize a complaint by members of a low-income neighborhood that they have a right to schools as good as their higher-tax-paying neighbors; the Court suggested that it would have found "far more compelling" a case in which the public school charged tuition, thereby preventing the poorest residents from having access to schooling at all.[23] This is arguably the case in the arena of transportation subsidies; roads are freely accessible to car-owners while fares discourage transit use.

As income inequalities in American society continue to grow, it is possible that the courts may grow more ready to recognize that poor people have as much claim to equal protection of the law as, for instance, ethnic minorities.

Persons with disabilities, one class of heavily transit-dependent citizens, may object to inadequate public transit facilities on the basis of the Americans With Disabilities Act.[24] The act provides a relatively clearcut right for access to public transit services by persons with disabilities.[25] However, the legal clarification of their rights may result in tension between their interests and those of other disfavored minorities with less clearcut remedies, especially during a time of declining funding for public transit.

Various citizens may raise objections to procedural flaws in the planning, allocation and administration of transportation funding under ISTEA (1991),[26] under the Due Process Clauses of the United States and state constitutions, under the Americans with Disabilities Act, and under various state "sunshine" and open-records laws against inscrutable public processes. ISTEA is perhaps the most promising method for assuring that transportation planners consider the interests of people who have traditionally been shoved aside at the transportation trough.

ISTEA was enacted only after years of growing public dissatisfaction with the ways in which federal transportation dollars were being spent. By 1991, broad consensus had gelled that transportation funding decisions are too often made for ad hoc reasons, rather than for reasons of sound public policy. ISTEA reflects popular and congressional dissatisfaction with business-as-usual in local and state transportation "planning." Among other things, ISTEA requires urban areas with populations more than 50,000 to conduct planning through an MPO in ways that weigh the "overall social [and] economic . . . effects of transportation decisions" and encourage the expansion and enhancement of transit services and other transportation alternatives.[27]

ISTEA provides an especially important but as yet untested basis for relief in common situations like the one in Macon, Georgia, where intermodal planning requirements have yet to be fully and fairly implemented. Indeed, ISTEA probably offers an important latent ground of relief for citizens around the country who have heretofore been effectively shut out of transportation planning in their respective communities. The U.S. Department of Transportation's new ISTEA regulations are designed to enforce the rights of such groups of citizens to fair treatment in transportation planning under ISTEA.[28]

Many of these legal theories have been elaborated with greater specificity and formality in a fairly comprehensive complaint, filed in 1994 with the U.S. Department of Transportation by the author, the Legal Defense Fund, and Georgia Legal Services, all on behalf of a class of carless citizens in Macon, Georgia. The U.S. Department of Transportation recognized that it has jurisdiction over the matter.[29] The case is apparently the first case nationally to implicate ISTEA in conjunction with Title VI and the Equal Protection Clause of the U.S. Constitution, and therefore may provide an interesting initial test of these theories.

Finally, the success or failure of any one case should be understood in broader perspective. In general, as the federal government's role in transportation declines, it will likely become necessary for the federal agencies and courts occasionally to step in at the local and state levels to ensure that the declines are not visited disproportionately on those least able to afford them. Moreover, the courts may also be obliged directly to supervise the decline in the federal government's role, to ensure that the resulting negative effects are not borne disproportionately by those least able to afford them. A revisitation of anti-discrimination law in transportation is apparently just beginning to unfold.

Empowering Communities of Color: Lessons from Austin

Susana Almanza and Raul Alvarez

People Organized in Defense of Earth and her Resources (PODER) is an Austin, Texas-based environmental justice group established to increase the participation of communities of color in corporate and government decisions that directly affect them. Austin is the state capital and has a population of over 465,000. The city's African-American and Latino-American residents are concentrated largely on the east side. For example, people of color make up over 88 percent of the seven census tracts in Central East Austin. Five of the seven census tracts have a poverty rate of 30 percent or higher, with two tracts having poverty rates that exceed 50 percent.

In Austin, only 21.5 percent of the population is sixteen years of age or under and 7.5 percent is over sixty-five. In Central Austin, however, over 30 percent of the population is sixteen years of age or under, and 14.2 percent of the population is sixty-five or over. Over 11.9 percent of civilian non-institutionalized persons between the age of sixteen and sixty-four in Central Austin are physically challenged, compared with 3.8 percent in the city at large. Thus, Central East Austin has a higher proportion of the poor, youth, elderly, and physically challenged.

PODER works to empower communities of color in the city through education, advocacy and action. We feel that all three of these elements are essential if we are to achieve the empowerment of our communities. While advocating for our communities is an important element of this strategy, it alone will not empower our communities. Communities become empowered only when they are able to advocate for themselves. This chapter will discuss PODER's efforts to work toward achieving community and youth empowerment through a better understanding of transportation.

Transportation and Community Empowerment

PODER is currently in the midst of a Transportation and Community Empowerment Campaign. The campaign is designed to raise awareness about the effects of transportation decisions on communities of color so that these communities may become active participants in the transportation decision-making process. PODER sees transportation as an important element in the struggle to create a sustainable community. Although improved transportation is only one element among the myriad of other challenges (i.e. housing, education, economic development, etc.) which must be addressed if our communities are to become livable places, it is a good place to begin.

Through our Transportation and Community Empowerment Campaign, PODER conducts workshops with neighborhood groups to help them identify the transportation needs of their community. At these workshops, PODER generally shows a video that presents the issue of transportation in terms of neighborhood impacts (i.e. road maintenance, bicycle and pedestrian safety, access to public transit, etc.), which is followed by a discussion about the transportation needs of their particular community. PODER helps the group compile information about transportation needs (through a neighborhood survey) and helps develop a plan to meet these needs. Communities are able to make intelligent decisions if they are provided with the proper tools for making these decisions.

Transportation and Our Youth

Young people are an important segment of our community. However, they have very limited options in terms of transportation. For the most part, young people are dependent on rides from family and friends to get from place to place — or they walk. If they choose to take the bus, their options are limited as to where they may travel and when they may travel. The issue of access to transportation will be further discussed in the following section, "Transportation and Youth Empowerment." In this section, we will focus on the issue of public safety for young people who choose to walk or bike.

One of the main focuses of PODER's Transportation and Community Empowerment Campaign addresses the issue of public safety. Our streets are not safe for those who do not (or cannot) travel by car. Of course, included in this group are kids who often play or ride their bikes on the street. The dangers were summed up by Librado Almanza (age 10) who is a victim of an auto-pedestrian accident:

"In many urban cities, the streets are our playground. We play football, baseball, ride our bikes and many other things in the street. On December 18th, 1994, my friends and I were walking to the corner store. We have to cross a six-lane street to get there. That day a truck ran a red light and struck me as I was crossing the street. My leg and collar bone were broken. The inside of my mouth was busted and my chin was cut. I had massive abrasions throughout my body. My mother says angels were guarding me and thanks the spirits for letting me live. Since my accident, five other children have been involved in auto-pedestrian accidents. Three of them died. Children have lost their right to their urban playground. The increased traffic in the inner city has become a death trap for children like me."[1]

Many other young people have not been so lucky. Streets are not safe places for our children. We must all work to make our neighborhoods safer by demanding that our communities have sidewalks, wheelchair ramps, bike lanes, as well as appropriate lighting, speed limits, traffic lights, traffic signs, and road markings. And we need adequate parks and playgrounds.

Traffic safety issues are especially crucial where elementary and middle schools are located. Many of the community concerns revolve around enforcement of the traffic laws. Many of the traffic safety problems in Austin's low-income and minority neighborhoods could be solved by strictly enforcing the speed laws. DOT has responded by building overpasses. However, the location of schools near major freeways and thoroughfares remains problematic.

In addition to traffic, inner-city children have to contend with noise and pollution from bus barns, refueling stations, and vehicles traveling the nearby freeways. Low-income people and people of color are usually left out of the planning process for the development of transportation facilities, and have had little or no control over the environmental and economic impacts they suffer as a result of placement of those facilities in their communities. Officials in charge of planning large-scale transportation systems give almost no consideration to the systems' potential impacts on low-income communities and communities of color. Few inner-city residents have a say in the location of local schools near freeways and highways that may pose risks to their children. Consequently, our children are exposed to disproportionately high concentrations of carbon monoxide and other pollution from automobile exhaust and congestion on the freeways that dissect our neighborhoods. At the same time, childhood asthma and other respiratory illnesses have reached an epidemic in the Latino and African-American community.

School busing, intended to eliminate discrimination in the school system, has become a system of hardship for youth of color. They very often must ride the bus for an inordinate amount of time to get to school. A look at the history of the educational system in Austin provides insight as to why this may be the case.

In 1954, the Supreme Court decision of Brown v. Board of Education ordered the communities of our nation, "to effectuate a transition to a racially non-discriminatory school system." The Austin school system did not comply with Supreme Court decision. In 1970, sixteen years after Brown, the U.S. government was compelled to file suit to eliminate racial discrimination in the Austin school system. In 1972, the Fifth Circuit Court of Appeals, upon appeal by the school district, ruled:

"We hold that the Austin Independent School District has, in its choice of school site locations, construction and renovation of schools, drawing of attendance zones, student assignment and transfer policies, and faculty and staff assignments, caused and perpetuated the segregation of black students within the school system."[2]

The Austin school system continued its fight within the legal arena, but in 1978 the Court of Appeals held for the fourth time that the Austin school system was discriminatory. The court remanded the case to the district court for continued monitoring. It was not until 1983 (twenty-nine years after Brown v. Board of Education, thirteen years after litigation began, and after having been told four times by the appellate court that the system was discriminatory) that the court was able to rule that the Austin school system had become a unitary system. Even today, we can see the long-term educational impact of this discriminatory system. Eight elementary schools, all located in East Austin, have been labeled "low-performing" or "clearly unacceptable" by the Texas Education Agency because less than one in five students who took the state achievement test in the spring of 1996 passed it.

The only high school, Anderson High School, located in the heart of the African-American and Mexican-American community, was relocated to west Austin. For youth of color, transportation became a very real issue with which to contend. Youth of color were forced to take on the burden of awakening early each morning to be bused to the opposite side of town. Youth missing the school bus were then faced with the dilemma of how to get from East Austin to West Austin. It was our youth who were bused from their neighborhoods to white neighborhoods in order to achieve desegregation. This practice has not changed much. As new schools are built further and further away from the inner city, black and brown kids are bused farther and farther away from their own communities.

Transportation and Youth Empowerment

This section on youth empowerment is dedicated to all of those individuals and organizations who are striving to breathe life into the tired souls of our communities through their work on issues related to education, employment, economic development, affordable housing, environment, health care, transportation, etc. We place great value on their work because these issues are at the heart of problems confronting our young people today. What is to stop a young person from becoming demoralized when they have to contend with outdated school curricula, a lack of quality employment opportunities, and a deteriorated living environment? These environmental factors coupled with negative images that young people are exposed to through television, movies and other media have a very negative impact on their psychological well-being. All of these factors contribute to the sense of hopelessness that many black and brown teenagers feel.

However, youth empowerment is not about hopelessness. It is about hopefulness. We are inspired by the work of Dr. Deborah Prothrow-Stith who has taken an environmental health approach to understanding and confronting the issue of violence in our communities. In her book, *Deadly Consequences,* she writes,

> "I am convinced that we can change public attitudes toward violence and that we can change violent behavior. What is required is a broad array of strategies - strategies that teach new ways of coping with anger and aggressive feelings. I believe that we can and must mobilize schools, the media, industry, government, churches, community organizations, and every organized unit within our society to deliver the message that anger can be managed and aggressive impulses controlled."[3]

A fundamental message in *Deadly Consequences* is that only when we achieve a fundamental understanding of the various factors that influence our behavior are we able to deal with these factors and thus make a change in our behavior. Similarly, it is only when we achieve a fundamental understanding of the various factors that affect our community that we are able to deal with these factors and thus make a change in our community. This is the basic idea on which PODER's community empowerment and youth empowerment efforts are based.

Youth Empowerment and the Environmental Justice Principles

A number of environmental justice principles (adopted at the First National People of Color Environmental Leadership Summit in 1991) are quite relevant to the issue of youth empowerment. A careful reading of these principles suggests the need for those of us involved in the environmental justice movement to work toward increased youth involvement in our activities. Although the environmental justice principles do not provide an outright mandate that our organizations focus on youth education and empowerment, this responsibility falls upon us since there are so few others out there who subscribe to these principles.

Environmental justice affirms the fundamental right to political, economic, cultural and environmental self-determination of all peoples (Principle Five). This principle could easily and accurately be made to read "political, economic, cultural and environmental self-determination for young people." The need for self-determination is based on our need to have the power to control our own destiny. We must fight for the basic right of self-determination because the dominant culture in this society
subsumes all other cultures. In fact, the dominant culture is able to remain dominant by denying those of different cultures access to economic and political power. Unfortunately, this culture of domination is ingrained in our minds at a very early age through our educational system, during a time in our lives when we lack the power (political and economic) and the awareness (social and cultural) to effectively question its validity.

Environmental justice demands the right to participate as equal partners at every level of decision-making (Principle Seven). This principle calls attention to the need for us to have a say regarding the issues affecting our lives. This is essential if we are ever going to possess the power to control our own destiny. Youth in particular are given little if no opportunity to influence decisions that have a direct impact on them. Programs are designed to address the "needs of young people" without so much as considering what types of program youth feel would best address their needs. In addition, there are many youth-oriented policies developed without taking into account (and very often ignoring) the opinions expressed by young people. Policies such as youth curfews and school dress codes aimed at dealing with the gang issue tend to impose strict rules on a vast majority of youth who are not involved in gang-related activities. These types of policies constitute injustices against young people.

Environmental justice demands that public policy be based on mutual respect and justice for all people, free from any form of discrimination or bias (Principle Two). One of the main reasons that young people are not allowed to participate in the decision-making process has to do with the lack of respect for their intellectual abilities. Decision-makers very often assume a paternal attitude when dealing with youth. They work under the assumption that young people are incapable of making intelligent decisions. Unfortunately, this lack of intellectual respect is commonly mirrored in the schools. Instruction in our schools tends to be carried out in a very top-down fashion; for the most part, the student is asked to accept the information presented and not to think about it critically. It is in this context that an evaluation of young people's behavior should be considered.

Environmental justice calls for education of present and future generations that emphasizes social and environmental issues, based on experience and an appreciation of diverse cultural perspectives (Principle Sixteen). This principle serves as a call to action in terms of the education of our youth. Some of us may choose to advocate for our youth in terms of the curriculum and investments in our schools. Others may choose to work directly with young people because our schools are not teaching them about the issues we feel are important. Others may not be in a position to choose either one. Whatever the case may be, it is important to realize that youth are disenfranchised in their own right and that, in the spirit of the principles of enviro- mental justice, they deserve to be treated with honor and respect in all that they do.

An Introduction to PODER's Summer Youth Program

In the summer of 1995, PODER made its first attempt at engaging youth on issues related to environmental justice. We had originally envisioned a two-to-three week summer program involving eight to ten students. As the summer approached, the opportunity to work within an established summer youth employment program arose. Our decision to collaborate with another organiza-tion on this project changed the complexion of the program we had envisioned. Instead of lasting for two to three weeks, the program would be eight weeks in duration, and instead of involving eight to ten students, the program would serve twenty-five students.

The vast majority of students (twenty-four out of twenty-five) who partici-pated in the program were African-American and Mexican-American. The pro-gram targeted students who were fourteen and fifteen years of age. Participants in the program worked twenty-five hours per week. Half the time was spent on work-related tasks and the other half was spent on academic-related tasks. The academic component, which was PODER's main focus, is described here.

Through collaboration, PODER had to help program participants conduct a public-opinion survey. With this in mind, PODER devised an eight-week cur-riculum focusing on the development of problem-solving and media-literacy skills. By mixing these two elements, PODER hoped to develop analytical and presentation skills as well.

Because PODER is committed to the principles of environmental justice, we structured the program so that participants would develop useful skills in an environment responsive to their interests. Our basic underlying premises are best summarized by Frank Stluka and Arnold H. Packer of the Institute for Policy Studies. In their model, "Developing Learning-Rich Tasks for Work-Based Learning Programs," they identify three premises of learning-rich work: honor the student; honor the work; and honor the learning.[4] One honors the students by helping them develop skills that will be useful to them. One honors their work by making sure the work has real value (to them, to society, or to the organization). Finally, one honors the learning by allowing the students to apply what they have learned to other aspects of their life.

Empowerment through the Development of Problem-Solving Skills

Students were given a framework to follow to complete the required public opinion survey; PODER presented a very standard problem-solving methodology of four components:
1. Identify the problem.
2. Study the problem.
3. Set goals for the purpose of addressing the problem.
4. Develop a plan to realize these goals.

Environmental Justice To put this methodology into practice, students were engaged in a number of discussions about issues related to environmental justice. To introduce the subject, students were asked to briefly discuss and then write about the concept of environment. Some students described environment in terms of conservation and global trends. Some looked at environment in terms of their surroundings, identifying trash, graffiti and violence as part of the environment in which they live.

Students were then asked to discuss and write about the concept of justice. A very prolonged discussion took place about various issues they considered to be injustices. They identified the Rodney King beating as an injustice. They identified the O.J. Simpson trial as an injustice (in terms of his being wrongly accused). When asked about issues they were faced with in Austin, they identified teen curfew, school dress codes and closed school campuses as injustices. Students were asked to write about what could be done to correct these injustices, mainly to stimulate their thinking about solutions, and not so much to evaluate the quality of their responses.

Next, we brought the terms environment and justice together and held a short discussion on the subject. Then we showed video case studies on environmental justice from around the country and invited speakers to talk about local environmental justice issues. With each case study, students were required to fill out a form, asking them:
1. What was the problem?
2. How did residents identify the problem?
3. How did residents study the problem?
4. What was their goal?
5. What did they do to try to achieve their goal?

Along with encouraging students to begin thinking systematically about problem-solving, we familiarized them with community struggles going on all over the country. Students had the opportunity to see that people of color were demanding that justice be served, and that in a few instances their demands had been met. In addition, they were able to learn about the history of struggle in their own community, and that people in their own neighborhoods were fighting for justice on a day-to-day basis. In this way, PODER showed students how other individuals and organizations dealt with unjust situations.

Transportation One of the issues covered in our discussion of environmental justice concerned transportation. PODER showed a video describing some of the issues related to transportation often not considered to be transportation-related issues. The video discussed transportation issues from a neighborhood perspective (i.e., sidewalks, bike lanes, lighting, road maintenance, bus services, etc.).

Students were given a neighborhood transportation survey and were asked to complete it based on the neighborhood in which they lived. Students were also engaged in a discussion of their specific needs in terms of transportation. Young people in general are transportation- disadvantaged since many do not have access to an automobile. When asked what some of their concerns were in terms of transportation, they mentioned that:

- Buses were very crowded after school and they often did not stop because they were too full.
- Bus service was very slow on weekends. Some said that they avoided using the bus on Sundays because the buses ran once per hour.
- Buses needed better lifts for handicapped people because they often broke, causing the bus to be stopped for a long time.
- Bus drivers should keep the homeless people off the bus because they ride around for a long time and sometimes bother people.
- The police should not give youth tickets when they ride their bicycles on the sidewalk because it is not safe to ride on some streets.

Some of the other transportation issues we discussed had to do with owning a car. When asked how they could get around easier, their first response was that they would like to have their own car. We briefly discussed the financial costs of owning a car (i.e., car payment, insurance, registration, inspection sticker, maintenance, fuel, etc.). We had them compute how much they would have to earn to be able to afford a car. We also had them compare the cost of owning a car to the cost of riding the bus, biking, or walking. Finally, we had them consider the external costs of owning a car (i.e., environmental, land use, etc.).

The Case of Light Rail: Who Benefits?

Clearly, residents of the mostly African-American and Latino Central East Austin have a much greater need for transportation services than the population at large.[5] A light rail system is planned for the Austin area. The jury is still out as to who will actually benefit from such a system. Light-rail systems run on routes (railways) specifically dedicated for their use. Unhindered by traffic signals and traffic congestion, they provide more efficient public transportation than traditional bus systems. However, light-rail systems, like so many other transportation improvements, are often designed to address the transportation needs of those traveling at peak periods (rush hour), and as a result fail to address the transportation needs of the disadvantaged.

The majority of the Austin light-rail system would service the area west of Interstate Highway 35. Only the short segment from the highway to Pleasant Valley Road provides direct access to the mostly African-American and Latino residents who live east of the interstate. Although the system would provide some access to Central East Austin residents, the majority of the population of this area would remain unserved by the system. Access to such a system may be further limited by the cost of use, which could be high.

The proposed system, while providing few benefits to Central East Austin, could have very significant direct, indirect and cumulative effects — environmental, economic and social impacts. The light-rail storage and maintenance facility is included within the short segment of the light-rail line that services Central East Austin. This facility would have to be of considerable size in order to accommodate the desired services.

People ask, why are these types of facilities always placed in our neighborhood? The location of the storage/maintenance yard is planned for a segment of Central East Austin that is blighted and in need of redevelopment, but it is doubtful that the yard would make an improvement. The increased noise and air pollution generated by such a facility would be a nuisance to nearby neighborhoods. In addition, the presence of the storage/maintenance yard would likely drive down property values in the surrounding areas — neighborhoods that already suffer from racial redlining by insurance companies, banks, and other financial institutions.

The light-rail system would also have a significant impact on pedestrian and bicycle circulation and local automobile traffic within the neighborhoods in Central East Austin. The proposed light-rail line runs along East Fourth and East Fifth Streets. Residents who live south of East Fourth would have to cross the railway each time they wanted to go to the grocery store, to a restaurant, or to church. Children who live north of East Fifth would have to cross the railway every day to get to school. Concerns about safety and simple inconvenience might lead people to find less direct routes, thus splitting the community. The rail line could become a barrier, isolating and cutting some residents off from the rest of the community, instead of increasing their mobility.

Light-rail may also have a direct impact on some residences and businesses in the surrounding neighborhoods. Commercial areas around light-rail stations have potential for increased business activity due to the influx of people. The proposed stations in Central East Austin are in a deteriorated area. There has been much talk about how light-rail can revitalize East Austin. However, talk is cheap.

A study on redevelopment was completed. Of concern is the potential that existing residences or businesses will be displaced. People of color and poor people in city after city know too well the history of urban renewal and displacement. Historically, the groups most vulnerable to displacement include the poor, people of color, elderly, and renters. Is such displacement necessary? What would be done about relocation? It is also important to consider what impact new businesses might have on those already established. Because they might take away from the customer base of existing businesses, new businesses should not overlap with the market of existing businesses. Existing businesses also should be given the opportunity to locate along the light-rail corridor, particularly if they are being displaced or would be otherwise adversely affected.

The issues raised by the light-rail proposal should be considered in all transportation system proposal evaluations. Ideally, they should be considered during the plan development process, but in the past this has seldom happened. This is due in large part to the fact that low-income communities and communities of color have not been represented at the table during the planning process. The involvement of these communities in transportation most often has had to be reactive and not proactive.

The Intermodal Surface Transportation Efficiency Act (ISTEA) is the first piece of legislation calling for increased public participation in planning processes; it requires the consideration of social and environmental issues in the development of transportation improvement programs and long-range transportation plans. Public participation is one of the cornerstones of environmental justice. ISTEA contains strong language about the need for public involvement. The act requires the metropolitan planning process to "include a proactive public involvement process that provides complete information, timely public notice, full public access to key decisions, and supports early and continuing involvement of the public in developing plans and TIPs [Transportation Improvement Programs]."

A further requirement of the planning process is that it "seek out and consider the needs of those traditionally underserved by existing transportation systems, including but not limited to low-income and minority households." This is a clear statement, and should be invoked when it becomes necessary to demand that Metropolitan Planning Organizations (MPOs) and State Departments of Transportation (DOTs) incorporate the concerns of people of color in their planning.

Unfortunately, ISTEA does not specify how MPOs and state DOTs will be held accountable to its requirements. Although the certification process is a potential avenue for addressing this shortcoming, certification is to a large extent at the discretion of the Federal Highway Administration and the Federal Transit Administration. Certification guidelines should be strengthened so that efforts to involve people of color will go beyond an ad in the newspaper or a name on a mailing list.

Although ISTEA does not state that considerations must be given specifically to low-income communities and communities of color, it does require that MPOs consider "the overall social, economic, energy, and environmental effects of transportation decisions (including consideration of the effects and impacts of the plan on the human, natural and man-made environment." Due consideration for such impacts on communities of color should be specified in the regulations.

For significant light-rail and roadway systems proposals, a major investment study is required. Current regulations specify that such a study "include environmental studies which will be used for environmental documents." They should specify, using similar language as that quoted from ISTEA, that the study must take into account social, economic, energy and environmental effects. Furthermore, section 3-301 (b) of Executive Order 12898 requires the agency to "identify multiple and cumulative exposures." In other words, the study should weigh the impacts of new transportation projects according to the negative social, economic, energy and environmental impacts already experienced by the affected low-income communities and communities of color.

ISTEA policy suggests that the transportation system should, "help implement national goals relating to mobility for elderly persons, persons with disabilities and economically disadvantaged persons." This policy should be translated into requirements for using access as a criteria for project evaluation.

Finally, social and environmental effects of the siting of transportation facilities are covered by the Environmental Justice Executive Order 12898. The order specifies that "to the extent practical and appropriate, federal agencies shall use this information [on environmental and human health risks borne by various populations] to determine whether their programs, policies, and activities have disproportionately high and adverse human health or environmental effects on minority populations and low-income populations."

Conclusion

Our communities need safe, efficient, and affordable transportation. Too often low-income and people-of-color communities are physically located on the "wrong side of the tracks." They are isolated from business and job centers with few transportation options. Freeways crisscross and cut through our neighborhoods, while few of our residents have cars. We breathe other people's automobile fumes and industrial pollution and pay the price in higher than average health problems.

Transportation facilities and systems can have major impacts on the areas in which they are sited, giving low-income communities and communities of color much to consider. Local residents and organizers need to begin seeking answers to key questions early in the process. Will the system provide transportation access to members of the community? Has there been meaningful involvement of the community in the decision-making process?

This case study used Austin to show how one might start thinking about education, empowerment, environment, and transportation. The connection between youth and transportation is of critical importance as we attempt to build a healthy and sustainable community. Transportation may be used as a basis for organizing and working with youth under the appropriate conditions.

Transportation regulations and laws can be used to demand more consideration of the issues of low-income communities and communities of color in planning processes, and these regulations can be strengthened. It is imperative that low-income communities and communities of color get involved in the planning of transportation systems. Concern for issues affecting our communities must become the rule, not the exception. Too long have tax dollars been used to subsidizetransportation systems, land-use policies, and development strategies that destroy our communities. PODER and other grassroots community groups around the nation are demanding an end to these unjust, destructive, and non-sustainable practices.

New Orleans Neighborhoods under Siege

Beverly H. Wright

Introduction

The City of New Orleans has had some form of public transportation since 1835. First came the mule-drawn omnibuses, which were succeeded by steam-powered rail cars, and then horse and mule-cars pulled on rails. By 1850, most of the street cars were powered by horses or mules. The first electric street car ran in New Orleans on February 1, 1893 and for many years serviced the whole city. One line still operates on St. Charles and Carrollton Avenues, from Canal Street to South Claiborne. This approximates a distance of six and a half miles. It is the oldest line in continuous operation in the world.

The St. Charles line has been placed on the National Register of Historic places. However, it is not just a tourist attraction. The St. Charles line carries thousands of residents to and from the business district daily. While the impact of the streetcar has made a positive imprint on the history of our city's development, what has been the impact of the development of an elaborate highway system to accommodate our rapid change to the automobile as our major source of transportation?

Our nation's highways have made travel easier by automobile from our urban centers to less populated areas, and made travel possible crosscountry. But our highways also have destroyed communities, displaced families, and in some cases, negatively impacted the social and economic viability of neighborhoods. This chapter investigates the impact of highway development on two communities in the City of New Orleans. The Vieux Carré, or French Quarter as it is popularly known, and the Treme community, or Sixth Ward, were both greatly impacted by the development of our nation's highway system. The results, however, were quite different for each of these communities. A major objective here is the review of the decision-making process and the extent of involvement citizens had on "final" decisions made on the construction of I-10, with emphasis on racial differences in the process, and resultant actions taken by the Highway Department. To fully comprehend the complexity of this phenomenon, it is necessary to review the early history and development of both communities.

Early New Orleans History

The history of New Orleans is intrinsically tied to the Vieux Carré. In fact, early New Orleans history is the history of the Vieux Carré. In 1718, Bienville, a French Canadian, and a small group of men left Mobile to establish a city on the banks of the Mississippi.[1] Located ninety miles from the Gulf of Mexico, this new city was to be named in honor of the Duke of Orleans. La Nouvelle Orleans was initially established to be a military outpost, a trading post, and an administrative center for French holdings in Louisiana. The new French settlement was located "on one of the most beautiful crescents of the river" and in time New Orleans became known as the Crescent City.[2] Adrien de Pauger, a French military engineer, was instructed to execute a plan for the city.[3] De Pauger laid out the streets in a "simple gridiron plan with the public square (Place d'Armes, later renamed Jackson Square) in the center with four square blocks extending in each direction above and below and six blocks back from the river.[4] The Vieux Carré has retained its original charm by maintaining its original street system (eleven blocks along the Mississippi River and six blocks deep), and also much of its colonial and antebellum character and charm. It also has a diversity of architectural styles, reflecting its multinational, cultural and historic evolution. Although the Vieux Carré is called the French Quarter, little remains from the French colonial period, due to a disastrous fire in 1788 that destroyed 850 buildings. This included all the business houses and residences of the most aristocratic families.[5] Although the rebuilding of the Vieux Carré was done under the Spanish Colonial period, most of the work was done by French architects, influenced by earlier French building styles and techniques. Although New Orleans was a Spanish colonial city for thirty-seven years, it remained essentially French. After the Louisiana Purchase, there was an influx of Americans, but because a majority of the new settlers lived outside the colonial city, the dominant character of the Vieux Carré remained French.

After 1820, the Vieux Carré experienced a transition from French to American style architecture. The use of red Philadelphia brick in building facades — a distinctly American influence — became increasingly popular. Many row houses, popular in Baltimore and Philadelphia, were built in the Vieux Carré. Cast-iron galleries were added to these structures and to many other buildings in the Quarter during the 1850s when wrought-iron balconies, a Spanish influence, were replaced by deep, cast-iron galleries. French Quarter galleries have since been recognized as "perhaps the most distinctive feature of New Orleans architecture." After the Civil War, expansion and development began occurring outside the Quarter and the Vieux Carré was neglected and eventually began to deteriorate. This neglect, however, preserved the flavor of the French Quarter, and it remains today very similar to what it was in the mid-nineteenth century, reflecting not one style, but a multiplicity of styles, each mirroring the cultural and historical period it came from.

Early Black New Orleans History

After the official launching of the American slave trade, blacks began to appear in large number in New Orleans. The 1726 census recorded only 300 slaves living in the city, but by 1732, there were nearly 1,000 slaves living in New Orleans.[6] New Orleans was not only unique because of its European inhabitants, uncommon in most southern cities, but it also had a significant number of "free colored people." The first free blacks were recorded in New Orleans in the 1720s; by 1803, there were 1,335 free blacks living in the city.

After the Civil War, New Orleans' black population experienced a dramatic increase. This resulted in the inability of many ex-slaves to find work or housing. Consequently, the poorest blacks lived where they could. They lived along the battures, or backswamps. Because the city of New Orleans was built facing the Mississippi River, her course followed the great crescent bend of the river. Hence, the batture was "the area on the riverside of the artificial levee without flood protection and without private ownership. The poorest blacks built shacks in the batture away from the dock area. These houses were, however, temporary because the river would periodically overflow and wash away the shacks.

Keeping in mind that New Orleans is a seaport town located at the mouth of the Mississippi and situated below sea level, with flooding her main problem, it is not surprising that whites occupied the highest and best land, protected by natural levees. Poor blacks lived in the backswamps, as P.F. Lewis describes it, "the demiland on the inland margin of the natural levee, where drainage was bad, foundation material precarious, streets atrociously unmaintained, mosquitoes endemic, and flooding a recurrent hazard." It is along this margin that a continuous belt of black population developed. Free blacks in New Orleans, many of whom were economically well off, originally lived and owned property in the French Quarter. After the Civil War and the onset of Jim Crow laws, however, they were pushed out of that section. Many of the blacks moved their families to the Treme, or Sixth Ward, an area adjacent to the French Quarter. As the Sixth Ward became crowded, many moved to the old Seventh Ward, an area that was contiguous to the Sixth Ward and represented a natural extension of the black community. These early black residential patterns developed over the years into longstanding, traditionally black neighborhoods, although early New Orleans's residential patterns were peculiarly integrated.

Several inventions influenced the racial geography of New Orleans in the twentieth century. These included the development of the Wood pump and the expansion of the city's public transportation system through use of the streetcar. The onset of World War I brought with it a virtual halt in the construction of housing. Black residents of New Orleans at this time lived in housing comparable to their white working class counterparts. But they were relegated to the less desirable homes in the backswamp area. There was also a large migration of rural blacks and whites, attracted by defense jobs in the city.

It became clear in the early 1920s that additional housing units were needed in the city. An apparent drive to improve housing conditions began when the 1920 census showed that New Orleans had dropped from twelfth to sixteenth place in popu- lation. The loss of population was blamed on the local authorities' inability to solve the housing problems of the city, resulting in many of the townspeople moving out beyond the city's boundaries.

South Carrollton Avenue was the focal point of the first systematic housing development in New Orleans. A second area of the Carrollton section, which consisted of more than 250 bungalows, was called Little California. The developer boasted that it was exclusively Caucasian and composed of only homeowners.

The Carrollton development probably marked the beginning of rigid residential segregation in the city. The onset of new housing brought with it heretofore nonexistent residential segregation paranoia. Ralph Thayer observes that "the more desirable renting and buying areas were correlated more and more with racial exclusivity from 1920 onward. The Wood pump that made the Carrollton development possible was truly a pervasive invention. It directly influenced the racial geography of the city.

The expansion of the city's streetcar system also affected its racial geography. As public transportation expanded, old black neighborhoods established in the nineteenth-century backswamp areas expanded into the newly drained margins of that area. The expanded transportation system made it possible for blacks to live in areas away from their jobs. The Wood pump, therefore, made it possible for whites to move to the suburbs and for blacks, with the aid of the expanded streetcar system, to move closer into the city. The black and white populations, it seems, were moving in opposite directions.

A discussion of the impact of Interstate 10 (I-10) on communities in the City of New Orleans requires two interrelated but separate discussions. In the 1950s, during which time I-10 construction decisions were first made, New Orleans was a completely segregated city, as was most of the U.S., but especially in the South. Consequently, the process and the results are completely different. The stories are clearly black and white.

A TALE OF TWO CITIES
The Vieux Carré: The White Tale

The years following World War II ushered a progressive spirit into the City of New Orleans. This spirit included a desire to rectify the city's chaotic transportation system. During this period, Robert Moses changed the face of New York City with the construction of parks, bridges, and expressways that catapulted the city into the twentieth century and the era of the automobile. He became the acknowledged leader of urban transportation planning.

Robert Moses was hired by the Louisiana Highway Department to develop an urban transportation plan designed to move people in cities. In 1946, Moses concluded that the principal traffic problem in New Orleans was "getting into and out of the heart of the city from the east and west, and expansion to the south, rather than getting straight through the city."[7]

In response to this problem, Moses advocated in his report, "Arterial Plan for New Orleans," the construction of an elevated riverfront expressway through the French Quarter. His plan sparked a debate that was to last for many years and has been referred to as the "Second Battle of New Orleans."

Moses' justification for building the freeway in the French Quarter was that it would reduce heavy traffic on Decatur Street in front of Jackson Square and make it easier for trucks to load and unload in the central business district. Despite the enormous presence that would surely loom over the French Quarter due to the prominence of the proposed elevated freeway, Moses believed that the historic flavor of the quarter and local treasures such as the St. Louis Cathedral and Jackson Square "would still be webbed to the Mississippi but would not be choked with needless through traffic (Second Battle, 32)."

Moses was keenly aware of the strong opposition that could arise from his plan. He responded to this anticipated criticism by proclaiming, "New Orleans' first duty and one which seems to be recognized is not only to preserve and restore the Vieux Carré, but to keep it alive by emphasizing and nurturing its kinship to the growing city which surrounds it, and particularly to the river which is still its lifeblood (Second Battle)."

Moses saw the freeway as "doing no harm" to the Vieux Carré as French Quarter preservationists prophesied its impending doom because of its construction. Moses proclaimed, "It is only necessary to give sufficient attention to progress, or if you prefer, change, to prevent the Vieux Carré from becoming a sterile museum with vital associations with the stream of life around it (Second Battle)."

Discussion around the development of the Vieux Carré expressway proposal dissipated and remained dormant for nearly five years. However, during that time, the city was involved in an impressive capital improvement program to modernize its rail transportation system.

Under the leadership of Mayor Morrison, the 1947 Union Passenger Terminal Agreement resulted in the consolidation of railroad tracks, the construction of grade separations, the abandonment of a number of existing railroads, and finally, the construction of the Union Passenger Terminal in central New Orleans. This massive project left little time for involvement in other transportation projects, but dramatically improved the city's transportation system.

The Vieux Carré expressway plan reappeared in 1951 with strong support from the Harland, Bartholomew and Associates Planning and Engineering Firm. However, for the next six years the city's major transportation efforts centered around the development of the Greater New Orleans Bridge that would link the central business district with the city's west bank and neighboring Jefferson Parish. Transportation efforts also included the construction of the Lake Pontchartrain Causeway, which consisted of a two-lane, twenty-four mile elevated causeway that would connect New Orleans on the south shore with Mandeville and Covington on the north shore.

In 1957, the Vieux Carré riverfront expressway regained center stage with the formation of the Central Area Committee of the Chamber of Commerce. The purpose of the committee was "to focus more attention on the particular needs of the central business district (Second Battle, 34)." A major goal of the committee was to find ways to provide better automobile access to and from the central business district.

Central Area Committee members represented the most powerful and prestigious institutions and organizations in the city. Moreover, the committee rapidly became one of the most powerful and influential special interest groups in the city. It was a power to be reckoned with on matters related to community affairs. Its thinking and philosophy dominated the policy and decision-making process in transportation planning in New Orleans during the 1960s.

Committee members were gravely concerned that population growth was more rapid in the suburbs than in the cities of the major metropolitan areas of the country. Moreover, between 1940 and 1950, that national trend could also be observed in New Orleans. Population growth in the city during that period was 15.3 percent, while the population of the total metropolitan area expanded by 24.1 percent.[8]

With this rapid population growth and development in the suburbs, the propotionate influence of the New Orleans central business district diminished. For example, retail sales in the central business district grew by 9.8 percent from 1958 to 1964; however, comparable sales in the metropolitan area increased by a staggering 32.3 percent during the same period.[9]

Concerned that the growing flight to the suburbs would cause a decline in the viability of the central business district, the Central Area Committee sought to develop long-range plans that would ensure healthy economic growth for the commercial and financial heart of the city. Moreover, the committee strongly believed that an integral part of any plan for the revitalization of the central business district was a system of high speed, limited-access freeways linking that district with the rapidly expanding metropolitan area.[10]

The Central Area Committee was committed to the development of a revitalization plan and was willing to financially support its development. To this end, they financed a trip to study transportation problems in twelve mid-western and eastern cities for the director-secretary of the City Planning Commission of New Orleans.[11]

The City Planning Commission's report, largely financed by the Central Area Committee, concluded that the "development of an outer belt [of freeways] consisting of the Pontchartrain expressway, the Mississippi River Bridge, the Claiborne Expressway, and Elysian Fields as [a] six-lane major street will provide facilities adequate to handle the anticipated increase in vehicles to the central business district to some date beyond 1990 (Prospectus)." The report further stated that "the missing link in the outer-loop from the foot of Elysian Fields to the Mississippi River Bridge must be supplied by development of an [expressway] route along the river front (Prospectus)." Until this missing link was constructed, the streets of the central business district would be filled with vehicles moving from one link of the freeway system to another. The existing surface routes, already loaded to capacity, could not absorb the increased traffic load that would be "dumped" into the central business district on completion of major segments of the outer loop of expressway. The prospectus concluded that "even conservative estimates of increased traffic loads indicate the inadequacy of any plans for arterial routes ringing the central business district which [do] not include a riverfront expressway (Prospectus, 26). The prospectus placed the City Planning Commission solidly behind the concept of a riverfront expressway from the moment of its publication in 1957. The commission was one of the principal advocates of a French Quarter freeway.

Riverfront Expressway on Major Street Plan

The New Orleans City Planning Commission held a public hearing in 1958 to determine whether the riverfront expressway should be placed on the city's major street plan. The hearing was opened by commission Director-Secretary Bisso who indicated that he favored the freeway. He rationalized that "with the construction of I-10 on North Claiborne Avenue, he saw a need for an Elysian Field-Vieux Carré Riverfront Expressway to close the loop in the proposed outer belt expressway in Central New Orleans." He also maintained that a freeway was needed along the French Quarter riverfront and that it would definitely be elevated.[12]

It was the general consensus of the expressway proponents that the riverfront expressway "would greatly stimulate the rejuvenation of this area, resulting in increased property values and greater tax return to the city (Public Hearing)."

The placing of the riverfront expressway on the major street plan received qualified support from two extremely important organizations that would be directly affected by its construction. The Vieux Carré Commission, the city agency charged with preserving the historic environment of the French Quarter, had passed no formal resolution supporting the freeway. Commission Chairman George M. Leake, nevertheless, wanted planning commission members to know that the Vieux Carré Commission wished "to go on record as approving the plan as well as the principles of the plan." He said that during the Vieux Carré commission discussion, "it was felt that, in general, getting the congestion out of the streets of the Quarter would far outweigh any detriment that some residents may feel would result (Public Hearing, 2-8)."

William J. Long, president of the Vieux Carré Property Owners and Associates, a 500-member organization of French Quarter owners and residents expressed conditional support for the expressway. He called the riverfront expressway "a great boom to the Quarter," but said his approval of the project was based on the concept of a grade-level facility rather than an elevated highway (Public Hearing, 2-9).

Martha G. Robinson, president of the Louisiana Landmarks Society (one of the largest and most respected preservation organizations in the state) said that she did not know whether she was in favor of the project. She did, however, note that "the Louisiana Landmark Society believed a grade-level expressway would be a great improvement because it would take heavy traffic out of the Vieux Carré." An elevated freeway, however, would mar the Quarter's beauty and its interests (Public Hearing, 2-12).

The City Planning Commission hearing to decide whether to include the riverfront expressway on the city's major street plan closed with Planning Commission Chairman J. Mort Walker, Jr. assuring those present that the commission "had no fixed opinion" on whether the expressway should be elevated or "at grade". He assured them that this issue would not be considered "until after the engineering studies have been made (Public Hearing, 2-16)."

On December 23, 1958, the City Planning Commission placed the Elysian Fields Vieux Carré" Expressway on the city's major street plan, thereby making the project eligible for construction.[13] This decision formally committed the commission to the riverfront expressway concept.

After the decision by the commission was made, the Central Area Committee of the Chamber of Commerce, as part of its effort to push the construction of the expressway, commissioned a number of influential studies underscoring the supposed need for the freeway and supporting an elevated structure. These included the Downs Report in April, 1959 and the Riverside Expressway Engineers report in 1960.

But despite numerous studies, preservationists remained unconvinced that an elevated freeway was in the city's best interest. Moreover, other studies conducted by the State Highway Department and the City Planning Commission convinced them that an elevated freeway was being planned for the Vieux Carré riverfront. Consequently, in 1961, the Louisiana Landmarks Society and the Vieux Carre' Property Owners and Associates passed resolutions opposing the elevated freeway. Both organizations urged greater consideration of a grade level facility. The Landmarks Society resolution read in part: "A survey of the land area between the existing floodwall and the river indicates that there is sufficient area to bring a four or six-lane elevated highway down to the level of the floodwall without impairing the use of the same area by the railroads and the dock board."[14]

Preservationists Mobilize as Expressway Plans Develop

In October 1962, newly elected Mayor Victor H. Schiro announced his support of the riverfront expressway project. He explained, however, that while the riverfront expressway would be constructed with state and federal funds, the city of New Orleans had to pay the cost of acquiring the right-of way for this essential project. The mayor then proposed in 1963 that $2.1 million should be provided for this purpose.[15] The capital budget for 1963 included the $2.1 million that Schiro had requested.[16]

Eight months later, New Orleans property owners went to the polls to vote on a $26.5 million capital-improvement bond issue. The $2.1 million earmarked for expressway right-of-way acquisition was included but was not specifically mentioned in the proposal.[17]

Institutional support for the freeway grew in 1963. The Louisiana Highway Department released "New Orleans Metropolitan Area Transportation Study" (NOMATS), an origin-and-destination traffic study justifying the need for the Vieux Carré Expressway. After the release of NOMATS II in 1963, the Highway Department placed the riverfront express on its State System of Urban Highways, thereby making the project eligible for construction.[18]

In April 1964, B.M. Dornblatt and Associates completed another preliminary engineering report on the expressway, this time for the Louisiana Highway Department. The Dornblatt study concluded that the surface expressway was undesirable and supported the elevated expressway concept. This study, coupled with the highway department's NOMATS I and II, justified the project's location and design.

With the publication of Dornblatt's 1964 report, preservationists realized that the study had persuaded most planning agencies and highway proponents that an elevated freeway along the river was the most reasonable and practical solution.

Expressway plans got their biggest boost on October 1, 1964, when U.S. Congressman Hale Boggs of New Orleans announced that the Bureau of Public Roads had decided to include the three and a half mile Vieux Carré expressway in the 41,000-mile interstate highway system. Inclusion of the freeway in this system made the freeway eligible for 90-10 funding; that is, the federal government would pay 90 percent of the cost of the project, while the state and local governments would pay the remaining 10 percent. Preservationists were incensed by the federal government's decision to include the freeway in the interstate highway system, but no formal protest was launched.

Because of the intense controversy over the expressway, on January 14, 1965, the New Orleans City Council unanimously adopted a resolution requesting the Louisiana Highway Department call a public hearing on the proposed expressway. The council's call for a public meeting sparked preservationists to action. Freeway opponents would finally have their day in court and it would be a matter of record. The momentum of the anti-freeway movement picked up with a mass meeting at Gallier Hall on January 29, 1965. More than 700 people crowded into the historic building to protest the elevated expressway. Preservationists asked George F. Stevenson of the Highway Department to address the audience. The highway official maintained that despite the objections, the riverfront expressway was badly needed.

The Gallier Hall meeting signaled a new stage in the Second Battle of New Orleans. In the past, protest had been sporadic and generally uncoordinated. Thereafter, freeway opponents became more aggressive and better organized. The issues were now clearly drawn and battle lines were carefully delineated. The Gallier Hall meeting resulted in an escalation in the New Orleans freeway war.

Preservationists wasted no time mounting an offensive and in a short period of time had garnered the support of some impressive organizations and individuals. Even the governor was said to have some doubts about the construction of an elevated freeway. With the Second Battle of New Orleans underway, preservationists were satisfied that they were holding their own at last.

Federal law required that any state highway department planning to penetrate a city with a federally-funded highway project certify to the U.S. Secretary of Commerce that the state highway department had either held public hearings or had provided the opportunity for such hearings to take place. Moreover, section 128(a) of Title 23 of the U.S. Code required that the economic effects of the highway's location be taken into consideration.[19]

On March 24, 1965, proponents and opponents of the freeway entered the auditorium of City Hall for the hearing. W. T. Taylor of the Highway Department opened what was to be a seven-hour meeting. Using charts and maps projected on a screen, Taylor explained the plans for the elevated freeway to connect downriver with the Claiborne Avenue leg of I-10.

What followed was an intense debate between proponents and opponents of the business community and preservationists that continued long after the hearing. In fact, expressway proponents more aggressively pursued the construction of the expressway. Freeway opponents organized even more aggressively against its construction and held a public meeting in the French Quarter on June 13, 1965. Protesters, as well as numerous public officials attended the meeting. The French Quarter protest meeting closed with a resolution opposing the project — the anti-freeway movement had come of age. Federal support however seemed solidly behind the construction of the freeway. Two events in history, however, would have a dramatic influence on federal decisions related to the construction of the freeway.[20] In November, 1967 James J. Howard introduced a bill in the U.S. House of Representatives permitting state highway departments to replace disputed links in the interstate highway system with non-controversial interstate highway projects located elsewhere.[21] The National Preservation Act of 1966 authorized the Secretary of the Interior to maintain a National Register of districts, sites, buildings, structures, and objects significant in American history, architecture, archaeology and culture.[22] The act also established the Advisory Council on Historic Preservation composed of seventeen members whose duties were, among others, to "advise the president and the Congress on matters relating to historic preservation. To ensure proper consideration of the value of National Register properties in the federal planning process, Congress gave the Advisory Council responsibility for review and comment.[23]

In section 106, the National Historic Preservation Act provided:

"The head of any federal agency having direct or indirect jurisdiction over a proposed federal or federally-assisted undertaking in any state and the head of any federal department or independent agency having authority to license any undertaking shall, prior to the approval of the expenditure of any federal funds on the undertaking . . . take into account the effect of the undetaking on any district, site, building,structure or object that is included in the National Register. The head of any such federal agency shall afford the Advisory Council on Historic Preservation . . . a reasonable opportunity to comment with regard to such undertaking."[24]

On January 28, 1969, it was released that federal approval of the riverfront expressway was withdrawn. The authorization had been retracted because the Advisory Council on Historic Preservation had not had an opportunity to fulfil the federal requirement that it comment on the project. On March 1, 1969, members of the council arrived in New Orleans. Executive Secretary Robert R. Garvey, Jr. told a reporter from *The Times Picayune*, "Our purpose is to evaluate the cultural heritage against possible destruction that might come about by building the highway."[25]

After a two-day investigation, the council released its report. The council concluded:

- The Riverfront Expressway would require the use of land from the banks of the Mississippi River, a part of the Vieux Carré Historic District;
- It would require the taking of grounds of the U.S. Mint that would curtail and seriously impair the use of the mint as a museum, the purpose for which it was transferred from the federal government to the state of Louisiana at no cost; and
- The introduction of visible, audible, and atmospheric conditions out of keeping with the historic and residential character and environment of the historic district would have a serious adverse effect upon that quality of the district, which has been described as the "tout ensemble," a quality of high importance.[26]

The battle between proponents and opponents of the riverfront expressway continued until July 1, 1969 when U. S. Secretary of Transportation John A. Volpe canceled the Vieux Carré Expressway. The environmentalists were exuberant. The Second Battle of New Orleans was over and the anti-freeway forces had staged a stunning upset. Many preservationists remained skeptical, saying they would not believe the news until they read it in the local newspaper, *The Times Picayune*. But if news of the cancellation was correct, the French Quarter waterfront, preservationists asserted, "had been saved from a swath of concrete and steel - a Chinese wall that would have separated the city from the river forever. Jackson Square had been spared irreparable damage. Saint Louis Cathedral would not be defaced."[27] The heretofore "invincible highway gang" had been stopped dead in its tracks on the banks of the Mississippi River in New Orleans." It was a great victory for the "little people", the preservationists believed.

The Times Picayune announced the cancellation of the riverfront expressway in its headline the next morning. It reported that Secretary of Transportation Volpe had advised New Orleans Congressman Hale Boggs of the cancellation on July 1. The secretary had told Boggs that Braman, assistant secretary for Urban Systems and Environment, was convinced that the conflict between opposing New Orleans groups was "irreconcilable" and that pending lawsuits would delay action on the project for years to come.

On July 9, 1969, Secretary Volpe formally announced the cancellation of the expressway. Volpe explained that the Vieux Carré expressway had been canceled because it "would have seriously impaired the historic quality of New Orleans' famed French Quarter." He continued, "A careful review of the highway proposal and the position of various interests convinced me that the public benefits from the proposed highway would not be enough to warrant damaging the treasured French Quarter." He further concluded that "the Riverfront Expressway would have separated the French Quarter from its Mississippi River levee and waterfront. Although that route had been approved by local highway and planning agencies, it had long been the subject of controversy at city, state and national levels." Despite strong local support for the riverfront roadway, the statement observed, "the President's Advisory Council on Historic Preservation, which includes Secretary Volpe and six other cabinet officers among its members, recommended either a new route for I-10, or, alternatively depressing that section of the highway which would traverse the French Quarter." A depressed expressway, Volpe indicated, was not acceptable "because of its disruptive effects, excessive costs and construction hazards which might cause damage to the levee protecting the entire city."[28]

The Volpe decision drew national attention the day after the official Department of Transportation announcement, and was reported on the front page of *The New York Times*. Washington correspondent William M. Blair wrote that Volpe's ruling "was believed to be the first denial of federal funds for a highway on the basis of preserving a historic area." The New Orleans decision has significance "far beyond historic preservation," he reported. On the basis of conversations with federal officials in Washington, Blair believed the secretary's ruling might signal a change in department policy and lead to a review of freeway crises in at least a dozen other cities that had plans affecting inner-city neighborhoods.[29]

Like *The New York Times*, support for the secretary's ruling continued to come from throughout the country. Similar opinions appeared the next day, for example, in the *Wall Street Journal, the Washington Post, Business Week,* and the *Delta Democrat Times* of Greenville, Mississippi.

Treme: The Black Tale

Treme is one of New Orleans' most historic communities. The importance of this neighborhood is best understood within the context of its history. The Treme community was created in 1810 when the city purchased a portion of the plantation of Claude Treme located behind the Vieux Carré between Orleans Street and Bayou Road for $40,000. One area was subdivided into lots for sale in 1812 by the city surveyor. This area of Treme is now Armstrong Park. The area was primarily developed with the construction of the house type known as the "Creole cottage."

The cottage was a one-storied, gable-roofed house with the ridge parallel to the street, a dominant chimney in the middle of each roof slope, four openings across the front, four main rooms, plus an attic, and built either of brick between posts, solid brick, or frame. This type of house continued to be built until past the mid-century when it was expanded to include more pretentiously scaled townhouses in the Greek revival and Italian styles, and somewhat later by the New Orleans bracketed and spindled "shotgun" type.[30]

Equal in importance to the housing stock were the people of Treme, who had inhabited the area since its earliest days and had maintained continuous bloodlines to the present.[31] Treme became a neighborhood united by common situation, interests, and interrelationships. It was settled in part by freemen of color and skilled black craftsmen who produced the finest of the city's architecture.

A major attraction of the Treme community was the Claiborne Avenue neutral ground. It originally extended from the Old Basin Canal to Esplanade Street and was paved in the center for promenading and lined with clusters of oak trees. Moreover, the trees served as a barrier to street cars that ran on both sides of the neutral ground.

Claiborne Avenue was a bustling business center for black New Orleanians, bolstering as many as 200 businesses in its heyday. A number of social activities also occurred on the neutral ground that promoted neighborhood stability: children played, people washed their cars, families picnicked or held games, clubs rallied there, and parades began there. This de facto park was a beautiful addition to the neighborhood. Its aesthetic value inarguably enhanced the neighborhood.[32]

The Treme neighborhood will long be remembered by locals as the home of Treme Market, Sunrise Bakery, Lucien's Bike Shop, the Gypsy Tea Room, black-owned pharmacies, the municipal auditorium, Congo Square, two-storied houses with sliding mahogany doors, and backyards with slave quarter-like structures lined with outdoor sinks and an occasional second-floor outhouse, sidewalks commonly referred to as "banquettes," made of bricks laid in beautiful geometric designs, and sights of local women using red or yellow ocher clay, a bucket of water and a broom to clean and change the colors of the banquette.[33]

In 1956, the Louisiana Highway Department announced that the I-10 expressway would be built on the North Claiborne Avenue neutral ground. The route was considered the most direct path from the central business district through eastern New Orleans, and it required moving the fewest homes. This median was the heart of the Treme community, one of the oldest neighborhoods in New Orleans. The Claiborne Avenue median, at that time, ran from Canal Street to St. Bernard Avenue. The median popularly referred to as the neutral ground by local residents measured 6,100 feet long by 100 feet wide with an area of thirteen and a half acres. It was lined with groves of live oak trees that were nearly forty years old. It was paved in the center for walking and was the central gathering place for black social life.

In 1956, Treme was generally seen by the white power structure as a run-down slum. This attitude was reflected in the demise which came with the destruction of the Claiborne Avenue neutral ground that was so clearly important to black economic development and black social life. In 1956, the black Treme community was not valued by the whites who were then running the city. Moreover, there clearly existed a careless disregard for Treme's architectural history, its black culture, and the aesthetic value of the neutral ground to the Treme community, a stark contrast to the value placed on the architectural history, culture, and aesthetic value of the French Quarter by preservationists. The neutral grounds or median partially paved and covered with grass and shaded by oaks served as a community park and front yard for communities bordering the street. The fine Creole cottages and neighborhood qualities of Treme were not valued by anyone except the blacks who lived there and whose voices were not heard by the white power structure.

As one reflects on the City of New Orleans today, with its black mayor, predominately black city council, school board and population, it is difficult to imagine that prior to 1950, even Mardi Gras was a segregated celebration. Claiborne Avenue traditionally served as the major gathering place for blacks on Carnival Day. The intersection of Dumaine and Claiborne was the place to enjoy the soul and excitement of Black Carnival.[34] It was here that one could experience Mardi Gras Indians, Skeleton Men, the Zulus, Second Line parades, Baby Dolls, Money Wasters, and a wealth of Black Masqueraders. All were a "must see" for black Mardi Gras revelers.

One must remember the time of the decision to construct I-10 on Claiborne Avenue and the place where that decision was made. Blacks in New Orleans in the 1950s did not have a strong political voice. Only during election time did politicians even recognize the community's existence. So certainly matters related to the development of highways to benefit the city and its future direction were not matters that the city fathers would discuss with the black community.

Unlike the hoopla that surrounded proposals for the construction of the Riverfront/Vieux Carré Freeway, no public hearings were held to inform the black community of the Claiborne Avenue section of I-10. Moreover, blacks in the city did not protest its construction when they were finally informed. This fact may puzzle some who are unaware of the conditions of black life or the degree of disenfranchisement of blacks in the South during the 1950s. However, these were not the times of black protest. In fact, the attitude of most blacks towards the construction of the I-10 was that its construction was imminent. As one resident of Treme so aptly put it, "You can't fight things like that."

There were no public hearings on the feasibility of the construction of I-10 in this area or its impact on the neighborhood and its people. There was no consideration of the economic impact the construction of the expressway would have on this community. There was no discussion of the aesthetic loss that would be suffered in the community, or the loss of cultural activities that promoted neighborhood cohesiveness and family stability.

What a contrast to the long-fought battle to keep I-10 out of the French Quarter. Preservationists fought a long and gallant battle to maintain the architectural history, culture and aesthetic value of the Quarter. But no one fought for the architectural history, culture, and aesthetic value of Treme. Families were displaced, neighborhoods were destroyed and some never recovered.

With the construction of the interstate, the oak trees were removed "and that strip of land, an essential element in the fabric of the community became a strip of sterile dirt."[35] Without a hint of protest and little fanfare, "a park measuring 6,100 feet by 100 feet with an area of thirteen and a half acres was removed from the community." Once the Claiborne section of the interstate was completed, "that same area and that same dirt were returned to the people covered now with a concrete roof 100 feet wide and 25 feet overhead (Claiborne, 43)."

The Claiborne median, once such an asset to the people, has become a blight. Those oaks, once so generous with their shade, are evidenced now only by the few survivors still existing near Elysian Fields (Claiborne, 43). With the construction of the I-10, the use of the Claiborne Avenue neutral ground was irrevocably changed. For many, its construction marked the beginning of ruin for Treme. The I-10 became a physical barrier that was unsightly and literally divided in half a beautiful neighborhood with strong social networks. In stark contrast to the clusters of tall oak trees that lined Claiborne Avenue and provided countless hours of pleasure for residents in the cool shade of the trees, there now appear tall, sterile concrete pillars. Here men now huddle under the hoods of parked cars talking over the noise of the traffic flow.

A view of I-10 from the ground, where residents are forever aware of its presence, is an ominous sight. From Gravier Street to Peoples Avenue Canal, I-10 is a six-lane facility entirely elevated on a viaduct structure. From Gravier Street to St. Bernard Avenue, the structure occupies the neutral ground of Claiborne Avenue, and from St. Bernard Avenue to Peoples Avenue, the highway is constructed on a new right-of-way. I-10 roughly parallels the right-of-way of the L & N Railroad from Elysian Fields to Peoples Avenue and measures 19,100 feet or 3.61 miles from Gravier Street to Peoples Avenue Canal (Claiborne, 45).

This once beautiful neighborhood has become host to an array of illicit and illegal activities. Drugs and prostitution run rampant in the community. Once the home of many businesses and great musicians such as Louis Armstrong and Mahalia Jackson, Treme was a very viable financial community. With the onslaught of urbanization, Treme lost its economic viability.

Tamborine and Fan

Tamborine and Fan, a black neighborhood-based education and cultural organization, working in the sixth and seventh wards of downtown New Orleans, was "oriented toward people generally bypassed or victimized for lack of participation in decisions or projects that seriously affect their lives (Claiborne, 14)."

A major goal of Tamborine and Fan was the restoration and improvement of neighborhoods in the I-10 Claiborne Avenue corridor. The Tamborine and Fan organization was a strong advocacy group that pushed hard for the survival of the community. One driving principle of the organization was the belief that with proper planning and resources, neighborhoods could be revitalized and self-sufficient in a manner which complemented the existing auto-oriented uses of I-10.

In early 1970, the organization began to organize around their concerns for the deterioration of the Treme area. Their concerns were delineated and addressed in the form of a proposal to City Hall for the revitalization of Claiborne Avenue. A series of meetings with the mayor's office and the city planning office ensued and resulted in the city seeking funds from the Bureau of Outdoor Recreation (U.S. Department of the Interior) to develop parks and recreational projects at the Canal and St. Bernard intersections of Claiborne Avenue.

Prior to meetings with the City of New Orleans, Tamborine and Fan's proposal for a feasibility study was brought to the attention of the Louisiana Department of Highways. In November 1973, the Louisiana State Department of Highways contracted the Claiborne Avenue Design Team to conduct a study of alternative plans for developing the public land under and adjacent to the I-10 Claiborne Avenue corridor. Implicit in this decision was the recognition by the Louisiana State Department of Highways that the I-10 structure had greatly changed Claiborne Avenue from an attractive boulevard of live oak trees and green neutral grounds, to a dusty trash-filled eyesore which blighted the surrounding neighborhoods.[36]

The objective of the I-10 multi-use study was to devise a comprehensive plan for redevelopment of the rights-of-way and of the neighborhoods adjacent to the I-10 expressway between Poydras Street and People Avenue.[37]

Expressway Impact

In 1976, a large-scale survey of neighborhoods impacted by the construction of I-10 (i.e., Claiborne area residents) asked residents whether any major changes had taken place in their neighborhood during the last ten years. In the Treme and Mid-City (Battlefield) neighborhoods, "yes" responses, particularly among home owners, reached 50 percent. Among persons with a "yes" response, 53 percent identified the construction of I-10 as the primary change.[38]

Fifty selected Claiborne area business establishments were surveyed to determine the impact I-10 had had on them. Many complained of the debris that was allowed to collect under and around the I-10 structure. Sixty-three percent of the respondents said they would not invest in another business venture in the area because the neighborhood was not conducive to trade, primarily because of the lack of physical attractiveness and the high crime rate. Twenty-seven percent of the business owners indicated that they would relocate their businesses if the option existed. There was a strong desire to move to a "better neighborhood."

Impacted residents were asked the question, "Do you feel that the structure is useful?" Eighty-nine percent of the respondents answered "yes" with 74 percent feeling that I-10 provides "faster access to other parts of town" as the reason for their "yes" responses."

The responses of residents who were critical of land-use changes, induced by construction of I-10, centered on the proliferation of blight, pollution, and neighborhood deterioration. In addition, they focused on relocation of friends and families, and changes in the volume of local street traffic.

Curiously, in 1976, some ten years after its construction, only about 28 percent of the area residents used the I-10 expressway every day. Thirteen percent never used I-10 and 25 percent seldom used the expressway. Moreover, some 40 percent of the local residents were infrequent users of the I-10 expressway. Early use of the expressway did not include to a great extent the people most impacted by the construction of the Claiborne Avenue Viaduct.

Vieux Carré Today

Slowly but steadily after World War I, the Vieux Carré slipped into a slum area until the early 1920s. At that time the renaissance of the French Quarter began. Newcomers to the city and farsighted New Orleanians were able to buy old houses, now worth a fortune, for little or nothing. The rehabilitation of the Vieux Carré was underway.[39] Another significant event in the architectural life of the French Quarter was the creation of the Vieux Carré Commission. The commission was charged with preserving the "quaint and distinctive character" of the French Quarter.[40]

For approximately eighty years, a string of metal-walled sheds blocked the public's view of operations on the river along the levee. Changing times have brought a rediscovery of the charm and economic value of having an exposed riverfront. The downtown riverfront area has been converted into a massive tourist, retail, and entertainment strip. This resurgence of efforts to restore the riverfront and thus enhance the Quarter began through private enterprise in the late 1970s. The old Jackson Brewery was converted into a retail tourist complex. This construction was followed by the 1984 Louisiana World Exposition (World's Fair) that stimulated later development. To accommodate the World's Fair, the New Orleans Convention Center, renamed the Ernest N. Morial Convention Center after the city's first black mayor, was constructed. The 800,000-square foot facility is presently being expanded to twice its original size to accommodate a growing tourist industry. Voters in 1986 authorized a special tax to help finance a $40-million aquarium that now overlooks the Mississippi River; and in 1986, the Riverwalk, which includes dozens of retails outlets, cafes, and restaurants housed in the converted warehouses, was opened along the wharves.[41] The riverfront has been revived and the French Quarter has been saved.

The preservationists, who in the early 1970s fought off the proposal to build the elevated expressway along the riverfront in the French Quarter, are also responsible for the revitalization of the riverfront and ultimately the rebirth of the Vieux Carré.

Following the defeat of the expressway proposal, Mayor Moon Landrieu, a strong supporter of the expressway, constructed with federal funds a twelve-foot-wide boardwalk on the levee at Jackson Square in the heart of the Vieux Carré. It immediately became a popular gathering place where people could view the river. The construction in the early 1970s of the boardwalk, or "Moon Walk" as it is popularly known, reintroduced New Orleanians to the river and stimulated its development. The expressway would have made it virtually impossible to redevelop the riverfront for recreational purposes. Redevelopment of the riverfront has been the single most important factor in the development and maintenance of the Vieux Carré.

Treme Today

Urbanization in the Treme community resulted in the destruction of twelve blocks of historic homes and thriving businesses for the construction of a major highway and later, a cultural center. Today, I-10 runs through the community. Treme is now the victim of voluminous highway traffic that spews toxins into the community, and old buildings that contribute to lead-paint problems.

The Treme community today consists of census tracts 39, 40, and 44.01. The total population for this community is 6,927 of which 97 percent is African-American. Census tract 39 is 51 percent female, census tract 40 is 54 percent female, and census tract 44.01 is 55 percent female.

Sixty percent of the households in census tract 39, 54 percent in census tract 40, and 43 percent in census tract 44.01 are headed by females. In census tract 39, 53 percent of those twenty-five years and older have received a high school diploma or higher, and 53 percent of those twenty-five years or older have received a bachelor's or higher degree. In census tract 40, 55 percent and 10 percent have received bachelor's or higher degrees.

Unemployment is high in all three census tracts. Of those individuals sixteen years of age and older, 47 percent in census tract 39, 48 percent in census tract 40, and 50 percent in census tract 44.01 are unemployed.

Low wages are another crippling factor in this community. Thirty-two percent of the households in census tract 39, 19 percent in census tract 40, and 30 percent in census tract 44.01 earn an income of less than $5,000. The median household annual income for census tract 39, 40, and 44.01 is $8,953, $12,000, and $8,173, respectively. In census tract 39, 56 percent of the families have an income below the poverty level. Forty percent in census tract 40 and 42 percent in census tract 44.01 have incomes below the poverty level.

Most of the housing units in this community were built before 1939, and are therefore causing concern regarding lead-based paint problems. In census tract 39, 80 percent of the housing units were built before 1939. Sixty-nine percent of the housing units in census tract 40 and 74 percent in census tract 44.01 were built before 1939.

Most residents in the community are renters. Eighty-four percent of the housing units in census tract 39 and 70 percent of the units in census tract 40 are renter-occupied. Seventy-five percent of the housing units in census tract 44.01 are renter-occupied. Vacant housing units in census tracts 39, 40 and 44.01 are 410, 329, and 340, respectively.

The median value of owner-occupied housing units is $47,800 for census tract 39, $53,400 for census tract 40, and $44,500 for census tract 44.01. The median rents for census tracts 30, 40, and 44.01 are $213, $251 and $213 respectively.

Here Comes the Casino

Treme's more recent history is mirroring the past, with it once again being targeted to bear the burden of urban growth and prosperity. In April 1995, Harrah's Casino opened its temporary headquarters in the Municipal Auditorium, which sits within the boundary of the Treme community. The heavy traffic of I-10 is a constant reminder of what outsiders can do to their neighborhood. Residents of Treme were wary as Harrah's opened for business.

Unlike the I-10 debacle, Treme community activists learned much from that experience and won some economic concessions from casino developers and promises of zoning and planning support from city officials. There were some, however, who still worried that the temporary gambling palace would cost the historic neighborhood its soul: "shotgun houses", Creole cottages, and music clubs.

Jim Hayes, a long-time community activist in Treme, was "apprehensive about the whole thing," noting how sudden economic growth and development can be too much of a good thing for an older neighborhood. Rising property values, according to Hayes, "can price longtime residents out of the market, while outsiders move in for the jobs and opportunities residents had hoped for."[42]

With the I-10 experience forever etched in their memory, Hayes and other neighborhood leaders went to work soon after plans for the temporary casino were announced to wrest commitments from the developers.

As part of its agreement with Treme, Harrah's created a $75,000 college scholarship program for Treme residents and a $75,000 summer job program for neighborhood children. Treme was also to receive about $200,000 from Harrah's for an economic development plan, part of which was aimed at minimizing the number of residents who would be displaced by property value increase.

According to Hayes, the cost of homes in Treme increased by $8,000 because of the casino, and some landlords were charging "ridiculous" rents of $500 per month. Hayes' organization increased home ownership in Treme, an area where the 1990 census showed an average annual income of $6,548.

The casino is not the first outside force to invade the 200-year-old neighborhood. Hayes said: "When the Interstate came through in the 1960s, it knocked out all our black businesses. It took away our neutral ground where we had the oak trees, where we'd promenade on Sundays and holidays, and cook from Lafitte Street all the way to People Avenue."

A few years later in the early 1970s, eight square blocks of homes near the auditorium were torn down to make room for a proposed cultural center that was to include the theater for the performing arts and several other buildings. Eventually, only the theater was built, which is now called the Mahalia Jackson Theater for the Performing Arts. Plans for the rest of the complex were scuttled after neighborhood opposition. The city then offered a park to the community in honor of Louis Armstrong. According to Hayes, the community "jumped at the chance." He said, "We thought it was for the community to appreciate and enjoy." But even the park came with indignities attached. The city built a fence around it, separating it from the neighborhood.

In 1980, Treme was finally designated a historic district, a designation that played a significant role in the decision to cancel the French Quarter Expressway. However, this designation has created both opportunities and problems for those who live in the old area next to the French Quarter. Upgrading of property means a more substantial neighborhood, but historically it has also meant higher rents and displacement of poor families. Treme, an important part of New Orleans heritage, is no exception.

For many old residents of Treme, a marriage between the community and preservationists is strained. For example, Hayes said, "I don't have too much confidence in preservationists. Not one preservationist spoke out when some of the finest homes this city ever had were torn down." Between 1956 and 1973, nine square blocks of a first-class nineteenth century neighborhood were demolished in Treme in order to build a cultural center. The financing fell through and Armstrong Park was developed instead.

In 1996, Harrah's Casino filed for bankruptcy, once again leaving Treme in its shadow. The large parking areas where houses were cleared for its development now stand as large empty spaces or holes in the fabric of the community. The towers where police would stand to guard casino clients from would-be attackers is a glaring reminder of the dangers that now exist in this community. And what of all the projects and promises made to the Treme community? They are gone, just as surely as the oak tree-lined neutral ground of Claiborne Avenue. Nearly 30 years since the construction of I-10, the community finds itself still reeling from its effects.

The Great Eastern Migration

Eastern New Orleans in the 1970s was the fastest growing section of the city. Riding high on the prosperity of the oil industry, construction was at an all-time high. Newly built moderate-to-expensive homes with comparable luxury apartments dotted the landscape of New Orleans' newest residential area. Unexpectedly, the "oil boom" turned to bust and the city likewise fell into decline. Banks that held the mortgage on large luxury apartment complexes were losing money because contractors overestimated housing needs and the ability of people to pay. At the same time, the city faced a housing shortage. The inner-city housing stock was dilapidated and becoming more so each year. Public housing was raggedy and in short supply. The city was in deep trouble and the city council was desperate for answers.

Special interest groups pressured city council to aid the bankers. On the other hand, the poor black population was very dissatisfied with the city's housing problems and demanded some recourse. Tenants organizations protested and marched on City Hall, demanding decent housing. For some members of the banking community and some councilmen, the solution was clear: city council should allow the Housing Authority of New Orleans and the Community

Improvement Association to give those residents in need of housing and who qualified for assistance rent certificates for the unoccupied rental units in eastern New Orleans.

A public hearing was held where proponents and opponents presented the pros and cons of the proposal. After some deliberation, city council made the decision to allow the luxury dwellings to be occupied by tenants under the Housing Assistance Plan. Consequently, public housing residents were eligible to move to the suburbs —and move they did, to the chagrin of many eastern New Orleans residents.

The construction of I-10 directly affected the migration of New Orleans residents. As earlier stated, a major reason for selecting Claiborne Avenue as a link of I-10 was its direct path from the central business district through eastern New Orleans.

Population patterns in the 1980s changed the race and class composition of eastern New Orleans. White residents very quickly migrated to St. Tammany Parish, a bedroom community across Lake Pontchartrain. Middle-class blacks bought more homes in the eastern suburb, and more and more luxury apartments were filled by poorer black New Orleanians on rent subsidies.

I-10 not only made it possible for middle-class black New Orleanians to move to the eastern suburbs; it also made it easier for white New Orleanians to move to St. Tammany Parish and drive into the central business district everyday for work, taking the city's tax dollars with them. The result of this new migration pattern has devastated the city's economy. New Orleans East, just like its inner city, has become increasingly black and poor.

The migration of poor blacks to the eastern suburb has brought with it some transportation woes. A car is nearly a necessity of life for those living in the suburbs. How then do poor people living in a suburban area without a car or the existence of a mass transit system transport themselves to work and maintain their everyday living activities? The answer to part of this question was made tragically clear. Several fatal accidents occurred as people tried to take short-cuts off the I-10 service road across the expressway to shopping centers.

Determining how poor people get to work became a serious transportation issue for city officials, not to mention those who needed transportation into the city. The New Orleans' bus transportation system, at one time hailed as one of the best in the nation, was in decline due to low revenue. To make matters worse, bus service in eastern New Orleans was grossly inadequate. Many residential areas had no access to bus transportation routes and those that did, had limited services. The situation intensified as the New Orleans Regional Transit Authority was forced to increase its fare to cover the increased cost of providing transportation to the community.

In a city where tourism is the major industry, with many of its citizens working in the service industry, the bus schedule in the eastern suburb only accommodated standard nine-to-five work schedules. But many of the working poor living in the eastern suburb did not have standard working hours. The Regional Transit Authority presently has attempted to address the transportation problems of eastern New Orleans. Bus schedules have been extended, but the service is not as readily available as in the city. Children and some adults continue their attempts to cross I-10 to avoid the long walk. The bus fare, however, has greatly increased to $1 plus twenty-five cents for a transfer. The legacy of I-10 continues.

New Orleans Today

New Orleans today, like most major urban centers, is a city in peril. Treme is but one story in the decline of a great city. New Orleans (Orleans Parish) has a total population of 496,938. Of this total, 62 percent are African-American, 34 percent are Caucasian, and 4 percent are of other races. Like many great cities, New Orleans also has its share of problems. Unemployment is steadily increasing and the city's murder rate continues to climb at an astounding rate. The economic structure of New Orleans makes it difficult to provide jobs with wages high enough to support a family. The city's economy might fairly be described as "pre-industrial," in that it has never provided large numbers of heavy manufacturing jobs.

The city has a median household income of only $18,477 with over 31 percent of the households having annual incomes under $10,000. Fifty-nine percent of the city's population is of traditional working age (between eighteen and sixty-four), 27.5 percent is under the age of eighteen, and 13 percent is age sixty-five or older. The overall unemployment rate is 12.4 percent. Despite efforts to combat poverty that focused on housing and community development, more than 50 percent of all families live at or below the poverty level in the city. Of this 50 percent, 81 percent are African-American families living in the older neighborhoods of the city. Forty-four percent of the city's inhabitants occupy dwelling units that are owner-occupied, and 16.6 percent of the city's housing units are vacant.

The juvenile homicide rate has doubled and juvenile arrests in many areas have shown an alarming increase, some over 100 percent. The city also has a high homeless rate, with 24 percent of the homeless population consisting of single women and 43 percent under the age of twenty-one. Although the city is home to numerous schools and universities, many of the residents remain illiterate, some lacking basic reading, writing, and math skills. Of all the adults in New Orleans, 40,404 (or 11.2 percent) have less than a ninth-grade education, and 56,804 (or 15.8 percent) of the adults never completed high school. Citywide, this means that 97,208 (or 27 percent) of the adults have not completed their high school education. More than 1,000 students are not enrolled in any school.

Health statistics are also discouraging. Fifty percent of children, by age two, have not received primary immunization shots. Forty-one percent of live births result from inadequate health care, with 25.3 percent of all live births from women age nineteen and under, many of whom are single-parent families. Low-weight babies account for 12.4 percent of all births and the city has an infant mortality rate of 14.7 percent. Of even greater significance are the environmental problems such as land, air, and water pollution that are created by the many chemical and industrial companies in New Orleans.

Conclusion

The struggle over the construction of the Vieux Carré Expressway was part of a larger conflict being fought in cities throughout the United States — a conflict between environmentalists and developers over the shape and design of the country's most important urban areas. One of the most dramatic clashes was the struggle waged over controversial links in the country's federal interstate highway system. In the 1960s, this conflict between developers and environmentalists was known as the "Freeway War." The Second Battle of New Orleans was a fight that began with efforts to preserve the integrity of Jackson Square, the site commemorating the first Battle of New Orleans in 1815.

The preservationists had been fighting for years to protect the character of the Vieux Carré. They believed that the proposed expressway was "an alien twentieth-century intrusion that would irreparably harm the fragile beauty of the old city." The downtown-business interest, however, thought the expressway was desperately needed to revitalize the central business district and thus prevent the decay and deterioration that had sapped the vitality and destroyed the integrity of so many other urban centers in America.[43] They suggested "the expressway would preserve the historic area by taking heavy, through traffic off the narrow streets of the old district."[44]

The Second Battle of New Orleans represented more than just a conflict between environmentalists and downtown developers. It represented a conflict of value and attitudes that reflected differences in priorities and perspectives about the character and personality of the city. At stake in the struggle was the integrity of the Vieux Carré, one of the most important historic districts in the United States. In the end, the preservationists/environmentalists won the Second Battle of New Orleans, but this was not to be the fate of historic Treme.

Ironically, the values and attitudes that resulted in a protracted and relentless struggle to preserve the integrity of the Vieux Carré was somehow not transferred to historic Treme. A close examination of the character of Treme reveals many of the same qualities found in Vieux Carré that ultimately protected it from the ravishes of urban renewal.

In reviewing the two most important historical events that influenced the 1969 decision to cancel the Vieux Carré Expressway, curious similarities and differences unfold. The National Preservation Act of 1966 and the Howard Bill of 1967 had profound impacts on government decisions. The National Preservation Act established the Advisory Council on Historic Preservation, whose duties in part were to advise the president and Congress on matters relating to historic preservation. But by the time the National Preservation Act of 1966 was authorized, many urban communities had already been destroyed by construction of controversial links to the interstate highway system.

The history and culture of many urban centers were already gone forever. The decision to cancel the expressway was based on review comments of the Advisory Council on Historic Preservation, that the Vieux Carré Expressway would "introduce visible, audible, and atmospheric conditions out of keeping with the historic and residential character and environment of the historic district that would have a serious adverse effect upon that quality of the district." Although historic significance was enough in 1969 to stop the construction of the

Vieux Carré link to the expressway, it was not enough to save Treme.

The historic significance of Treme was not formally recognized until the early 1980s when the city established the Esplanade Ridge Historic District. This designation was twenty years too late to stop the first act of desecration to this community with the construction of the Claiborne Avenue link to I-10, and the destruction of nine square blocks of historic housing stock. Once the interstate was present, it was easier to justify destroying its housing. According to the Historic District Landmark Commission, the houses that were torn down were some of the most architecturally significant houses in the city. The commission found 49 percent of Treme's housing to be of architectural or historical importance. Twenty-six of the area's 704 buildings were of major architectural importance and 315 fell into the second highest category of architectural or historical importance. Only fifty-six of the buildings had no significance.[45]

The historic significance of Treme in 1980 was strongly supported by the Historic District Landmarks Commission. But many of the city's great craftsmen, artisans and musicians also lived in Treme. It is not uncommon to hear people say that Louis Armstrong is "spinning in his grave" over what has happened to Treme. The media termed it "the urban sin of the century."[46] Not only were those who lived in the area displaced, but also many whose ancestry was rooted in Treme pulled up stake, traumatized by the "sight of the landmarks of their long colorful history turned to rubble and carted away in dumptrucks."[47]

Second only to the Vieux Carré, Treme is one of the most culturally rich neighborhoods in the city. Using the Advisory Council on Historic Preservation criteria, in retrospective, Claiborne Avenue I-10 link introduced visible, audible, and atmospheric conditions out of keeping with the historic and residential character and environment of the historic Treme district that have had a serious adverse effect upon that quality of the Treme district, which has been described as the "tout ensemble," a quality of high importance.

The Howard Bill of 1967 also strengthened the preservationists' cause to stop the Vieux Carré Expressway. The bill called for the replacement of disputed links in the interstate highway system with noncontroversial interstate highway projects located elsewhere. What cannot be disputed is the fact that the Vieux Carré link was controversial. The battle raged for nearly twenty years. But there were no preservationists in 1956 protesting the construction of the Claiborne Avenue link. There were no residents of Treme protesting the construction of the link.

Moreover, the Vieux Carré preservationists, all of whom were white, were not at all concerned about a poor black neighborhood. Racism was the silent killer in the death of Treme. No voices were raised in protest because one group was politically locked out of the process and could not speak. The other group, unconcerned about this segment of the population, would not speak.

An old adage of the South was true: "If you want to find the black community, just cross the railroad tracks." The railroad tracks formed a physical barrier between the races, reflecting deep-rooted segregation that resulted in Jim Crow laws. More recently, both solid and hazardous waste landfills are also a part of the black communities' landscape. Now that old adage can be expanded to: "If you want to find the black community, follow your nose to the nearest landfill."

Yet another insult is the building of elaborate highway systems through black communities to accommodate our rapid change to the automobile. The old adage may once again be expanded to: "If you want to know where the black community is, just follow your ears to the noise of the freeway."

The South Lawrence Trafficway: Environmental Justice Guidance for Native Americans

Charles E. Haines

The impact of the South Lawrence Trafficway on Haskell Indian Nations University (HINU) campus in Lawrence, Kansas reveals a complexity of issues — including environmental, cultural, ethical, economic and practical — surrounding transportation, as they relate to Native American communities and the National Environmental Policy Act (NEPA).[1] Many of the trafficway issues confronting HINU students and alumni in the last five years directly concern natural and cultural resources of tribal governments.[2]

Much more is needed, however, than a mere list of issues. The overriding theme of this chapter is the more important challenge to minority groups: to develop credible strategies and make a concerted effort to address environmental injustice. We live in a society that is profoundly and violently at odds with the natural world. From this perspective, the social, economic, and cultural aspects of environmental justice must address each of our freedoms and rights to live in a healthy and sustainable environment.

Reality Check

Use of the terms "NEPA process" and "environmental impact statement" (EIS) in this chapter refers to the same bureaucratic process of evaluating impacts to the environment. This process consists of two interrelated working levels. The first level involves federal agencies and their policies and/or statutory responsibilities in formulating or commenting on an environmental assessment of a proposed transportation project in accordance with NEPA. The second level is somewhat ambiguous, but related to proponents of the project. It may involve consulting firms as well as officials from local and state governments. The project may also begin with a lead federal agency proposing the undertaking. The selection of the "players" in the project, whether local, state, or federal officials, determines in large part the tone of the NEPA process. The political situation may be ambiguous. However, a combination of federal, state, and local political issues often determines the thrust or energy of the project.

Minorities and members of low-income groups who participate in the NEPA process can appreciate the meaning of the term "Catch-22." Participation in the

NEPA policy process may often lead to unexpected and unpleasant consequences. The source of this problem is rooted in the very heart of the democratic and social forces that govern our country. In many situations, any potential solution to the problems raised by a transportation project is ultimately denied by circumstances inherent in the problems.

As minority groups and low-income populations understand, communities can be adversely affected by transportation projects if they are not actually involved at much higher levels of decision-making. For example, the lead federal agency involved in an EIS does not consider the public as part of the decision-making process for its agency. That's the Catch-22. Federal transportation projects involve consulting firms,
politicians, and bureaucrats in federal agencies who make the decisions, but who are often not affected by or seriously concerned with the environmental, socioeconomic, and cultural impacts to the local communities. Secondly, the affected communities are generally treated by the federal agencies and/or the NEPA political process as adversaries rather than partners. The critical issue facing these communities is having the resources and time to participate in the process. The new policies to address these issues, such as environmental justice, only float on the surface of the very deep circumstances inherent in the social and cultural problems and concerns of affected minorities.

One of the most disturbing aspects of the trafficway project was the condescending attitude and divisive nature demonstrated by the local media. A number of editorials in the local newspaper referred to opponents of the South Lawrence Trafficway in stereotypical, sometimes racist, terms. The events that led to the draft supplemental EIS (DSEIS) did not occur in a vacuum, but in a charged atmosphere. The negative journalism fostered mistrust, distorted the issues and concerns that HINU and local environmental groups had raised, and prejudiced the process of open discussion.

To counteract misleading news reports and assist other minority groups who face similar environmental issues, this case study recounts Native American experience with EIS. Specific difficulties in the NEPA process will be identified, and cultural differences between Native Americans and federal regulators addressed.

Assessment of the Project

The South Lawrence Trafficway is a project providing a new four-lane divided roadway linking the Kansas Turnpike (Interstate 70) west of the city of Lawrence to Kansas Highway 10, east of Lawrence. The route of the trafficway was designed to improve transportation efficiency for Lawrence and improve access to major local attractions: the University of Kansas and Clinton Lake. The draft EIS was issued in 1987 and the final EIS was released in 1990. A DSEIS covering new issues was initiated by the Federal Highway Administration in October, 1994 and completed in 1995.[3]

The preferred alignment for the trafficway crosses the southern portion of the HINU campus. Haskell is a national intertribal university located on a 320-acre campus in Lawrence, supported by the Bureau of Indian Affairs within the Department of the Interior. Its student population of approximately 900 American

Indian students represent tribes from every state in the nation. The campus area where alignment of the trafficway is proposed is part of a larger wetland complex used for Haskell's science courses. In addition, the wetland area serves as a site for sweatlodges and spiritual "earth work" (Medicine Wheel) used for prayer and other ceremonial purposes.

Protection of this wetlands area was the catalyst for HINU's original 1992 notice to county and federal officials. Several HINU students and faculty voiced their concerns that the EIS did not consider the multiple impacts upon Haskell. (Eventually, a few members of this group formed the Wetlands Preservation Committee to represent student interests in 1993).[4] In fact, the EIS stated that the campus was not affected by the trafficway. In 1994, two years after the Federal Highway Administration was notified of this serious error, they issued a Notice of Intent to conduct a supplement EIS to address the impacts of the trafficway on educational, cultural, historical, and spiritual issues associated with Haskell's campus.

However, both the final EIS and DSEIS fell short of providing the comprehensive analysis of environmental impacts required under NEPA. Specifically, the analysis of Native American spiritual, cultural, academic, and enviro mental issues presented in the DSEIS did not fully disclose, but trivialized, significant information.

The DSEIS presented HINU's concerns in a fragmentary fashion, although the Wetlands Preservation Committee had emphasized that all things are connected and that the issues and concerns cannot and must not be fragmented. Further, the DSEIS analysis of spiritual and cultural issues showed a lack of understanding and a patronizing attitude. Therefore, the Wetlands Preservation Committee recommended that the Federal Highway Administration withdraw the document in place of a comprehensive and complete analysis of all issues.

A fundamental issue the DSEIS failed to address was the impact of the trafficway on the interconnected historical, spiritual, cultural, educational, social, and environmental/ecological values of the wetlands. The DSEIS did not recognize that these interconnected values cannot be replaced — the wetlands is inextricably linked to Native American culture, spiritual practices, education, ancestors and history. Federal, state, and local agencies cannot replace these values with a new complex of wetlands a few miles down the road, as had been suggested.

The following issues not evaluated in the DSEIS would have significant environmental consequences if the proposed trafficway is completed. Although specific to this project, many of these concerns can be applied to almost every transportation project in the United States.

1. The DSEIS did not include real estate and commercial development within the trafficway corridor as one of the purposes and needs of the trafficway. As a result, the supplemental EIS inadequately analyzed the effects of direct, secondary, and cumulative impacts to the environment. Even preliminary work on the trafficway has already seriously impaired land-use controls for the area, resulting in developmental trends causing significant indirect effects. The extent and nature of urban growth andresultant environmental impacts were not acknowledged.

2. The DSEIS did not provide a complete alternative analysis, thus limiting

the ability of the public and decision-makers to fully assess all potential highway alignments. It failed to consider a full range of alternatives as defined in section 1502.14 of the Council on Environmental Quality regulations that implement NEPA.

3. The DSEIS did not appropriately analyze the significant cumulative environmental impacts on the floodplain. Preliminary construction of the trafficway and real estate development occurring have already caused significant damage; critical changes are now occurring due to loss of biological corridors, impairment of water quality, and habitat fragmentation.

4. The DSEIS did not adequately consider effects on water resources, soil, wildlife, air quality, vegetation, visual quality, land use and other related transportation proposals (e.g., widening U.S. Highway 59, probable demographic shifts to the south of the Wakarusa River, and related developments).

5. The DSEIS did not address cumulative environmental change.[5] In fact, the DSEIS narrowed the impact focus and overlooked environmental change involving indirect and secondary impacts, including:

- significant reduction in prime agricultural land;
- increased requirements for services and wastewater treatment and disposal facilities;
- net increase in costs for improvements and maintenance of municipal services for correcting problems with the storm water drainage system and the wastewater disposal system (already strained to meet service requirements);
- analysis of major traffic generators, e.g., the University of Kansas and the 23rd Street business district, and the new business district along South Iowa Street (U.S. Highway 59), encompassing 31st to 35th Streets;
- an increase in freight traffic intensity related to expanding real estate development;
- significant changes in residential and commercial land development and growth of a new large commercial development outside the central business district;
- the negative impact on the downtown business district, which was designated in the city's urban plan (Plan 95) as Lawrence's strongest regional shopping and business center;
- increase over the normal trend in property value, assessed land values, and changes in resale value (e.g., the cost of the right-of-way of the trafficway from Interstate 70 to U.S. Highway 59 has had a tremendous ripple effect on the local economy through increased property values.); and
- meeting all requirements under ISTEA.[6]

The Value of Qualitative Data: Cultural Resources and Environmental Justice

In addition to the serious ecological concerns involved in transportation issues, experience demonstrates that federal agencies usually do not utilize social science methodologies in their assessment of data. Due to this deficiency, one important strategy, which must be developed by environmental justice centers, should focus on bureaucratic assessments based solely upon standard engineering and environmental analysis. Generally, federal agencies overlook NEPA's explicit recommendation to use non-quantitative methods and relevant information. For example, historical, social, and cultural information often remains invisible and insignificant in procedural documents (42 USC section 4332(b)],[7] becoming background issues in both quality and substance.

For example, in 1996, the Wetlands Preservation Committee presented a detailed response to the Federal Highway Administration on the DSEIS. The committee was particularly concerned that the draft did not address the historical importance of Haskell Institute, which was designated a national historic landmark on July 4, 1961.

Historical Significance of Haskell Wetlands

Current efforts to protect Haskell's old farm are directed at documenting the significant historical and cultural transformations occuring at Haskell Institute between 1884 and 1935. Evidence demonstrates that the Haskell wetlands were utilized by Native American ancestors, much as the area is used today.

The founding mission of Haskell Institute in 1884 was to enforce an educational policy on American Indians based upon European agricultural traditions and farming methods. Government policy-makers were consumed with directing every aspect of the American Indian's life. This need to control and to define the lives of American Indian people excused all manners of cultural destruction. At the very heart of the government's American Indian policy was the belief that turning American Indians into farmers would end their dependence on the vagaries of the chase and the starvation cycle of Native subsistence systems. Policy-makers believed that reservation agriculture and allotment policies were the best steps in accomplishing those goals.Thousands of American Indian children who went to Haskell between 1884 and 1933 were forced to go through the agrarian-based education program. The purpose and intent of the agrarian program was to civilize and assimilate American Indians into the mainstream of American society as self-supporting yeoman farmers and farm families.

Boarding schools such as Haskell were devoted to the cultural quarantine of children, keeping them away from their homes and families. This policy represents a historic cultural change and transformation because as tribal relations were broken up, the children lost many of their cultural traditions and ways of life.

For at least the first twenty-five years of Haskell existence, many of the children were forced to attend because of the policies exercised by agents at the reservations. Reservation superintendents forced parents or guardians to sign contracts for their children's attendance at school. Initially, parents who resisted this effort were penalized by having their allotment of rations terminated.[8] Eventually, reservation superintendents turned to taking legal guardianship of the children themselves or selecting white families to be guardians to enforce the mandatory school attendance policy. American Indian parents who did not support the superintendent's efforts were declared incompetent; guardianship of their children was automatically granted to American Indian agents or persons of the agent's choice. Many children were orphans and agents quickly achieved guardianship, sending the children to off-reservation boarding schools.[9] Whatever method the agents used, their goal was to separate children from their families, especially American Indian families who maintained rich cultural traditions.

Starting with 280 acres in 1884, Haskell's land base grew to 1011 acres by 1902. Acquisition of the land was directly related to the agrarian education program, which consisted of the school's farm and livestock operation. On the farm, children were taught the full range of farm and garden operations: wagon and harness-making, dairy production, blacksmithing, field drainage, crop and fruit production, and harvesting. The children also did well-digging, stone-quarrying, hauling, excavating for buildings, draining, masonry and mortar work, and carpentry. From 1884 to 1933, children were the labor force that constructed the beautiful stone buildings, farm and instruction buildings, and staff residences on campus. The farming and industrial nature of the institution was Haskell's main focus and goal, with most of the campus and the farm built and maintained by the children.

Many of the children were overworked and suffered from malnutrition, dysentery, and communicable diseases such as tuberculosis, trachoma, typhoid, and pneumonia. Students with communicable diseases were not segregated or put on special treatment until the 1910s. Because the school was inadequately funded for the first twenty years, children were often fed hardtack rations turned in from army units and some butter from the school's dairy cows. During the wet season, children did not have raincoats or overshoes, and government field inspectors cited Haskell numerous times for keeping children in the cold or rain.

Dormitory life consisted of overcrowded barracks with mattresses aligned side by side; windows were nailed down and fire escapes were locked. In the boys' dormitory, two to four boys had to share one 36-by-40 inch mattresse. Inadequate toilet facilities and sewage disposal resulted in numerous illnesses.[10]

Documentation in the National Archives, U.S. Senate Subcommittee Hearings[11] and the Meriam Report demonstrate a number of areas of concern, including malnutrition and harsh punishment. For example, to segregate students with behavior problems, disciplinarians locked children in confinement rooms located in the dormitories or in the guardhouse, which was used from 1884 to 1910. (A new three-room jail was built in 1910 and was in use until the early 1930s.) In the early years, if the guardhouse was full, punishment for delinquent behavior resulted in being locked in an empty root cellar overnight. Corporal punishment for major violation of the rules resulted in floggings with a belt or harness strap administered by staff; however, sometimes a student supervisor administered the flogging. Children who ran away or repeat offenders of rules were severely punished by confinement in chains, which were sometimes placed so tightly, their hands, arms or upper torsos were mutilated. Metal rails along the walls of the dormitory sleeping areas were used to chain problem children to their mattresses. There are also reports of enforced sterilization for young adults who exhibited what the authorities considered vulgar behavior.

Although children worked long hours on the Haskell farm, they could freely talk to each other during work. Numerous stories from Native family histories reveal parents or relatives sneaking across the Wakarusa River to visit children at the south end of the farm. Parents or relatives also buried ceremonial material along the river levee for the children to use. Thus, the Haskell wetlands served a vital role as a place of refuge and retreat for generations of Haskell students.[12]

Spiritual Considerations

The trafficway impacts are primarily spiritual issues for many (but certainly not all) Haskell students and alumni.[13] Native American spiritual and cultural concerns about the environment, history, and education must be viewed holistically and not as fragmented pieces of information, separate from one another. The history of the American Indian people, their historical connections with the wetlands, and the history of Haskell Institute play a critical role in forming their spiritual viewpoint. Throughout the process of opposing the trafficway, HINU students learned about the boarding school experience of the early years of Haskell Institute, and the government policy of cultural genocide.

The Wetlands Preservation Committee struggled to find a way to explain concepts that incorporate ecological thinking as part of the process to bring about harmony and balance between people and their environment. Common sense suggests that spiritual issues are impossible to quantify because they involve a viewpoint of holistic relationships and interconnections of a people, their history, and the way they view the earth. A spirituality based upon connections and respect for the earth and all living things is given little credibility within the process of NEPA and its bureaucratic structure.

On numerous occasions, the committee attempted to convey that spiritual and cultural practices cannot be separated from the physical environment. Embedded in the biophysical environment is a set of values and functions that are not quantitative. Spiritual and cultural practices conducted in the area impacted by the trafficway and the wetland fill include traditional Native American ceremonies (e.g., pipe and sunrise ceremonies), Native American Church services, the collection of medicinal plants, and the use of sweatlodges for spiritual purification.

Indeed, core members of the committee found strength in their Native American spiritual traditions as they attempted to communicate their concerns about the trafficway's direct, secondary, and cumulative impacts. Repeatedly, the Committee spoke at public forums as well as with HINU students to discuss the variety of elements —aesthetic, recreational, cultural, historical, and ecological issues — that would be directly and adversely impacted by the trafficway. Public discussions of ecological threats to the wetlands proved to be a very positive experience, as the committee was supported by hundreds of non-Native members of the Lawrence community. Native and non-Native joined forces in candlelight vigils, moonlight tours of the wetlands, and nonviolent protest demonstrations along the proposed route.

Spiritual and cultural practices of Native Americans, which take place in the landscape, must be recognized under NEPA. Federal agencies follow internal guidance policies under NEPA guidelines that generally regard the physical environment and spiritual practices as separate functions and values. Yet this issue of the land and its use lies at the heart of American Indian traditions and cultural practices. Many federal agencies fail to address the embodiment of American Indian spiritual and cultural practices in the physical environment and the feeling of sacredness for the land.

The central question is, "How can traditional (i.e., spiritual) Native American knowledge and concerns function in the NEPA process as relevant knowledge?" Currently, NEPA guidance fails to incorporate Native American knowledge in the decision-making process.

Ecological Issues and the USACOE

Haskell and local environmentalists agreed that the proposed trafficway would cause or contribute to significant degradation of American waters and migratory bird habitat. They insisted that potential effects of the trafficway on human use be examined with regard to the Clean Water Act, section 404(b) (1) guidelines.[14] In correspondence with the U.S. Army Corps of Engineers (USACOE), the committee urged that attention be paid to recreation, education, historic sites, cultural resources, spiritual sites and practices, and aesthetics involving water resources and, accordingly, rescind a wetlands fill permit which would allow construction of the trafficway. The committee suggested that USACOE does not know or understand what values will be lost if the Haskell wetlands are filled in to allow trafficway construction. Therefore, HINU asked the USACOE to analyze present and future use of the Haskell wetlands with and without the wetland fill and trafficway. This request was made in an effort to follow the NEPA process, and ensure that presently unquantified environmental amenities and values be given appropriate consideration in decision-making.

The cooperation of the USACOE is critical to ensure the inclusion of Native American spiritual, cultural, and environmental concerns for equity in decision-making. Once again, the problems are related to differences in cultural perceptions and attitudes between decision-makers and American Indian people on environmental issues.

Trust Obligations and Responsibilities The government has a fiduciary obligation under federal American Indian law, known as the trust responsibility, to protect the tribes' property, treaty rights, and way of life. Generally, tribes are often directly and severely impacted by environmental degradation, and fulfilling this trust responsibility may require environmental protection above and beyond the standards set by statutory environmental law. However, these standards are tailored to the needs of the dominant society and are usually minimal in nature. The trust responsibility also defines the federal duty to protect cultural resources and the Native way of life from intrusions of the dominant society. Educational institutions such as Haskell provide a sacred place for time-honored cultural traditions to continue and flourish.

In the environmental context, the trust obligation to protect tribal resources is often translated into a higher level of ecological protection than required when solely non-Native interests are affected. Each federal agency is bound by this trust responsibility and obligations in carrying out statutory programs affecting tribes and their natural and cultural resources. The courts have expressed that federal agencies must deal with tribes according to the most exacting fiduciary standards. The duty of protection is a substantive one and is properly interpreted to include an affirmative duty to take action when necessary to protect American Indian property. The case law indicates that federal agencies cannot abrogate or extinguish the trust relationship or violate treaty rights, although Congress still holds such power.

Lessons Learned

Although the struggle is not over for HINU, there are some important lessons that can be learned from the experience.

1. People of color and low-income groups should expect to be treated as adversaries by federal and state agencies who are not part of the political network. Therefore, they should make every effort to demonstrate their positive desire to participate in the process, rather than merely complain.

2. First discover the most appropriate regulatory authority of the state and federal agencies, then determine how these agencies apply the "public interest balancing process" to fulfil their statutory responsibilities. Do not let your group be intimidated by the bureaucracy, but always remember that federal agencies are required to undergo the burden of inquiry into the public interest. Beware, however, that agencies define the "purpose and need" of a project so narrowly that they are strongly reluctant to consider any alternative to their proposed action.

3. Be prepared to read and know the regulations. If you don't understand a regulation, ask questions and continue to ask questions. Request a time-line schedule and copies of all documents developed on the project from all agencies, including local, state, and federal agencies involved in the project. Typically, private consulting firms perform most of the evaluation and assessment for a project. To acquire this information, channel your request through the state or federal agency that has contracted the firm. Remember, private firms do not have to follow the same rules and regulations as government agencies. Sometimes it's important to understand the personal connections between the private consultants and the local, state, and/or federal agencies. Remember that all politics are local.

4. Do not file your own response to the agencies until you are certain that you have obtained all necessary information from every agency involved. Your group has the legal right to request time extensions in preparing your own response to the agencies, especially if you are waiting for complete files and full disclosure statements from these agencies.

5. The key issue in NEPA is the term "scoping." This term refers to the agency's obligation to identify all the important issues involved in their assessment of environmental impacts. This becomes the most critical factor in projects because scoping occurs early in the NEPA process and new issues, which come up late in the process of assessment, are typically ignored. If a project was not scoped properly and a significant environmental impact was not identified, agencies are required to evaluate and assess the new information.

6. Scoping of the issues is a key element in NEPA and underscores and establishes an agency's commitment to the process. Scoping meetings should include

American Indian people or any minority group in the affected area from the very beginning of a project. Lobby the Council on Environmental Quality, which is part of the Executive Office of the President, to broaden the scoping guidance and to incorporate and establish a tracking mechanism for environmental justice issues and concerns. More importantly, a broader scoping definition ensures the incorporation and appropriate avenues of analysis of environmental justice issues. Tracking issues is part of the process to ensure their inclusion for equity in decision-making. This broader definition is a two-step process: first, assess the issues with the affected peoples themselves; and second, incorporate appropriate material, issues, and analysis for decision-makers. Perhaps HINU's present problems would not exist today if NEPA had included a definition that broadens scoping and if NEPA had a section that directly addresses the inclusion of issues with proper analysis. In HINU's case, the supplemental EIS fails to accurately and rationally portray the issues, leaving decision-makers with inadequate and incomplete information upon which to base a decision.

7. Although NEPA is a process for environmental assessment, the concept of process is vaguely defined and each agency may view the process differently because of unique statutory responsibilities peculiar to the agency. For example, the Federal Highway Administration and the Environmental Protection Agency often have opposing statutory responsibilities. Each federal agency has developed its own set of rules and policies for NEPA guidance. Acquire from all the federal agencies their particular NEPA guidance policy.

8. Document every action and information exchange on a calendar of events and keep copies of careful records. Expect a mountain of paperwork.

9. Expect unpleasant surprises, even betrayal by members of your coalition. Threats of retaliation, offers of bribes (both monetary and non-monetary) have been known to change the minds of even the staunchest allies and the highest level of administrators. Members of the Wetlands Preservation Committee are still recovering from a number of such shocks. Nevertheless, they take comfort in remembering the tremendous acts of heroism and self-sacrifice that have surfaced in some of the darkest times.

10. Don't give up. Expect a long, hard battle. Be patient.

11. Seek common ground without compromising your ideals. In an era of increasing global pollution, shrinking natural resources, and a demand for equal rights in the area of environmental justice, it is more critical than ever before to integrate traditional Native American knowledge with the environmental sciences and federal regulations, forming a bridge of mutual respect between different peoples. Any environmental project based solely upon standard engineering and environmental analysis overlooks NEPA's explicit statements for the use of non-quantitative methods (42 USC section 4332[b]). Native and Western perspectives are generally distinct from each other, especially in the dichotomy between quantitative and qualitative analysis. Nevertheless, although Native and Western environmental scientists often manifest different value systems, both strive for harmony with nature. Therefore, both sides must seek to facilitate mutual understanding and to link these two very powerful forms of environmental awareness and stewardship.

Suggestions for Community Leaders and Federal Agency Collaboration

- Be creative in seeking ways to ensure effective outreach, education, and collaboration for community involvement.
- Expand the scoping process to ensure the incorporation of issues and concerns of minorities by coordinating and integrating public participation to cooperate in identifying major issues.
- Assess the capacity and available resources and, if necessary, provide technical assistance aimed at solving specific environmental, cultural, or historical problems.
- Develop methods by which to assess local problems and use the assessment method as a basis for community education and involvement.
- Document gaps in critical information.
- Compile and document the extent of the environmental impact or problem.
- Develop usable information for minority communities for effective outreach, education, and risk communication.
- Determine the most effective methods to expand the amount and scope of information on environmental impacts.
- Provide ongoing monitoring and evaluation of activities and issues relevant to addressing a community's concerns.
- Ensure that efforts lead to enhanced community empowerment and involvement in addressing environmental impact issues.
- Provide opportunities for meaningful participation before making decisions that will affect the community.

Civil Rights and Legal Remedies: A Plan of Action

Bill Lann Lee

Claims of environmental injustice arise not only because of the activities of private entities, but because government regulatory agencies, whether wittingly or unwittingly, provide environmental protection in a racially and economically disparate manner. As a result, the historic tendency of private actors to impose disproportionate environmental burdens on minority and poor communities is often not restrained by the responsible regulatory agencies.

The environmental justice movement, in some respects, is a response on various levels — grass roots community activists, local governments, environmental organizations and civil rights groups — to the failure of the federal government in providing equitable regulatory enforcement.

This chapter discusses the remedies available for claims of civil rights violations and cases brought by the NAACP Legal Defense and Education Fund on behalf of minority community groups and individuals. Tips are included for community activists and others interested in prosecuting civil rights complaints. Finally, details of a community's legal fight to block a freeway in Los Angeles provides a useful case study.

The Problem of Discriminatory Regulatory Enforcement

Two approaches have emerged to address discriminatory regulatory enforcement. One approach is to improve enforcement of environmental laws and regulations in minority and poor communities by enhancing community participation in the regulatory and enforcement processes; requiring governmental scrutiny of the impact and bases of decision-making on minority and poor individuals; and increasing citizen suit environmental enforcement. The Environmental Justice Executive Order, Executive Order 12898 (February 11, 1994), is an example of this approach; its provision of federal administrative programs and actions address environmental justice in minority and low-income communities. Another example is environmental law administrative or judicial proceedings brought by minority communities.

The second approach is to address directly the problem of disparate governmental enforcement by invoking civil rights laws and regulations, which require even-handedness in governmental operations. Federal, state or governmental agencies historically have been prohibited from racially discriminatory enforcement under the Constitution or civil rights laws. In Brown v. Board of Education, for instance, the Supreme Court ruled that local Southern school districts were required to desegregate public schools according to the Fourteenth Amendment's guarantee of equal protection of the laws. The lower courts later ruled that federal funds could not be used to support unconstitutional segregation (Adams v. Richardson, 480 F.2d 1159 [D.C. Cir. 1973]; Simkins v. Moses Cone Memorial Hosp., 323 F.2d 959 [4th Cir. 1963], cert. denied, 376 U.S. 938 [1964]). Examples of this approach in the environmental justice context are complaints brought against regulatory agencies for violating their obligation under the civil rights laws to provide even-handed environmental protection.

These two approaches are complementary. Often they should be combined in a single effort. Thus community activists should participate in environmental decision-making processes as stakeholders. Because discriminatory governmental regulation may result, community activists should invoke not only environmental law protections but also the requirements of civil right laws in enforcement proceedings. An early case illustrating this synthetic approach of combining environmental and civil rights claims in a single proceeding is Keith v. Volpe, 858 F. 2d 467 (9th Cir. 1988), aff'g 618 F.Supp. 1132 (C.D. Cal. 1986); 506 F. 2d 696 (9th Cir. 1974), aff'g 352 F.Supp. 1324 (C.D. Cal. 1972). On behalf of several residents and community organizations, including the local chapters of both the Sierra Club and the NAACP, the case challenged the construction of the Century Freeway in Los Angeles County on environmental and civil rights grounds.

The Civil Rights Laws

The civil rights laws address both intentional discrimination and unjustified disparate impact. The Fourteenth Amendment and post-Civil War civil rights laws (e.g., 42 U.S.C. sections 1981, 1982 and 1983) prohibit intentional discrimination by government. Often proof of intentional discrimination is difficult to obtain. Factfinders have great latitude in assessing intentional discrimination claims, often deferring to the policy choices or decisions of state or local governmental officials. Generally, such claims have been unsuccessful in the environmental justice context because of the difficulty of proving intentional discrimination.

An intentional discrimination case, however, does not necessarily require "smoking gun" evidence. Systemic discrimination can be demonstrated by a showing of circumstantial evidence of disparate impact, historical background, departures from normal procedural sequence and substantive departures, such as in the fair housing case, Arlington Heights v. Metropolitan Housing Corp., 429 U.S. 252, 266-67 (1977). Minority communities that suffer from the cumulative effects of years of arbitrary environmental impositions should consider using the Arlington Heights paradigm in particular.

The modern Civil Rights Act enacted in 1964 and afterward correct some of the shortcomings of the earlier legal framework. The modern statutes often prohibit not only intentional discrimination but unjustified disparate impact. As a practical matter, disparate impact claims usually supplement, rather than replace, intentional discrimination claims.

In order to prove disparate impact discrimination, a plaintiff must show that the challenged policy or practice has a significant adverse effect on a protected group. Examples are the location of an environmentally hazardous facility in a minority community rather than in a nearby white community, or the allocation of mitigation or other benefits. If a plaintiff proves adverse impact, the burden shifts to the defendant to justify the adverse effect by showing business necessity through expert evidence of validity. Such a showing may be difficult for a defendant to meet because it cannot rely on the deference courts ordinarily accord a defendant's discretionary decision-making and policy choices. Even if the defendant carries that burden, a plaintiff may still prevail by showing that a nondiscriminatory alternative exists that the defendant erroneously rejected.

The modern civil rights laws also generally require federal agencies to promulgate implementing regulations and to establish compliance review and complaints procedures. As a result, the modern civil rights statutes usually can be enforced not only judicially, but also by the action of an administrative agency. Administrative enforcement is often inexpensive and more informal. The administrative agencies may have expertise, but may also be too attuned to the interests of the state and local agencies they regulate or fund. It remains to be seen how effective administrative enforcement will prove to be.

Title VI and its Regulations

A modern civil rights act relevant to many environmental justice claims is Title VI of the Civil Rights Act of 1964, 42 U.S.C. section 2000(d), which broadly prohibits the use of federal funds by recipients to discriminate on the basis of race, color, or national origin.

Under the coordinating authority of the U.S. Department of Justice, Executive Order 12250; 28 C.F.R. section 42.401 et seq., each federal agency has promulgated enforcement regulations (e.g., 49 C.F.R. Part 21[DOT]; 23 C.F.R. section 710.400 et seq. [FHWA]). The Supreme Court has ruled that while the intentional discrimination standard applies in cases brought to enforce only Title VI, the disparate impact standard applies in Title VI administrative proceedings or court cases brought to enforce the Title VI implementing regulations that incorporate such a standard (Alexander v. Choate, 469 U.S. 287, 293 [1985]). All the agencies have declared regulations that incorporate a disparate-impact standard for assessing claims that Title VI has been violated.

The attorney general reaffirmed these principles on July 14, 1994, the thirtieth anniversary of the passage of Title VI, in a memorandum to all heads of federal departments and agencies, entitled "Use of the Disparate Impact Standard in Administrative Regulations Under Title VI of the Civil Rights Act of 1964." The attorney general stated that:

"Enforcement of the disparate impact provisions is an essential component of an effective civil rights compliance program. Individuals continue to be denied, on the basis of their race, color, or national origin, the full and equal opportunity to participate in or receive the benefits of programs assisted by federal funds. Frequently discrimination results from policies and practices that are neutral on their face but have the effect of discrimination. Those policies and practices must be eliminated unless they are shown to be necessary to the program's operation and there is no less discriminatory alternative."

Fair Housing Act

Environmental justice claims can also be raised under the Fair Housing Act, Title VIII of the Civil Rights Act of 1968, 42 U.S.C. section 3601 et seq., which prohibits discriminatory conduct affecting fair housing opportunities. As in cases using Title VI and its implementing regulations, it is not necessary to prove discriminatory intent to prevail under Title VIII. Plaintiffs must initially prove that the challenged conduct results in discriminatory impact; if the defendant can prove that the conduct is justified, plaintiffs must then illustrate that a less discriminatory alternative exists (Huntington Branch NAACP v. Town of Huntington, 844 F.2d 926 [2d Cir.], review declined in part and aff'd, 109 S. Ct. 276 [1988]; Betsy v. Turtle Creek Assoc., 736 F.2d 983 [4th Cir. 1984]).

Title VIII is a useful supplement to Title VI because, unlike Title VI, it reaches private defendants and governmental defendants whether or not they receive federal funds (e.g., United States v. Real Estate Develop. Co., 374 F. Supp. 776 [D.C. Mass. 1972]). However, for Title VIII to apply, the challenged conduct must involve fair-housing opportunities or the provision of services associated with housing, like police and fire protection and garbage collection (e.g., Campbell v. City of Berwyn, 815 F. Supp. 1138 [N.D. Ill. 1993]). A proposed land use involves fair housing opportunities if, for example, it affects access to housing by people of color — such as a case in which housing in minority communities will be demolished or displaced by a freeway or bus repair facility — or results in increased segregation (United States v. City of Parma, Ohio, 494 F. Supp. 1049 [N.D. Ohio 1980] aff'd, 661 F.2d 562 [6th Cir.1981], cert. denied, 456 U.S. 926 [1982]).

Community Development Block Grant Program

The Community Development Block Grant program of the Housing and Community Development Act of 1964, 42 U.S.C. section 5301 et seq., like the general Title VI provision, specifically bars discrimination in state or local government use of federal block grant funds. The disparate impact standard applies to complaints brought under the Community Development Block Grant program. In addition to race, color, or national origin, the act prohibits discrimination on the basis of sex and religion. While employment issues may be difficult to raise under the Title VI regulations, such issues may be raised under the act.

Comparing Civil Rights and Environmental Enforcement

The civil rights and environmental claims of a minority community can often be presented in tandem. Pursuing civil rights claims, moreover, may offer distinct benefits unavailable under environmental statutes. As a substantive law matter, application of the disparate impact standard results in less deference to state and local agency policy and decision-making than may occur under an environmental statute. Meeting the expert business-necessity standard and rebutting the existence of nondiscriminatory alternatives entail substantial effort. The two inquiries inevitably result in greater judicial scrutiny of agency policies and practices. Under a disparate impact analysis, "it is an insufficient response to demonstrate some rational bases for the challenged practices"; the standard "involves a more probing judicial review of, and less deference to, the seemingly reasonable acts of administrators and executives" than is usual (Washington v. Davis, 426 U.S. 229, 246-48 [1976]).

The civil rights statutes may also offer procedural benefits. As noted above, the modern civil rights statutes are usually implemented by agency regulations and procedures separate from those offered by environmental law enforcement schemes. Thus, Title VI administrative complaints can be filed with the offices of civil rights of the particular federal agencies that administer federal funds to the state or local agencies whose conduct is being challenged. Title VIII and Community Development Block Grant administrative complaints can be filed with the Office for Fair Housing and Equal Opportunity of the U.S. Department of Housing and Urban Development.

Civil rights enforcement may also be more "user-friendly" than environmental enforcement. Administrative exhaustion requirements are usually less stringent than under environmental laws. Neither Title VI nor Title VIII administrative claims need to be exhausted before a lawsuit can be filed to enforce the Title VI statute, its regulations or Title VIII. The statute of limitations is often longer than in many environmental enforcement processes, although such limitations should be carefully adhered to, no matter what their duration. As a result, fewer claims should lapse as a result of the passage of time, a common problem for poor and minority communities.

Perhaps the most striking procedural benefit is that civil rights claims are tried de novo by courts so that plaintiffs potentially can conduct discovery, engage in trial preparation, and present witnesses and evidence in open court. Unlike judicial proceedings, under many environmental statutes in which the courts merely review an administrative record compiled by an agency, courts hearing civil rights claims are not limited to the administrative record. In some cases, therefore, a civil rights lawsuit may approximate a "second bite at the apple."

Legal Defense Fund Cases

A recent administrative complaint filed by the NAACP Legal Defense Fund in a California case illustrates the use of civil rights protections in Mothers of East Los Angeles, El Sereno Neighborhood Action Committee, El Sereno Organizing Committee, et al. v. California Transportation Commission, et al. (before the U.S. Departments of Transportation and Housing and Urban Development). The administrative complaint filed under both Titles VI and VIII by community groups and individual families who live on the proposed route alleges that the state agencies seek to construct a four and a half mile freeway extension in East Los Angeles through El Sereno, a Latino neighborhood of Los Angeles and the predominantly white cities of Pasadena and South Pasadena.

The state agencies, however, propose that mitigation measures be discriminatorily distributed by proposing that all of the freeway in Pasadena and 80 percent in South Pasadena be below ground level, thus diminishing noise, air and visual pollution, while most of the proposed route in El Sereno will be placed above grade with undiminished pollution.

While a mile of the freeway in white areas will be covered over, little of the El Sereno portion will be covered. All of the historic preservation measures are limited to the white areas, in spite of many historic structures in the El Sereno area. The state agencies intend to accommodate a private school in Pasadena and a public schoolin South Pasadena with cut-and-cover tunnels over the adjacent freeway but the freeway will run above grade adjacent to El Sereno's Sierra Vista public elementary school.

Discriminatory siting and mitigation disparities were issues in Clean Air Alternative Coalition v. U.S. Department of Transportation (N.D. Cal. C-93-0721-VRW), another highway case settled by plaintiff community organizations, churches and individuals for enhanced mitigation measures along the route of the Cypress Freeway in West Oakland, California. The same issues are raised in James City Historical Society v. North Carolina Department of Transportation (before the Federal Highway Administration, U. S. Department of Transportation), involving a highway bridge proposed for James City, North Carolina, a predominantly African-American town, instead of adjacent white areas.

The Legal Defense Fund is also litigating two cases concerning funding decisions by state agencies. In Labor/Community Strategy Center v. Los Angeles Metropolitan Transportation Authority (C.D. Cal.CV 94-5936 TJH [Mcx]), the Legal Defense Fund sued local agencies on behalf of a class of 350,000 minority, poor bus riders represented by the Labor/Community Strategy Center, the Bus Riders Union, Southern Christian Leadership Conference, Korean Immigrant Workers Advocates and individual bus riders. Plaintiffs challenged inequitable funding and operation of bus transportation used by poor, minority Los Angeles residents.

The lawsuit followed two years of organizing by the Strategy Center and the Bus Riders Union. One of the key issues is the plaintiffs' allegation that the Transit Authority used federal funds to pursue a policy of raising the cost to riders of bus service and reducing the quality of bus service in order to fund rail and other projects for predominantly white, suburban residents. In September, 1994, the federal district court preliminarily enjoined the elimination of a low-cost $42 monthly bus pass and a hike of the basic fare. The parties then stipulated retention of a still affordable $49 bus pass along with a fare hike pending trial on all issues. This case was settled in October, 1996.

Nettie L. Thomas, et al. v. City of Macon, Georgia, et al. (before the U.S. Department of Transportation) concerns a similar set of issues arising out of the long history of discriminatory allocation of funds by Macon and Bibb County authorities. Representing African-American individuals, the Legal Defense Fund and Georgia Legal Services have challenged the local officials' practice of spending funds on highways that principally serve white residential areas, while starving the bus system exclusively used by black Macon residents. Both the Macon and Los Angeles MTA cases involve not only Title VI of the Civil Rights Act of 1964, but also related ISTEA (1991), 49 U.S.C. App. section 1607 obligations.

These cases demonstrate not only the variety of issues that can be addressed under the civil rights laws, but also suggest larger issues, such as failure to document possible adverse impacts on minority groups, failure to impose ISTEA and business necessity justification requirements, and failure to consider nondiscriminatory alternatives.

Moreover, none of these cases would have arisen, had federal agencies been more vigilant in discharging their obligation to guarantee the nondiscriminatory use of federal funds under Title VI and duties imposed by other civil rights measures. The level of federal environmental justice enforcement should increase if the Environmental Justice Executive Order is faithfully implemented.

Tips for Prosecuting Administrative Civil Rights Complaints

The following tips for filing and prosecuting administrative civil rights complaints uses the El Sereno complaint as a case study.

1. Why file? The practical effect of the Environmental Justice Executive Order is to make federal agencies (that fund many of the projects raising environmental justice concerns) potential allies for minority communities. It is as yet unclear whether the federal agencies will actually utilize this Title VI authority to enforce Title VI and the environmental justice executive order in a meaningful fashion. This is a period of some flux. How agencies treat early complaints is obviously an indication of their commitment, as is the level and quality of staffing of the enforcement effort.

2. A checklist of what to file:

- Complaints should state why a federal agency has jurisdiction: Does the agency fund the work of the state or local governmental agency or other entity whose conduct is being challenged? Does Title VI and its regulations or the Community Development Block Grant Program apply? Are fair housing opportunities affected? Does the Fair Housing Act apply? Does the· Environmental Justice Executive Order apply?
- Whose conduct is being challenged? Is the entity a federal fund recipient under the Title VI regulations and/or the Community Development Block Grant program? Does the entity's conduct affect housing opportunities of minorities?
- When did the challenged conduct occur? Is it within the 180 day Title VI regulatory complaint period? If the conduct occurred earlier, is the challenged conduct part of a larger course of conduct that is continuing, and did some part of the course of conduct occur within the 180 day period? Is there any other reason the agency should excuse a late submission?
- What is the conduct being challenged? What happened? How are minority persons or other groups protected by the civil rights statutes adversely affected by the conduct? How are white persons favored?
- What remedy do you want? What do you want the state or local governmental entity to do? What do you want the federal agency to do?

3. How do we file? Environmental justice administrative complaints are rare. No one yet has very much experience with them. Generally, agency officials most familiar with the Environmental Justice Executive Order and civil rights remedies are at agency headquarters rather than regional, district or local offices, which are often criticized for working "hand in glove" with state and local agencies receiving federal assistance. Complaints should generally be sent to the head of the agency with copies to other officials.

4. Do we need a lawyer? A knowledgeable lawyer should be consulted, even though the complaint process is informal. Optimally, a lawyer should assist in preparing the complaint and monitoring its progress. A lawyer should also be consulted about alternatives such as court litigation.

5. What should we do after the complaint is submitted? The agency may not have sufficient resources to properly investigate the complaint. A complete investigation should be pressed for. Documents, witnesses or other assistance should be provided to assist the agency investigation.

The Case Study: El Sereno and the Long Beach Freeway

The NAACP Legal Defense and Educational Fund, the Natural Resources Defense Council and the National Health Law Program, acting on behalf of the complainants (Mothers of East Los Angeles, the El Sereno Neighborhood Action Committee and the El Sereno Organizing Committee), filed an administrative complaint to challenge the proposed Long Beach Freeway Extension Project (California Route 710), which, if built, would violate the complainants' rights to environmental justice and fair housing.

The project, as proposed by the California Transportation Commission and the California Department of Transportation (Caltrans), does not comply with controlling environmental justice and fair housing mandates because it disproportionately imposes environmental and housing burdens on minority communities, and those communities are denied mitigation measures that are accorded predominantly white communities elsewhere along the freeway route. As a result, minority residents are exposed to greater risk of environmental harm and denied equal availability to housing opportunity.

Mothers of East Los Angeles, El Sereno Neighborhood Action Committee and El Sereno Organizing Committee believe that the proposed freeway is inequitable because El Sereno would be disproportionately impacted both environmentally and in terms of fair-housing opportunities. The route of the proposed freeway traverses both predominantly white and wealthier communities in Pasadena and South Pasadena, as well as El Sereno. Most of the proposed freeway is planned to be below grade with extensive cut-and-cover tunneling in Pasadena and South Pasadena. In contrast, the proposed freeway is planned to be above grade or at ground level, with only minimal cut-and-cover tunneling in El Sereno.

While schools adjacent to the proposed Freeway in both Pasadena and South Pasadena would be accommodated by the provision of a below-grade route and tunneling, a similarly-situated public school in El Sereno would not be so accommodated. All of the historic preservation mitigation is allocated for Pasadena and South Pasadena. Notwithstanding the fact that a number of El Sereno homes, some dating back to the beginning of this century, are eligible for the National Register of Historic Places, the commission and Caltran have declined to recognize their historic significance. As a result, El Sereno residents would disproportionately bear the environmental and housing burdens that will be imposed by the proposed freeway extension.

Jurisdiction

This complaint involves claims arising under Title VI of the Civil Rights Act of 1964, 42 U.S.C. section 2000(d), Title VI implementing regulations, 49 C.F.R. section 21.5(b) (2) and (3); 23 C.F.R. section 710.405(c) (2) and (3), and Executive Order 12898. This complaint also involves claims arising under the Fair Housing Act of 1968, 42 U.S.C. section 3601 et seq., and Executive Order 12892.

Pursuant to 49 C.F.R. section 21.11, the Secretary of Transportation has jurisdiction to investigate claims of discrimination in programs that receive federal assistance from the Department of Transportation. Pursuant to 49 C.F.R. section section 21.1 and 21.13, the secretary additionally has the power to effect compliance with the mandate that programs receiving federal funding do not subject any person to discrimination on the grounds of race, color, or national origin. The secretary therefore has jurisdiction to hear and adjudicate this administrative complaint.

Pursuant to 24 C.F.R. section 4100.91, the Secretary of the Department of Housing and Urban Development has the authority and responsibility to administer and effectuate the Fair Housing Act and its implementing regulations. The secretary therefore has jurisdiction to hear and adjudicate this administrative complaint.

Complainants

Mothers of East Los Angeles is a community organization of residents of East Los Angeles, including the Los Angeles neighborhood of El Sereno. East Los Angeles is a substantially low-income community with a principally Latino population that has been severely and disproportionately impacted by the location of many forms of environmental pollution by both governmental and private actors, including the largest concentration of freeways in Los Angeles County. Mothers of East Los Angeles was founded a decade ago to combat degradation of the environment and quality of life in East Los Angeles, and has led efforts to resist the further disproportionate location in East Los Angeles of incinerators, prisons, and other facilities that impose environmental burdens.

The El Sereno Neighborhood Action Committee is a grassroots group of residents of El Sereno, an almost completely Latino Los Angeles neighborhood that will be severely impacted by the proposed freeway. Fully 47 percent of the housing units to be removed for the freeway are located in El Sereno. Although the Neighborhood Action Committee was founded in 1984 to advance the interests of El Sereno on a broad series of issues, the Neighborhood Action Committee believes the proposed freeway is the major threat to the integrity of El Sereno.

The El Sereno Organizing Committee is a grassroots group of residents of El Sereno formed to oppose the proposed Long Beach Freeway Extension. Most of the Organizing Committee's members reside in the northern part of El Sereno, where most of El Sereno's historic structures are located. The Organizing Committee, which grew out of the Maycrest Neighborhood Watch Association, has opposed the Freeway Extension before the California Transportation Commission and other public bodies. Last year, the Committee gathered - in only eight hours - over 800 signatures of El Sereno residents opposed to the proposal. The Organizing Committee was also instrumental in obtaining the opposition of the Los Angeles Times editorial board to the proposed Freeway Extension.

Don Justin Jones, Hugo Garcia, and Jesse Granados are individuals who reside in the path of the proposed freeway extension project and who would be adversely affected by the practices described here.

This complaint is filed on behalf of over 30,000 predominately Latino residents of El Sereno, a neighborhood located in the city of Los Angeles, California.

Facts

Failure to Enforce Environmental Justice and Fair Housing Mandates
On September 14, 1994, the California Transportation Commission adopted the meridian variation alignment of the Long Beach Freeway Extension proposed by Caltrans. The project consists of the construction of a four and a half mile extension at an estimaed cost ranging between $670 million and $1 billion in current dollars.

In approving the proposal, the commission failed to perform any analysis of whether the proposal complied with the environmental justice mandates of Title VI, its implementing regulations, and the Environmental Justice Executive Order or the fair-housing mandates of Title VIII, its implementing regulations or the Fair Housing Executive Order. The commission failed altogether to acknowledge either mandate or the environmental justice or fair housing executive orders.

The U.S. Environmental Protection Agency, Region IX, in a recent letter to the Federal Highway Administration, noted that the failure to address environmental justice concerns requires reconsideration.[1]

The Existing Record on Unjustified Disparate Impact   Although the California Transportation Commission's decision to approve the freeway project was rendered September 14, 1994, and Caltrans' environmental impact statement was released in 1992, the commission and Caltrans relied on 1980 census data. This existing record, however, indicates that a strong case of unjustified disparate impact exists.

The commission documents and Caltrans' environmental impact statement reveal that the level of mitigation along the proposed freeway appears to vary inversely with the level of minority population in the adjoining community.

Census Data   The 1980 census indicated that the total area affected by the freeway is home to 82,300 persons who were 56 percent minority (45 percent Latino, 9 percent Asian-American and 2.5 percent African-Americans and others) and 43.5 percent white. However, the communities along the proposed freeway are racially and economically stratified. This is clearest from a comparison of the three areas in which Caltrans expects the most displacement: El Sereno (47 percent of the total housing units removed); South Pasadena (42 percent of the total) and Pasadena (11 percent of the total).

The seven El Sereno census tracts of 29,309 residents, 36 percent of the total affected population, were the tracts with the highest nonwhite population. White population ranged from 5 percent to 15 percent. The Latino population in the El Sereno census tracts ranged from 68 percent to 91 percent. (Tables 1-3). El Sereno is the poorest area affected by the proposed freeway. While the 1980 countywide median family income was $20,000, the income in the affected El Sereno areas was considered well below, ranging from $12,700 to $16,500.

Table 1: Seven El Sereno Census Tracts, 1980		
1980 Census Tract	**%White**	**%Minority**
2017	15	85
2016	9	91
2015.2	10	90
2015.01	13	87
2011	13	87
2012	5	95
2013	12	88

Table 2: Four South Pasadena Census Tracts, 1980		
1980 Census Tract	**%White**	**%Minority**
4807.02	58	42
4807.01	74	26
4805	83	17
4806	81	19

Table 3: Two Pasadena Census Tracts, 1980		
1980 Census Tract	**%White**	**%Minority**
4639	85	15
4637	77	23

The four South Pasadena census tracts, with a total 1980 population of 22,681, had populations ranging from 58 percent white to 83 percent white. The average white population in the four tracts was 76 percent. Median family income was above the countywide average, ranging from $24,031 to $32,917. The two Pasadena tracts affected, with a 1980 population of 6,000, were more than 80 per cent white, ranging from 77 percent to 85 percent. The 1980 median family income in the Pasadena tracts ranged from $38,500 to $42,000, or twice the countywide average.

Discriminatory Placement of Mitigation Measures According to the environmental impact statement: "Manmade objects such as concrete structures are intrusive. Open-cut slopes and high embankments reshape the natural landscape with long flat broad areas that are visible for great distances. Elevated freeways have a greater impact on aesthetics than a depressed facility, as the depressed facility is out of sight from most normal human activities."[2] The commission noted that a below-grade highway also results in less noise.

The commission and Caltrans acknowledged that beneficial freeway mitigation measures are concentrated in Pasadena and South Pasadena. While 80 percent of the freeway would be below grade in South Pasadena and all of it in Pasadena, almost all of the freeway would be at or above grade level in El Sereno. According to the commission, construction of the freeway "below the adjacent terrain through about 80 percent of the City of South Pasadena and all of the City of Pasadena . . . will reduce the levels of freeway/transitway generated noise for adjacent receptors."[3] According to Caltrans:

"This feature will have the ancillary effect of lessening any perceived neighborhood disruption by placing the facility below the level of sight for most observers. An added benefit of a depressed freeway is a facility that is less visually intrusive than one that is at-grade or elevated."[4]

This feature would lessen any perceived neighborhood disruption by placing the facility below the line of sight for most observers. Other significant mitigation measures are cut-and-cover tunnels. According to the commission:

"A cut-and-cover tunnel will completely cover the freeway/transitway at [certain] locations and will provide space for the relocation of dwelling units (historic structures in particular), recreational areas, or other community uses. It will also allow for the construction of a realigned north-south local street and facilitate continued access between alternate sides of the freeway/transitway. These features will serve to mitigate the perception of a divided neighborhood and provide for a continuum of the urban fabric."[5]

As adopted by the commission, the proposed freeway would have six tunnels. Five tunnels, totalling 5180 feet, or almost a mile in length, would be located in Pasadena or South Pasadena. Only one tunnel of 980 feet is planned for El Sereno. The disproportionate construction of tunnels in Pasadena and South Pasadena largely restricts to those areas the ability to reduce residential dwelling losses by locating units on or near the tunnels. The above-tunnel replacement housing program is, in fact , limited to Pasadena and South Pasadena. It also largely restricts to Pasadena and South Pasadena above-tunnel "landscaping [that] will also help to blend into the community."[6]

In 1980, the South Pasadena School District had a 76-percent white student population, while El Sereno had a 5-percent white student population. The commission stated that a 1,160-foot long cut-and-cover tunnel was planned in the vicinity of the South Pasadena High School in order to reduce noise levels.[7] Caltrans noted that this tunnel "will completely cover the freeway at this location and will provide space for recreational areas or other community uses."[8] The commission and Caltrans also plan a similar accommodation for a private school in Pasadena, Westridge School for Girls. On the other hand, the commission and Caltrans plan for the proposed freeway to be above-grade alongside the Sierra Vista Elementary School in El Sereno, notwithstanding environmental justice concerns raised by the Board of Education of Los Angeles:

> "The Sierra Vista Elementary School is 'immediately adjacent' to the proposed freeway and Caltrans has stated that the freeway is above grade in this area. A depressed freeway has not even been considered for the El Sereno community, yet the high school in South Pasadena which is 'immediatelyadjacent' to the freeway will be depressed. If each school along the Route 710 corridor is to be treated equitabl[y] . . . , I believe more consideration, has to be given to our school children attending this elementary school . . . Our children deserve the best education possible when attending school; they should not have to face the additional disadvantages of noise pollution and poor air quality that will accompany this freeway."[9]

The commission also acted before historic assessment was complete, and without resolving the request of the National Trust for Historic Preservation that a historic district in El Sereno be declared eligible for the National Register.[10] As a result, the freeway project includes absolutely no preservation measures for El Sereno's intact historic community. In contrast, Caltrans and the commission have purported to mitigate the loss of dozens of historic properties affected in South Pasadena and Pasadena. Because virtually all of the historic properties throughout the corridor of the proposed freeway serve as residences, the disparate impact on historic properties in El Sereno would adversely affect housing availability and community integrity in El Sereno.

The EIS admitted that the meridian variation of the proposed freeway extension "would disrupt the communities and neighborhoods of El Sereno, Pasadena and South Pasadena,"[11] and that the only mitigation measures to lessen the disruption are those limited to Pasadena and South Pasadena. The report stated that "disruption of communities and neighborhoods will be lessened by maximizing vehicular and pedestrian circulation across the freeway, using a less intrusive depressed freeway design where feasible, and cut-and-cover tunnels at key residential locations."[12] The commission and Caltrans, in short, plan to mitigate community disruption in Pasadena and South Pasadena, but not in Latino El Sereno.

As a result of unmitigated disruption, a significant part of the cohesive El Sereno community would be orphaned by the proposed freeway extension as an urban island, separate from the rest of the area. These Latino residents would be denied access to community and cultural institutions, such as churches, markets, and recreational facilities, to a much greater extent than the predominately majority residents of comparable areas in Pasadena and South Pasadena.

Moreover, El Sereno residents would additionally suffer environmental harms as a result of the proposed freeway extension. To date, the commission and Caltrans have made minimal efforts to reduce and manage decades-old traffic congestion in the El Sereno area resulting from the terminus of the present 710 Freeway in the area, and they are making little effort to reduce existing air pollution, noise and other environmental harms in the very area of the proposed freeway extension with the largest minority population. While Caltrans has not generally maintained very well the properties it has taken to date for the freeway extension, it particularly has failed to maintain and operate residences and structures that have been taken for freeway construction in El Sereno. If the proposed project is implemented, El Sereno residents will have to deal with both existing conditions as well as new harmful impacts, including the removal of trees and other vegetation that contribute to the health and beauty of the community.

Necessity The commission and Caltrans simply have not advanced any reason rising to the level of necessity (which was recognized by the attorney general's July, 1994 memorandum), to justify the evident disparity between allocation of mitigation measures between predominantly-white Pasadena and South Pasadena and Latino El Sereno.

Nondiscriminatory Alternatives The commission and Caltrans did consider nondiscriminatory alternatives to the discriminatory allocation of mitigation measures. But the commission failed to consider approaches such as the multimode, low-build alternative proposal of September 1993; this proposal suggested the diversion of traffic to other modes of transportation, diffusion and management of traffic, and a short extension of the freeway through an existing industrial zone. These alternatives would relieve congestion in and around El Sereno while avoiding the destruction of hundreds of homes. If such alternatives are pursued, analyses can and should be conducted to assure that mitigation measures are allocated on a nondiscriminatory basis. (One of the concepts utilized in the multi-mode proposal is the development of a Blue Line rail project connecting downtown and Pasadena. The efficacy of this project is questionable in light of issues raised in Community/Labor Strategy Center v. Los Angeles County Metropolitan Transit Authority, C.D. Ca. CV 94-5936 TJH [Mcx]. A far better option, consistent with the multi-mode approach, is enhanced bus transportation.)

Legal Claims

The California Transportation Commission and Caltrans are recipients of federal funds, making Title VI and its implementing regulations applicable. The disproportionate impact of the proposed Freeway on housing opportunities and benefits in minority communities along the freeway's route also makes Title VIII of the Civil Rights Act of 1968, 42 U.S.C. section 3601 et seq., applicable.

Environmental Justice Title VI provides that "no person in the United States shall, on the ground of race, color, or national origin . . . be subjected to discrimination under any program or activity receiving federal financial assistance." Caltrans and the Federal Highway Administration issued implementing regulations providing that:

> "In determining the types of services . . . or other benefits, or facilities which will be provided under any . . . program [receiving federal financial assistance] . . ., a recipient may not, directly or through contractual or other arrangements, utilize criteria or methods of administration which have the

effect of subjecting persons to discrimination because of their race, color . . . or national origin, or have the effect of defeating or substantially impairing accomplishment of the objectives of the program with respect to individuals of a particular race, color . . . or national origin."

In determining the site or location of facilities, a recipient (of federal assistance) may not make selections with the purpose or effect of excluding persons or denying them the benefits of, or subjecting them to discrimination under any program to which this directive applies, on the grounds of race, color or national origin; or with the purpose or effect of defeating or substantially impairing the accomplishment of the objectives of Title VI of the Civil Rights Act of 1964 or this directive (21 CRF section 21.5[b] [2] and [3]; 23 CFR section 710.405[c] [2] and [3]).

On February 11, 1994, President Clinton issued Executive Order 12898 to clarify the need for federal administrative actions to address environmental justice in minority populations and low-income populations under Title VI. The Environmental Justice Executive Order reaffirmed that:

"Each federal agency shall conduct its programs, policies, and activities that substantially affect human health or the environment, in a manner that ensures that such programs, policies and activities do not have the effect of excluding persons (including population) from participation in, denying persons (including populations) the benefits of, or subjecting persons (including population) to discrimination under, such programs, policies and activities, because of their race, color, or national origin." (Executive Order 12898, section 2-2)

The order also states that:

"to the greatest extent practicable and permitted by law . . . each federal agency shall make achieving environmental justice part of its mission by identifying and addressing, as appropriate, disproportionately high and adverse human health or environmental effects of its programs, policies, and activities on minority populations and low-income populations."

Disparate Impact Standard   Attorney General Janet Reno issued a memorandum for heads of departments and agencies that offered guidance on the enforcement of the Title VI implementing regulations. The attorney general stated that:

"Enforcement of the disparate impact provisions is an essential component of an effective civil rights compliance program. Individuals continue to be denied on the basis of their race, color, or national origin, the full and equal opportunity to participate in or receive the benefits of programs assisted by federal funds. Frequently, discrimination results from policies and practices that are neutral on their face but have the effect of discrim-ination. Those policies and practices must be eliminated unless they are shown to be necessary to the program's operation and there is no less discriminatory alternative."[13]

According to the attorney general, "racially neutral policies and practices that act as arbitrary and unnecessary barriers to equal opportunity must end."

Fair Housing The Fair Housing Act declares that "it is the policy of the United States to provide, within constitutional limitations, for fair housing throughout the United States" (42 U.S.C. section 3601). The act makes it unlawful for governmental entities to "make unavailable or deny a dwelling to any person because of race, color . . . or national origin" (42 U.S.C. section 3604[a]).

On January 17, 1994, the president issued Executive Order 12892 to further fair housing in all federal programs and activities relating to housing and urban development. This fair housing executive order required that "the head of each executive agency is responsible for ensuring that its programs and activities relating to housing and urban development are administered in a manner affirmatively to further the goal of fair housing as required by [the Fair Housing Act]" (Executive Order 12892, section 2-202). The order also declared that "in carrying out the responsibilities in this order, the head of each executive agency shall take appropriate steps to require that all persons or other entities . . . who are supervised or regulated under, agency programs and activities relating to housing and urban development shall comply with this order." The order also established the President's Fair Housing Council, on which the Secretary of Transportation serves.

Like Title VI, a disparate impact standard is used to enforce the protections of the Fair Housing Act.[14] Largely restricted to predominantly white Pasadena and South Pasadena, the mitigation measures of a below-grade freeway path, cut-and-cover tunnels, accommodation for public school students and historic preservation programs exacerbates the already disproportionate environmental burden on El Sereno residents in terms of air quality, noise, preservation of community integrity and visual intrusion. This disproportionate allocation, along with the failure to provide replacement housing, raises serious issues under Title VI regulations. The California Transportation Commission and Caltrans, however, failed to enforce the environmental justice mandate by analyzing the disparity and assessing whether any disparity was justified by necessity or whether nondiscriminatory alternatives existed.

Complainants Mothers of East Los Angeles, El Sereno Neighborhood Action Committee and El Sereno Organizing Committee submit that the Commission's failure even to recognize and apply environmental justice and fair housing requirements is a fatal defect, a position already taken by the Environmental Protection Agency. The department, consistent with its obligations to enforce Title VI and the environmental justice executive order should not permit the commission and Caltrans to proceed with the project without a comprehensive analysis of whether the proposal has disparate impact on minority residents; whether any disparity is justified by business necessity; and whether nondiscriminatory alternatives exist. Fair Housing dictates also require no less.

Even the existing record provides compelling evidence that the mitigation disparities have the clear and unmistakable effect of subjecting El Sereno's minority residents to discrimination because of their race, color or national origin; and defeating or substantially impairing accomplishment of the objectives of the Long

Beach freeway extension project with respect to El Sereno minority residents. The record reveals neither anything approaching a necessity justification nor the absence of nondiscriminatory alternatives.

After the environmental impact statement was prepared in 1992, the Route 710 Mitigation and Environment Advisory Committee was appointed to identify further mitigation and enhancement measures. However, Caltrans refused to seat grassroots El Sereno community representatives who requested to serve on the panel, depriving El Sereno of representation.

Pursuant to the environmental justice executive order as well as Title VI regulations, Caltrans is obliged to ensure that its programs, policies and activities substantially affecting human health or the environment do not exclude persons from participation or deny them benefits because of their race, color or national origin. Approval of the Long Beach freeway extension would violate that obligation.

The failure to properly assess the mitigation disparities also denies El Sereno residents equal housing opportunity guaranteed by the Fair Housing Act and the fair housing executive order.

The El Sereno housing that would be destroyed by the proposed freeway extension is affordable to low- and moderate-income families and individuals. Such housing, as the environmental impact statement admits, is not readily available in El Sereno or nearby communities,[15] and those displaced would not be able to obtain replacement housing anywhere near their present homes. In Pasadena and South Pasadena, on the other hand, the displaced would not face such severe barriers. Remaining El Sereno residents not displaced by freeway construction would live in a community whose integrity and vitality would be compromised to a much greater degree than Pasadena and South Pasadena areas.

The unjustified discriminatory mitigation measures "make unavailable or deny dwellings" because of race, color or national origin directly through disparate historic preservation mitigation or maintenance of Caltran-owned housing in El Sereno compared to Pasadena and South Pasadena. The measures fail to provide an above-tunnel replacement housing program or measures to compensate for adverse effects on El Sereno.

The inevitable result is that, unless remedied, Latino El Sereno residents would end up with less opportunity for housing than Pasadena and South Pasadena residents. The affirmative fair housing goal of Title VIII and the Fair Housing Executive Order would thus be frustrated.

Conclusion

Complainants respectfully request that the departments deny approval of the Long Beach freeway extension project pursuant to the civil rights statutes and executive orders that the project as proposed would violate. Complainants request preliminary relief, in the form of an order staying approval of the proposed freeway extension, until environmental and fair housing violations are redressed.

Epilogue

Robert D. Bullard

All transportation modes are not created equal. Federal transportation policies, taxing structure, and funding schemes have contributed to the inequity between the various transportation modes, i.e., private automobile, rail, bus, and airplane. Funds are dispensed on an unlevel playing field. State departments of transportation have become de facto road-building programs that buttress the asphalt and construction industry. On the other hand, funding for efficient, clean urban mass transportation systems has been spotty, at best.

Transportation decision-making — whether at the federal, region, state, or local level — often mirrors the power arrangements of the dominant society and its institutions. In reality, affluent suburbanites do not want inner-city bus riders "invading" their communities. Millions of Americans voted with their feet, accelerating the political power shift to the suburbs. The end result is transportation apartheid.

Some transportation policies distribute the costs in a regressive pattern, while providing disproportionate benefits for individuals who fall at the upper end of the education and income scale. Central cities and suburbs are not equal. They often compete for scarce resources. One need not be a rocket scientist to predict the outcome between affluent suburbs and their less affluent central city competitors. Freeways are the lifeline for suburban commuters, while millions of central-city residents are dependent on public transportation as their primary mode of travel. But recent cuts in mass-transit subsidies and fare hikes have reduced access to essential social services and economic activities. Nevertheless, road construction programs are booming — even in areas choked by air pollution.

Clean air appears to be everyone's dream. This sentiment cuts across race, class, gender, and geographic lines. The air quality impacts of transportation are especially significant to low-income persons and people of color (especially children) who are more likely to live in urban areas with reduced air quality than affluent individuals and whites. No doubt, clean and energy-efficient public transportation could give millions of Americans who live in polluted cities a healthier environment and possibly longer lives.

Even after years of government regulations and mandates, people of color and the poor are still exposed to greater health and environmental risks than the

173

society at large.[1] Pollution from multiple sources (smokestacks, incinerators, refineries, hazardous waste dumps, bus barns, freeways, lead in drinking water and paint, etc.) endanger the health and safety of millions of urban residents.

Something must be done. The country took the lead out of gasoline. The switch to unleaded is a success story — illustrating what this country can do when it decides to do the right thing. However, lead is still around — mostly in older homes, on playgrounds, and near freeways that dissect inner-city neighborhoods — from South Bronx to South Central Los Angeles. Lead affects 3-4 million children in the United States - most of whom are African-American and Latinos living in urban areas. Among children five years old and younger, the percentage of African-American children with excessive levels of lead in their blood far exceeds the percentage of whites at all income levels.[2]

The public health community has insufficient information to explain the magnitude of some of the air pollution-related health problems. However, persons suffering from asthma are particularly sensitive to the effects of carbon monoxide, sulfur dioxides, particulate matter, ozone, and nitrogen oxides.[3] African-Americans and Latinos, for example, have a significantly higher prevalence of asthma than the general population.[4] The leading cause of emergency childhood hospital visits in most major cities is not gunshot wounds or drive-by shootings — it is asthma. Children are literally running out of clean air. This is not ethical, just, or fair, and some advocates are challenging the legality of these conditions.

Grassroots groups are not sitting back and complaining about these problems. They are acting. Their battle cry is: "It's not about whining, it's about winning." They have forced government agencies to take a closer look at their policies and practices, especially as they impact the poor and people of color. In May 1995, for example, a national environmental justice transportation conference was held in Atlanta, Georgia.[5] The conference was co-sponsored by the Federal Highway Administration, Federal Transit Administration, Federal Railroad Administration and the Environmental Justice Resource Center at Clark Atlanta University. The 1995 meeting was attended by over 250 grassroots environmental justice leaders, civil rights advocates, legal experts, planners, academicians, and government officials from thirty states. Many of the contributors to this book participated in the meeting. The conference included over eighty presenters, keynote speakers, moderators, and panelists. Conference highlights and on-the-ground struggles are captured in the 1996 Just Transportation video.[6]

Representatives from the grassroots environmental justice network were an integral part of conference speakers. Over half of the presenters represented grassroots groups and other nongovernmental organizations. Conference participants were charged with defining new approaches to foster greater public participation of impacted populations to create healthy and sustainable communities through wise transportation investments. The conference provided a forum for leaders to present their views on transportation decision-making. The following recommendations emerged from the meeting:

1. Ensure greater stakeholder participation and public involvement in transportation decision-making. Public involvement is essential to effective transportation planning. Statewide transportation agencies and metropolitan planning organizations (MPOs) are challenged with the task of involving culturally diverse stakeholders early in the planning process and during project development. Specific recommendations include:

- Design strategies to identify culturally diverse stakeholder groups, high-impact populations, and facilitate their involvement in decision-making.
- Design culturally-sensitive outreach, communication, and training programs, manuals, guidebooks, videos, and other educational materials in collaboration with impacted communities.
- Target transportation resources to address existing needs of underserved populations.
- Expand involvement of historically black colleges and universities/minority academic institutions and other nongovernmental organizations in university transportation centers.
- Conduct training workshops for planners and decision-makers on public participation and environmental justice provisions under Executive Order 12898 and the Proposed DOT Order.
- Provide funds for grassroots groups to conduct evaluations of public participation process and outcomes.
- Collaborate with environmental justice and other community-based groups in design of public involvement strategies and outreach programs.
- Provide public input in the design of requests for proposals and review processes.
- Integrate public involvement requirements into the MTO-certification process.
- Provide training, technical assistance, and research in public participation.
- Conduct public hearings on underfunded areas and underserved populations.
- Coordinate ongoing dialogue of environmental justice and community stakeholders to design a broad-based transportation advocacy agenda.
- Fund public involvement partnership pilots involving impacted communities, grassroots groups, minority academic institutions, MPOs, and state DOTs.

2. Direct resources to identify and address discriminatory outcomes, disproportionate impacts, inequitable distribution of transportation investments, and their civil rights implications. Discriminatory practices, policies, and outcomes need to be addressed under existing laws and regulations such as Title VI of the 1964 Civil Rights Act and NEPA. Some policies and practices have disproportionately and adversely affected low-income and people-of-color communities. Moreover, while some investment strategies may be effective in reducing congestion and improving overall mobility, they can also have significant equity impacts. The conference participants recommended the following actions:

- Provide equal enforcement of existing environmental, civil rights, housing, and health laws.
- Compile annual report cards of state DOTs and MPOs Title VI compliance.
- Conduct training workshops for federal and state DOTs and MPOs enforcement and compliance of Title VI, Executive Order 12898 and the DOT Order, and environmental justice guidance in NEPA.

- Design studies to assess the possible regressive and discriminatory impact of new strategies (congestion pricing) and technologies (intelligent vehicle highway systems).
- Survey and analyze Title VI transportation discrimination complaints against federal and state DOTs and MTOs.
- Promote state DOTs, MPOs, and community groups that have been success ful in providing equitable transportation services, programs, investments, and public-private partnerships.

3. Improve research, data collection, and assessment techniques. Negative environmental and health impacts often fall heaviest on the poor, Native and indigenous communities, and people of color. Data gaps exist in areas of distributive impacts of the Clean Air Act Amendment, congestion control, energy conservation strategies, contracting, facility siting, transport and routing of hazardous and radioactive materials, investments, program funding, quality and availability of service, and relocation actions. Recommendations were grouped under assessment and data collection:

Assessment:

- Finalize and approve the proposed DOT Order and provide guidance for the order to be integrated into state DOTs and MPOs.
- Develop tools to identify and assess the impacts of transportation policies on low-income and people-of-color communities.
- Conduct analysis on interaction of transportation, land use, and economic-disinvestment outcomes.
- Conduct transportation investment studies that assess equity and environmental justice implications.
- Assess impact of existing transportation-investment strategies on residential segregation and growing inequity between central cities and suburbs.
- Integrate environmental justice principles into the NEPA process and assess their impact on equity.
- Provide feedback on environmental, health, and socioeconomic impacts.
- Establish monitoring and mitigation programs that involve impacted communities as partners.
- Conduct analysis of model transportation partnerships or success stories that could be replicated elsewhere.
- Improve designs, methodologies, and measures to assess and mitigate disproportionate health effects (including multiple and cumulative impacts) of DOT or DOT-funded programs, policies, and activities under NEPA and other environmental laws.

Data Collection:

- Require impact assessments to include qualitative and quantitative data.
- Conduct training in Geographic Information System for use in Title VI and NEPA compliance.
- Design mechanisms to improve accuracy of highway and transit usage data and data requirements of diverse customers.
- Design methodologies to assess community impacts (environmental, human

health, socioeconomic, cultural, etc.), existing risk burdens (multiple and cumulative impacts), and vulnerable populations (low-income, children, elderly, workers, etc.) before facilities are sited.

- Document progress of State DOTs and MPOs in developing nondiscriminatory policies, practices, and outcomes.

4. Promote interagency cooperation in transportation planning, development, and program implementation to achieve livable, healthy, and sustainable communities. An interagency approach offers great promise in addressing social equity and distributive issues, location decisions, land use, investment and development strategies, and strategies to foster partnerships among local, state, tribal, and federal stakeholders. Some solutions require many agencies working together with the public. This can be accomplished through the following:

- Use Executive Order 12898 as a vehicle to coordinate enforcement and compliance on environmental justice concerns across program areas (i.e., Title VI of the 1964 Civil Rights Act, National Environmental Policy Act, Intermodal Surface Transportation Efficiency Act, American Disability Act, Community Right-to-Know, Community Reinvestment Act, Home Mortgage Disclosure Act, Federal Fair Housing Act Amendment of 1988, and Uniform Relocation Assistance and Real Property Acquisition Policies Act).
- Provide technical assistance and training in intergovernmental coordination.
- Support the continuation and expansion of interagency funding of hazardous material training for urban inner-city youths.
- Design model interagency projects in empowerment and enterprise zones, and other targeted redevelopment areas.
- Design assessment tools and training program in conflict and dispute resolution.
- Conduct training in Title VI for state DOTs and MPOs.
- Provide resources for coordination of Native transportation programs with state DOTs and federal agencies.
- Conduct evaluation of state DOTs and MPOs in compliance with Title VI.

Grassroots groups and community leaders are demanding a place at the table with MPOs as equal partners in transportation decision-making, especially on issues that have direct impact on their communities. It is not enough to be sitting at the table, but those most affected by transportation policies must have a voice, and this voice must be respected.

The contributors in this book have shown us that race and class barriers still persist in transportation. Through their critiques and case studies spanning the nation from New York to California, the multidisciplinary and multi-ethnic team of activists, academics, lawyers, environmentalists, and civil rights advocates clearly articulate the urgent need for American society to address social inequities. Many of these social ills related to racial segregation, residential apartheid, and institutional racism have been swept under the rug or superficially buried.[7] Transportation must become a bridge — not a barrier — to carry us forward into the twenty-first century.

Endnotes

Introduction

1. See Joe R. Feagin and Clairece B. Feagin, *Discrimination American Style: Institutional Racism and Sexism* (Malabar, Fl.: Krieger Publishing Co., 1986); Robert D. Bullard and Joe R. Feagin, "Racism and the City," in *Urban Life in Transition* , eds. M. Gottdiener and C.V. Pickvance (Newbury Park, Ca: Sage, 1991). pp. 55-76.

2. See J. M. Jones, "The Concept of Racism and Its Changing Reality." *Impact of Racism on White Americans* (Beverly Hills: Sage, 1981), p. 47.

3. See Robert D. Bullard, ed., *Confronting Environmental Racism: Voices from the Grassroots* (Boston: South End, 1993); Robert D. Bullard, "The Threat of Environmental Racism," *Natural Resources and Environment 7* (Winter 1993): 23-26; Bunyan Bryant and Paul Mohai, eds., *Race and the Incidence of Environmental Hazards* (Boulder, Co.: Westview Press, 1992); Regina Austin and Michael Schill, "Black, Brown, Poor and Poisoned: Minority Grassroots Environmentalism and the Quest for Eco-Justice," *The Kansas Journal of Law and Public Policy* 1(1991): 69-82; Kelly C. Colquette and Elizabeth A. Henry Robertson, "Environmental Racism: The Causes, Consequences, and Commendations," Tulane Environmental Law Journal 5 (1991): 153-207; Rachel D. Godsil, "Remedying Environmental Racism," Michigan Law Review 90 (1991): 394-427.

4. Michael Omi and Howard Winant, *Racial Formation in the United States: From the 1960's to the 1980's* (New York: Routledge and Kegan Paul, 1986), pp. 76-78.

Chapter 1: Just Transportation

1. John Hope Franklin, *From Slavery to Freedom: A History of the Negro in America*, 4th ed. (New York: Alfred A. Knopf, Inc., 1974), p. 276.

2. Aldon D. Morris, *The Origins of the Civil Rights Movement: Black Communities Organizing for Change* (New York: The Free Press, 1984), pp. 17-25.

3. Ibid., p. 51.

4. See Bunyan Bryant and Paul Mohai, *Race and the Incidence of Environmental Hazards* (Boulder, Co: Westview Press, 1992).

5. Council on Environmental Quality, The Second Annual Report of the Council on Environmental Quality (Washington, D.C.: U.S. Government Printing Office, 1971).

6. Dee R. Wernette and Leslie A. Nieves, "Breathing Polluted Air: Minorities are

Disproportionately Exposed," *EPA Journal* 18 (March/April 1992): 16-17.

7. See Robert D. Bullard, *Unequal Protection: Environmental Justice and Communities of Color* (San Francisco: Sierra Club Books, 1996).

8. U.S. Environmental Protection Agency, Draft Guidance: EPA Environmental Justice in EPA's NEPA Compliance Analyses (Washington, D.C.: U.S. EPA, 1995).

9. U.S. Department of Transportation, Community Impact Assessment: A Quick Reference for Transportation (Washington, D.C.: Federal Highway Administration, 1996).

10. See Eric Mann, *L.A.'s Lethal Air: New Strategies for Policy, Organizing, and Action* (Los Angeles: Labor/Community Strategy Center, 1991).

11. Bill Lann Lee, "Civil Rights Remedies for Environmental Injustice" (Paper presented at the Transportation and Environmental Justice: Building Model Partnerships Conference, Atlanta, Ga. (11 May 1995), p. 9.

12. Richard Simon, "Settlement of Bus Suit Approved," *Los Angeles Times*, Tuesday, 29 October 1996.

Chapter 2: Just and Sustainable Communities

1. Steven Alexander, *The Need for Rural Transportation* (Little Rock: Arkansas State Highway and Transportation Department, 1994).

2. The Urban Habitat Program (UHP) is a nonprofit social justice and environmental organization led by people of color. UHP works to create socially just and ecologically sustainable communities in the San Francisco Bay Area by cultivating multicultural leadership among African, Native, Chicano/Latino, Asian/Pacific Islander and European-Americans. UHP is a project of Earth Island Institute.

3. Martha Naomi Alt, "Does Access to Jobs Affect Employment Rates and Incomes of Inner-City Residents?" (Paper prepared for the Urban Habitat Program of Earth Island Institute, December, 1991).

4. Urban Habitat Program, Bayview Hunters Point Social and Ecological Justice Transportation Plan (San Francisco: Pittman & Hames Associates for the Urban Habitat Program, 1994), p. 1.

5. Peter Calthorpe et al., The Ahwahnee Principles (Sacramento, CA: Local Government Commission, 1991).

6. Created by participants of the Defining Sustainable Communities Conference, Oakland, CA, 2-4 June 1994.

7. Urban Habitat Program, *Sustainability and Justice: A message to the President's Council on Sustainable Development — An Urban Habitat Program Reader* (San Francisco: Urban Habitat Program, April, 1995).

8. Urban Habitat Program, *On the Right Track: The Bayview Hunters Point Third Street Light Rail Project — A Handbook for Transportation and Land Use Planning, Community Action and Neighborhood Revitalization* (San Francisco: Urban Habitat Program, 1995).

9. Low-floor vehicles create a more pedestrian-friendly environment; access is at street level and no high boarding platforms or lifts are required. Because access by disabled and elderly people is made easier, compliance with the American Disabilities Act is facilitated for existing and future transit expansions in a more cost-effective manner.

Chapter 3: Linking Social Equity with Livable Communities

1. Robert Cervero, *Suburban Gridlock* (New Brunswick, New Jersey: Center for Urban Policy Research, 1986).

2. Rick Wartzman, "Good Connections: New Bus Lines Link the Inner-City Poor With Jobs in Suburbia," *The Wall Street Journal,* 24 September 1993. In a reverse commute program sponsored by the National Center for Neighborhood Enterprise, it was estimated that 30 percent of people participating in the program would not have worked at all.

3. Since some agencies have been lax about enforcing this regulation, groups such as the Conference of Minority Transportation Officials have been working to ensure that contracts are awarded more equitably to promote racial and economic justice, and community economic development. For more information, contact the Conference of Minority Transportation Officials in Washington, D.C. at (202) 775-1118.

4. The American Public Transit Association (APTA) estimates that low-income transit riders constitute 28 percent of total riders, which is twice the national level of 14 percent of people living below poverty line. If the New York City Transit Authority is not considered, the percentage increases to 38 percent. Definitions of poverty differ slightly between the APTA study (below $15,000 annual income per household) and the Census Bureau ($13,924). See Americans in Transit: A Profile of Public Transit Passengers (American Public Transit Association, December 1992).

5. Pisarski, Alan E., *Travel Behavior Issues in the 90s* (U.S. Department of Transportation, Federal Highway Administration, July, 1992).

6. Ibid. In fact, all trip increases between 1983 and 1990 can be attributed to increased car trips.

7. 1000 Friends of Oregon is perhaps the most active environmental group pushing this notion.

8. For more information, contact the Surface Transportation Policy Project, at (202) 939-3470.

9. Michele Herman, *Bicycle Blueprint: A Plan to Bring Bicycling into the Mainstream in New York City* (New York: Transportation Alternatives, 1993).

10. According to the National Center for Neighborhood Enterprise, only roughly 18 percent of Chicago's poor people have access to cars.

11. John Holtzclaw, Explaining Urban Density and Transit Impacts on Auto Use (Natural Resources Defense Council, 15 January 1991, in California Energy Commission Docket No. 89-CR-90).

12. According to Michael Cameron of the Environmental Defense Fund, a fifty-cent per vehicle mile traveled (VMT) charge in Southern California will achieve an 11-percent reduction in VMT. Of this, there will be a 29-percent reduction in driving among low-income people, compared with a 9-percent reduction in driving for high-income people.

13. Between 1983 and 1990, for example, vehicle trips and VMT grew by 25 and 40 percent, respectively; both more than double associated person-travel trends.

14. Several studies place the degree of study between $300 billion and $750 billion per year. See John Moffet, The Price of Mobility (Natural Resources Defense

Council, October 1993); Jim MacKenzie, Roger Dower, and Don Chen, *The Going Rate: What It Really Costs to Drive* (World Resources Institute, July 1992); Charles Komanoff and Brian Ketcham, *Win-Win Transportation: A No-Losers Approach to Transportation Planning* (San Francisco: Natural Resources Defense Council, 1992).

15. Michael Cameron, "A Consumer Surplus Model for Roadway Pricing" (Environmental Defense Fund, July, 1991).

16. Jeffery Tumlin and Patrick Siegman, "The Cost of Free Parking," *Urban Ecology* (Summer 1993).

17. Conversation with Martein Hernandez of Watchdog in Los Angeles.

18. See Don Chen, "Remembering Cynthia Wiggins: A Lesson in Transportation and Community Revitalization," *Environmental Action* 28 (Spring/Summer 1996): 31-32.

Chapter 4: Tale of Two Cities

1. See R.D. Bullard, J. Eugene Grigsby, and Charles Lee, *Residential Apartheid: The American Legacy* (Los Angeles: UCLA Center for African American Studies, 1994).

2. R.D. Bullard, "The Legacy of American Apartheid and Environmentalism," *St. John's Journal of Legal Commentary* 445 (1994).

3. National Advisory Commission on Civil Disorders, Report of the National Advisory Commission on Civil Disorders (New York: E.P. Dutton, 1968).

4. *American Rivers, North America's Most Endangered and Threatened Rivers of 1994* (Washington, D.C.: American Rivers, 1994).

5. Office of Policy and Evaluation, District of Columbia Government, Indices: A Statistical Index to District of Columbia Services (December 1992).

6. See generally African American Environmentalist Association, et al., *Our Unfair Share: A Survey of Pollution Sources in Our Nation's Capital* (June 1994).

7. See R. D. Bullard, ed., *Confronting Environmental Racism: Voices from the Grassroots* (Boston: South End Press, 1993), pp. 60-75.

8. Robert D. Bullard, "The Legacy of American Apartheid and Environmental Racism," St. John's J.L. Comm. 9 (1994): 445,451.

9. Executive Office of the President of the United States, Budget of the United States Government for Fiscal Year 1995, 144 (1994). As a result of the investment of over $1 billion in restoration funds, the Potomac River now is restored for fishing and swimming.

10. U.S. Environmental Protection Agency, Chesapeake Bay Program Office, *The Restoration of the Anacostia River, The Report to Congress* 5 (9 July 1992).

11. Both of the remaining projects, the Children's Island theme park and the Barney Circle Freeway, have been challenged in court by community groups. See Anacostia Watershed Society, et al., v. Babbitt, et al., 871 F. Supp. 477 (D.D.C.), appeal filed, D.C. Cir. No. 95-5115; Anacostia Watershed Society, et al., v. Peña, et al., Civ. No. 94-1051 (PLF) (D.D.C.); D.C. Federation of Civic Associations, et al., v. Peña, et al., Civ. No. 94-1101 (PLF) (D.D.C.); Anacostia Watershed Society v. Kelly, et al., Civ. No. 7136-94 (D.C. Super. Ct.).

12. Stephen C. Fehr, "Metro Board Raises Bus, Subway Fares," *The Washington Post*, D-1, 5 May 1995; Stephen C. Fehr, "D.C. Crisis Jeopardizes Metro Finish,"

The Washington Post, A-1 19 March 1995.

13. Keary, "Bus Route Cuts, Fare Rises Hit Anacostia Hard," *The Washington Times,* 13 March 1995.

14. See generally D.C. Federation of Civic Associations v. Volpe, 450 F.2d 1231 (D.C. Cir. 1972).

15. Opponents of the freeway include Advisory Neighborhood Commissions 6A, 6B, 6C, 2D; Barney Circle Neighborhood Watch; Citizens Committee to Stop It Again; D.C. Federation of Civic Associations; Far Northeast/Southeast Council; Fairlawn Citizens Association; Ives Watch; Kingman Park Civic Association; North Lincoln Park Civic Association; Southeast Neighborhood Association; Urban Protectors; Anacostia Watershed Society; Audubon Naturalist Society; American Rivers; Friends of the Earth; New Columbia Sierra Club; and Committee of 100 on the Federal City.

16. The Sierra Club Legal Defense Fund's clients in Anacostia Watershed Society, et al., v. Peña, et al., Civ. No. 94-1051 (PLF) (D.D.C.), are the Anacostia Watershed Society, Kingman Park Civic Association, Barney Circle Neighborhood Watch, Urban Protectors, Committee of 100 on the Federal City, American Rivers, and Friends of the Earth.

17. Statement of Deeohn Ferris, Washington Office on Environmental Justice, at the Federal Highway Administration's Environmental Justice and Transportation Conference in Atlanta, Georgia, 12 May 1995.

18. See Testimony of Dr. Robert D. Bullard, "In the Matter of Louisiana Energy Services (Claiborne Enrichment Center)" before the Atomic Safety and Licensing Board, Dkt. No. 70-3070, 24 February 1995.

19. For a history of this period, see Joe A. Mobley, *James City: A Black Community in North Carolina* (Raleigh: N.C. Dept of Cultural Resources, 1981).

20. See David S. Phelps, et al., An Archaeological-Historical Study of the Bryan Cemetery and Site 31CV25, Simmons-Nott Airport, New Bern, North Carolina, No. 19 (Raleigh: N.C. Archaeological Council, 1979).

21. Ibid.

22. See Implementation of the DOT Title VI Program, DOT Order No. 1000.12, at IV-2, 19 January 1977.

23. FHWA and DOT Title VI regulations and Executive Order 12,898 prohibit the use of federal aid for projects that have the effect of discriminating on the basis of race: 49 C.F.R. sections 21.5(b)(2), (3) (DOT); 23 C.F.R. sections 710.405(c)(2), (3) (FHWA); Executive Order 12,898, section 2-2, reprinted in 42 U.S.C.A. section 4321, at 477. As explained by the attorney general of the United States in her memorandum entitled, "Use of the Disparate Impact Standard in Administrative Regulations Under Title VI of the Civil Rights Act of 1964," the Title VI regulations' disparate impact standard dictates that "policies and practices [having discriminatory effects] shall be eliminated unless they are shown to be necessary to the program's operation and there is no less discriminatory alternative." Memorandum from Attorney General Janet Reno (July 14, 1994). The attorney general's interpretation of the Title VI disparate impact standard is binding on the federal agencies since, under Executive Order 12,250, the president delegated authority to the attorney general to implement Title VI.

24. See Memorandum from Attorney General Janet Reno to Heads of Federal

Agencies.

25. Ibid.

26. See FHWA Region 6 Implementation Plan.

Chapter 5: Transportation Efficiency and Equity in Southern California: Are They Compatible?

1. Excluding walking trips.

2. Southern California is defined here as the four counties of Los Angeles, Orange, Riverside and San Bernardino.

3. All table figures in this paper excerpted from "Efficiency and Fairness on the Road: Strategies for Unsnarling Traffic in Southern California" (Environmental Defense Fund, 1994), p. 7.

4. The California Supreme Court in Serrano v. Priest (5 Cal. 3d 584, 1971) held that the "right to an education in public schools is a fundamental interest which cannot be conditioned on wealth." Judicial findings in these cases refer to the equal protection clause of the U.S. Constitution.

5. Figures for combined automobile and transit travel.

6. These figures do not mean that travel is less important to lower-income individuals. These estimates of mobility benefits are based on people's willingness to pay, which in turn is based on people's ability to pay. In 1991, the median income per capita for the lowest income group was $4,100, for the middle income group it was $11,900; and for the highest income group it was $37,950 per person.

7. The health damage estimate excludes the effects of carbon monoxide emissions, which come primarily from vehicles. Given that lower-income residents are more likely to live near major roads where CO hot-spots occur, they are probably exposed to more health damages than individuals with higher incomes.

8. Actual hours of delay are distributed more evenly: the 20 percent of people in the lowest income group incurred roughly 9 percent of all hours lost to congestion, compared to 19 percent of hours lost by the middle income group, and 32 percent of hours lost by the highest income group. In light of the wage-based values of time estimated by the Southern California Association of Governments, which assign the value of $15.10 per travel hour to high-income travelers, $5.26 to middle-income travelers and $1.99 to low-income travelers, the distribution of the value of lost hours is weighted heavily toward high-income individuals: 56 percent of the lost value from congestion was incurred by the highest income group, 12 percent by the middle-income group, and 2 percent by the lowest income group.

9. Data for Chicago to be published by Environmental Defense Fund in the Winter of 1996. The data stems from an analysis of Chicago's transportation system very similar to the one performed for Southern California and on which this chapter is based.

10. Assuming the average car gets twenty-five miles per gallon.

11. The TRIPS model was developed by Greig Harvey of Deakin, Harvey, Skabardonis. The full documentation for the model is included as an Appendix in the full report of "Efficiency and Fairness on the Road."

12. The discrepancy between the percentage reduction in emissions (10-11 percent) and the percentage reduction in health costs (40 percent) is explained by the fact that, for purposes of this study, the health damages are associated with emissions over the federal health-based standard only. Thus total emissions are reduced by 10-11 percent, but the emissions over the level needed to attain federal standard are reduced by 40 percent.

13. Congestion is a nonlinear problem. That is, it is the last few cars on a crowded roadway that bring speeds way down. Conversely, removal of those few cars can restore free flow. Hence a small reduction in VMT can yield a significant reduction in congestion.

14. The discrepancy between the percentage reduction in hours (29 percent) and percentage reduction in cost of congestion (26 percent) is due to the fact that the estimated value of each hour saved depends on the wage-rate of the person driving.

15. The model used to estimate these impacts is based on highly debatable assumptions about the value that people place on their travel, on their time, and their health. Given the wide band of uncertainty that surrounds these assumptions, the margin of error is fairly large. The assertion that low-income individuals would probably be worse off as a result of the five-cent per mile fee, while the model shows a modest improvement, is a way of saying that the model results fall within the error band for low-income individuals and therefore are not reliable.

Chapter 6: Confronting Transit Racism in Los Angeles

1. See Bill Boyarsky, "MTA's Rude Behavior Shows it is Out of Touch with its Riders," *Los Angeles Times*, 17 July 1994.
2. For an in-depth discussion of these issues see Eric Mann, *A New Vision for Urban Transportation: The Bus Riders Union Makes History at the Intersection of Mass Transit, Civil Rights, and the Environment* (Los Angeles: Labor Community Strategy Center, 1996).
3. Richard Simon, "Settlement of Bus Suit Approved," Los Angeles Times, 29 October 1996; David Bloom, "Bus Riders Beat MTA on Fares, Service," Daily News, 29 October 1996.

Chapter 7: Race and the Politics of Transportation in Atlanta

1. Ivan Allen, Jr., *Mayor: Notes on the Sixties* (New York: Simon and Shuster, 1971).
2. See Faye Goldberg and Marymal Williams, *Transportation Needs of the Atlanta Black Community* (Atlanta University Urban Transportation and Urban Affairs Project, School of Business Administration, April, 1972); Abraham Davis, *An Analysis of the Decision-Making Process of the Metropolitan Atlanta Rapid Transit Authority* (Atlanta University Urban Transportation and Urban Aff airs Project, School of Business Administration, April 1972); and Abraham Davis, *An Analysis of the November 9, 1971 Referendum Vote on Rapid Transit in Fulton County* (Atlanta University Urban Transportation and Urban Affairs Project, School of Business Administration, March, 1973).

3. Atlanta Regional Commission, MARTA Residential Displacement and Relocation Activity: August 1973 through March 1978 (Atlanta: Atlanta Regional Commission, April, 1979).

4. Richard Lovelace, Director of Real Estate, Metropolitan Atlanta Rapid Transit Authority. Personal communication, 14 March 1994.

5. Metropolitan Atlanta Rapid Transit Authority, FY'94 Adopted Operating and Capital Budgets (Atlanta, MTA), p. 16.

6. Atlanta Regional Commission, *Atlanta Regional Transportation Improvement Program FY 1994 - FY 1999* (Atlanta: Atlanta Regional Commission, June 1993) Executive summary.

7. George Hoyt & Associates, Inc., *Final Report On-Board Bus and Rail Survey RFP# 135* (Atlanta: Metropolitan Atlanta Rapid Transit Authority, October, 1990).

8. Ibid.

9. Bureau of Labor Statistics, *Consumer Expenditure Survey 1990-1991* (U.S. Department of Labor, September, 1993), Table 7, pp. 38-41.

10. Metropolitan Atlanta Rapid Transit Authority, Awards of Contracts: FY1989 - FY1993 (Office of the General Manager). Unpublished internal report.

11. Federal Transportation Administration, Report of DBE Awards and Commitments (Office of the General Manager, Assistant for Equal Opportunity). A quarterly report to the Federal Transportation Administration.

12. Georgia Department of Transportation, DBE/WBE Participation in Contracts (Georgia: Office of Equal Opportunity).

13. Robert L. Bradley, Georgia Department of Transportation, Office of Equal Opportunity. Personal communication, 11 March 1994.

14. Georgia Department of Transportation, State and Local Government Information (EEO)-4 (Office of Equal Opportunity). Data for employment as of June 1993; U.S. Bureau of the Census, 1980 Census of Population and Housing; U.S. Department of Commerce; 1990 Census of Population and Housing, Public Use Microdata Sample "B". Special data extract prepared by the University of Georgia.

Chapter 8: The Legacy of Jim Crow in Macon, Georgia

1. This account is drawn primarily from the author's telephone interview with Rosa Parks on July 1, 1994. However, Ms. Parks has also relayed her story in two other recent books: Rosa Parks with Jim Haskins, *My Story* (Dial Press 1992); Rosa Parks with Gregory J. Reed, *Quiet Strength: The Faith, Hope and the Heart of a Woman Who Changed the Nation* (Zondervan Publishing).

2. Montgomery served again as a forum for that struggle when, in 1960, the Supreme Court struck down the conviction of a young African-American bus passenger for sitting at a bus station luncheon counter in Montgomery reserved for whites, Boynton v. Commonwealth of Virginia, 364 U.S. 454 (1960).

3. Labor Community Strategy Center et al. v. L.A. County Metropolitan Transportation Authority et al., U.S. District Court for the Central District of California, Civ. Act. No. 94-5936 (filed Aug. 31, 1994).

4. A lawsuit challenging a planned fare increase on New York's subway system was filed in November, 1995 on behalf of transit riders. The suit was predicated on an asserted violation of Title VI. Although the district court initially enjoined the increase, however, a panel of the Second Circuit Court of Appeals vacated the injunction on the grounds that the plaintiffs had failed to adequately demonstrate a likelihood of success on the merits in the unique factual circumstances of that case. New York Urban League v. State of New York, No. 95-9108 (2d Cir., Dec. 7, 1995), reversing Civ. Act. No. 9001, filed in the Southern District of New York in November, 1995.

5. The Philadelphia suit challenged the public transit authority's alleged over-allocation of funds to rail primarily serving white suburban commuters, and likewise challenged the alleged under-allocation of funds to the city transit system on which minority and poor people depended. The suit led to settlement negotiations, but was later dismissed on the transit authority's motion for summary judgment (Committee for a Better North Philadelphia v. Southeastern Pennsylvania Transportation Authority, 1990 Westlaw 121177 [E.D. Pa. 1990]).

6. See generally David Oedel, "An Independent Study of Public Transit in the City of Macon and Bibb County, Georgia." Unpublished report, 1993. See also "Some Results of an Open Public Forum on Public Transit in Macon and Bibb County, Georgia, held on March 31, 1994." Unpublished report.

7. See Mitch Clarke, "Leaders: Limit tax plan to road work," *Macon Telegraph*, 11 May 1994.

8. For instance, an employee of GDOT charged with considerable responsibility for transit matters has repeatedly proclaimed in public that Macon's transit system is "the best in the state." In the context of the demonstrably deplorable state of public transit service in Macon, statements like that can only mean that the authorities are applying a radically different standard when measuring the value of the transit service than they are when measuring the value of roads, streets and highways. According to the GDOT measure, the bus system is valued by how little it costs, while the roads are valued by how many and how well they serve.

9. In fact, there is good reason to believe that this underestimates the number of people with disability limitations in Macon and Bibb County who need paratransit service. For instance, according to the 1990 census, 10,405 Bibb County residents aged sixteen to sixty-four had mobility limitations.

10. See Washington v. Davis, 426 U.S. 229 (1976).

11. Village of Arlington Heights v. Metropolitan Housing Development Corp., 429 U.S. 252, 264-265 (1977); East Bibb Twiggs Neighborhood Association v. Macon-Bibb County Planning & Zoning Commission, 706 F. Supp. 880, 884 (M.D. Ga. 1989).

12. Title VI of the Civil Rights Act of 1964, Public Law 88-352, is now codified at 42 U.S.C. section 2000d, and is implemented by numerous agency regulations.

13. Guardians Association v. Civil Service Commission, 463 U.S. 582, 584 n. 2, 608 n. 1 (1983); Alexander v. Choate, 469 U.S. 287, 292-94 (1985); U.S. Attorney General's Memorandum, "Use of the Disparate Impact Standard in Administrative Regulations Under Title VI of the Civil Rights Act of 1964," 14 July 1994.

14. See Sidney D. Watson, "Reinvigorating Title VI: Defending Health Care Discrimination - It Shouldn't Be So Easy," 58 Fordham L. Rev. 939 (1990).

15. Public Law 102-166, 105 Stat. 1074.

16. President Clinton issued the Environmental Justice Executive Order, Executive Order 12,898, on February 11, 1994. The order calls on each federal agency to "make achieving environmental justice part of its mission by identifying and addressing, as appropriate, disproportionately high and adverse human health or environmental effects of its programs, policies, and activities on minority populations and low-income populations," section 1-101. The U.S. Department of Transportation has proposed an order that would implement the executive order by identifying procedures for identifying and addressing disproportionately high and adverse impacts (60 Fed. Reg. 33,899 [June 29, 1995]). The DOT's proposed order had not yet been finalized by December, 1995, and has been criticized by representatives of state highway planners and others.
17. See Corfield v. Coryell, 6 Fed. Cas. 546, 551-552 (No. 3230) (C.C.E.D. Pa. 1823), "the right of a citizen to pass through or reside in any other state, for purposes of trade . . . or otherwise" is "fundamental." "The right of interstate travel has repeatedly been recognized as a basic constitutional freedom," Memorial Hospital v. Mariocopa County, 415 U.S. 250, 254 (1974). The court listed a variety of cases for the same proposition in Dunn v. Blumstein, 405 U.S. 330, 338 (1972).
18. Laurence H. Tribe, American Constitutional Law 1773 (1988).
19. See Oklahoma Tax Commission v. Jefferson Lines, Inc., 63 U.S.L.W. 4233 (April 3, 1995), upholding state sales tax on interstate bus travel in the state in which the ticket is sold and in which travel originates.
20. Public Law 91-190, 83 Stat. 852 (1969), codified at 42 U.S.C. sections 4321-4347.
21. See William H. Rodgers, Jr., *Environmental Law* 800-1023 (1994).
22. Edwards v. California, 314 U.S. 160 (1941).
23. 411 U.S. 1, 25 n. 60 (1973).
24. Public Law 101-336 (passed July 26, 1990), 104 Stat. 327, mainly codified at 42 U.S.C. sections 12101-12213.
25. The general non-discrimination provision of the Americans with Disabilities Act (ADA) holds that "no qualified individual with a disability shall, by reason of such disability, be excluded from participation in or be denied the benefits of services, programs, or activities of a public entity, or be subjected to discrimination by any such entity" (Section 202 of the ADA, codified at 42 U.S.C. section 12132). The ADA also obliges public entities operating fixed-route transit systems to purchase only vehicles that are accessible to individuals with disabilities (42 U.S.C. section 12142). Moreover, public entities providing fixed route systems must also provide paratransit service to individuals with disabilities, including point-to-point service, that is comparable, in terms of both level of service and response time, to the services provided to individuals without disabilities (42 U.S.C. section 12143).
26. Public Law 102-240 (passed December 18, 1991), 105 Stat. 1914.
27. 49 U.S.C. App. section 1607(f)(13), (14).
28. Initially adopted in 58 Fed. Reg. 58064 (Oct. 28, 1993), the regulations implementing ISTEA are now codified at 49 C.F.R. Part 450. See, e.g., 49 C.F.R. Part 450.316(b), stressing the need for MPO planning to proceed only on the basis of proactive public involvement of all persons (especially including disfavored minorities), timely and adequate public notice, and explicit consideration of public input.

29. For developments in this case, contact the author at (912) 752-2629, Mercer University Law School, Macon, Georgia.

Chapter 9: Empowering Communities of Color: Lessons from Austin

1. Statement presented by Librado Almanza at the Environmental Justice and Transportation-Building Model Partnerships Conference in Atlanta Georgia, May 11-13, 1995.
2. See United States v. Texas Education Agency (AISD), 467 F.2nd 848, 870 fn. 36.
3. Deborah Prothrow-Stith, *Deadly Consequences* (Chicago: Harper Collins Publishers, 1991).
4. Arnold H. Packer and M. Frank Stluka, *Developing Learning-Rich Tasks for Work Based Learning Programs* (Baltimore: John Hopkins University, Institute for Policy Studies, 1995).
5. This section of the chapter is a condensed version of Susana Almanza and Raul Alvarez, "The Impact of Siting Transportation Facilities in Low-Income Communities & Communities of Color," *Transportation: Environmental Justice and Social Equity Conference Proceedings* (Washington, D.C.: July, 1995), pp. 34-37.

Chapter 10: New Orleans Neighborhood under Siege

1. Regional Planning Commission of Orleans, Jefferson and St. Bernard Parishes, History of Regional Growth of Jefferson, Orleans, and St. Bernard Parishes, (November 1969), p. 13.
2. Braubbach, Raid, Borah E., *The Second Battle of New Orleans: A History of the Vieux Carré Riverfront Expressway Controversy* (Alabama: University of Alabama Press,1981), p.5.
3. Regional Planning Commission, History of Regional Growth, p. 13.
4. Bureau of Government Research, "The Vieux Carré New Orleans: Its Plan, Its Growth, Its Architecture" (December, 1968), p. 44. Samuel Wilson, Jr. wrote this report under a subcontract with Marcu, O'Leary and Associates.
5. Ibid., p. 44. Subsequent citations indicated in text by "Plan, Growth."
6. See B.H. Wright, "Black in New Orleans: The City That Care Forgot," *In Search of the New South: The Black Urban Experience In the 1970's and 1980's*, ed. Robert Bullard, 1989, pp. 45-74. Subsequent citations indicated in text by "New Orleans."
7. The Second Battle, p. 30. Subsequent citations indicated in text by "Second Battle." City Planning Commission of New Orleans, *A Prospectus for Revitalizing the New Orleans Central Business District* (October, 1957), p. 18.
8. City Planning Commission of New Orleans, "A Prospectus for Revitalizing the New Orleans Central Business District" (October, 1957), p.18.
9. Ibid.
10. See Louis D. Brown, Central Area Committee of the Chamber of Commerce of the New Orleans Area, memorandum, "Notes Regarding the Development of the Riverfront Elysian Fields Expressway and the Role of the Central Area Committee."
11. City Planning Commission, Prospectus for Revitalizing New Orlean's Central

Business District, p. vi. Subsequent citations indicated in text by "Prospectus."
12. Transcript of public hearing concerned with placing the riverfront express-way on the major street plan of New Orleans (held by the City Planning Commission of New Orleans, 19 November, 1958), p. 2-2; hereafter referred to as major street plan. Subsequent citations indicated in text by "Public Hearing."
13. City Planning Commission of New Orleans, Resolution 23 (December 1958), p. 2.
14. Vieux Carré Courier, 23-29 December 1961; see "Vieux Carré Property Owners and Associates, Inc.: Its Purpose, Its Goals and Accomplishments," brochure by Vieux Carré Property Owners and Associates.
15. *The Times Picayune*, 21 July 1961.
16. Ibid.
17. New Orleans State Item, 16 July 1963.
18. B.M. Dornblatt and Associates, Inc., "Preliminary Engineering Report, Riverfront Expressway and Elysian Fields Avenue" (April 1964), p. 1.
19. The Second Battle, p. 52.
20. The National Preservation Act of 1966 and the Howard Bill of 1967.
21. H.R., 90th Cong., 1st sess., Congressional Record (20 November 1967) 113: 33, 227-28.
22. National Historic Preservation Act of 1966, Public Law N.O. 89-665, 80 Stat. 917 as amended 16 U.S.C. 470 (F) Supp. V 1975.
23. Ibid.
24. Ibid.
25. Advisory Council, Comments Upon the Proposed Expressway, I-310, adjacent to the Vieux Carré, New Orleans, La., 2 March 1969, p. 2.
26. Ibid.
27. U.S. Department of Transportation, Department of Transportation News, Office of the Secretary, 9 July 1969; New York Times, 10 July 1969.
28. Ibid.
29. Ibid.
30. Labouisse, Monroe, Jr., "Architecture . . . The Ironical History of Louis Armstrong Park," *New Orleans Magazine*, July, 1974, p. 74.
31. Ibid.
32. Claiborne Avenue Design Team, 1976, p. 32.
33. Ibid.
34. Ibid.
35. Claiborne Avenue Design Team, p. 43. Subsequent citations indicated in text by "Claiborne."
36. Claiborne Avenue Design Team, p.15.
37. Claiborne Avenue Design Team, p.13.
38. Ibid.
39. See W. C. Cowan, C. Dufour, J., et al., *New Orleans Yesterday and Today* (Louisiana State University Press, 1988).
40. Ibid.
41. Ibid.
42. *Times Picayune,* 28 April 1995, A-1.
43. See Metropolitan Area Committee, resolution re: Statement on Riverfront Expressway," 11 March 1969, p. 2; Advisory Council on Historic Preservation,

"Comments upon the proposed Expressway, I-310, adjacent to the Vieux Carré, 18 march 1969, p. 4.
44. Ibid.
45. Ibid.
46. Ibid.
47. Ibid.

Chapter 11: The South Lawrence Trafficway: Environmental Justice Guidance for Native Americans

1. The National Environmental Policy Act of 1969, 42 U.S.C. 4321-4347.
2. The information presented here is a synthesis of several volumes of material (letters to federal, state, and local agencies; reports to HINU administration; historical research; and press releases) which I wrote between 1992 and 1997 while serving as faculty sponsor of the Wetlands Preservation Committee.
3. South Lawrence Trafficway: HHWA-KS-EIS-87-01-D; FHWA-KS-EIS-87-01-F; FHWA-KS-EIS-95-01-D-S. The NEPA process involves the circulation of a draft EIS, which is written by private consulting firms or the lead federal agency. This document should identify and evaluate the environmental impacts of the proposed project (e.g., road or airport), and made available to the affected community and state and federal agencies who have statutory responsibilities under the law to analyze and comment on the environmental impacts identified in the draft. As a general rule, there is a forty-five day comment period for the public and agencies to comment. Following the comment period the sponsors of the project will issue the final EIS, which addresses the comments to the draft, and issue a record of decision. Once the final EIS is published and circulated, the project can begin construction.
4. Given the transitory nature of a college environment, it was inevitable that membership in this committee would wax and wane. Nevertheless, the following students formed the heart and soul of the committee over the course of several years: Josephine Fire Lame Deer, Sleepy Eye LaFromboise, Stephen Luck, Anna Wilson, and Angie Bitsie. These students demonstrated tremendous courage, tenacity, self-sacrifice, and rare insight in the face of tremendous obstacles. The enormous contributions and encouragement of Dr. Henrietta Mann, Stan Ross and Thomasine Ross, Dan Wildcat, and Bill Welton (faculty and alumni advisors) also proved an inspiration to each of us.
5. Assessing cumulative impacts is a key provision in NEPA.
6. The Intermodal Surface Transportation Efficiency Act of 1991. ISTEA establishes fifteen factors which must, at a minimum, be considered in the development of transportation plans and programs in cities and counties.
7. NEPA rules allow for the analysis to consider factors "which will insure that presently unquantified environmental amenities and values may be given appropriate consideration in decision-making along with economic and technical considerations."
8. In 1891, Congress passed a provision for regulations to enforce compulsory school attendance (Act of March 3, 1891, 26 Stat. 989, 1014, 25 U.S.C. 284. This translated into the Secretary of Interior giving Indian Agents the right to withhold

a family's annual rations or subsistence. (See also Act of July 13, 1892, 27 Stat. 120, 143, 25 U.S.C. 284 and Act of March 3, 1893, 27 Stat. 612, 628, 635, 25 U.S.C. 283.)
9. In Oklahoma, lawyers and land speculators dominated the ranks of professional guardians. In many cases, guardians sold the land of a minor on the pretext of paying for their education, which usually was at federal boarding schools (U.S. Commissioner of Indian Affairs, Annual Report 1908, 2:192-194; 1910, 1:47; 1912, 2:486-487; 1913, 2:8; 1914, 2:54-56; 1915, 2:33, 370, 412-413.
10. L. Meriam, *The Problem of Indian Administration.* The Institute for Government Research (Baltimore, Maryland: The Johns Hopkins Press, 1928).
11. U.S. Senate (1928-1944), Subcommittee on Indian Affairs. Survey of Conditions of the Indians in the United States, Government Printing Office.
12. At the present time, the number of children who died at Haskell can only be estimated because of the lack of complete records. Health records and official death certificates from the early years have apparently been lost. The current estimate is that 700 children died at Haskell between 1884-1935. Part of this information is based upon tribal records and correspondence from Haskell to reservation agents. Some of these deaths involved runaways and were reported in the local newspapers of local cities, such as Topeka, Kansas City, and Ottawa. There are reports of wagon trains leaving Haskell and traveling to reservations carrying small caskets. To date, documentation has been found on only one of the 103 children buried in the cemetery.
13. It must be emphasized that the population of HINU, as of most other institutions, is culturally diverse. In truth, only a handful of HINU students, faculty, and administrators became actively involved in the spiritual issues of the trafficway struggle, although the historical and educational significance of the Haskell wetlands were unanimously appreciated. Furthermore, the tremendous contributions of non-Native members of the community, such as Bill and Laurie Ward, Bev Worster and Sylvie Ruth - good people who value Native American spiritual traditions as manifested in environmental preservation — must not go unrecognized.
14. Section 404 of the Clean Water Act, 33 U.S.C. 1344, is a permit to fill wetlands and is regulated by the United States Army Corps of Engineers and the Environmental Protection Agency.

Chapter 12: Civil Rights and Legal Remedies: A Plan of Action

1. Letter of January 6, 1995 to Jeffrey R. Brooks, Director, FHWA Program Development Office from Deanna M. Wieman, Director, Office of External Affairs, EPA, Region IX ("[FHWA's] reevaluation should consider and reflect the requirements of Executive Order 12898."
2. California Department of Transportation and Federal Highway Administration, California 710, Final Environmental Impact Statement (1992), p. II-14.
3. Ibid., pp. IV-45, 3, 5.
4. Ibid., pp. IV-45, 5.
5. Ibid., p. 6.
6. Ibid., p. IV-46.
7. Ibid., p. 3.

8. Ibid., p. IV-45, IV-46.

9. Letter dated January 5, 1993 to Thomas Larson, FHWA Administrator from Leticia Quezada, President, Board of Education of the City of Los Angeles.

10. See Portia Lee, "Evaluation of Historic Significance Short Line Villa Tract District," (prepared for Los Angeles Conservancy & National Trust for Historic Preservation, 21 February 1995).

11. California 710, Final Environmental Impact Statement, p. S-10.

12. Ibid., p. S-11.

13. Memorandum from Attorney General Janet Reno to head of departments, Use of the Disparate Impact Standard in Administrative Regulations Under Title VI of the Civil Rights Act of 1964 (14 July 1994).

14. See Memorandum from Roberta Achtenberg, Asst. HUD Secretary for Fair Housing and Equal Opportunity, Applicability of Disparate Impact Analysis to Fair Housing Cases (17 December 1993).

15. California 710, Final Environmental Impact Statement, p. S-10.

Epilogue

1. See Robert D. Bullard, "Solid Waste Sites and the Black Houston Community," *Sociological Inquiry* 53 (Spring, 1983): 273-288; United Church of Christ Commission for Racial Justice, *Toxic Wastes and Race in the United States: A National Study of the Racial and Socioeconomic Characteristics of Communities with Hazardous Waste Sites* (New York: Commission for Racial Justice, 1987); Dick Russell, "Environmental Racism" *The Amicus Journal* 11 (Spring, 1989): 22-32; Eric Mann, *L.A.'s Lethal Air: New Strategies for Policy, Organizing, and Action* (Los Angeles: Labor/Community Strategy Center, 1991); Leslie A. Nieves, "Not in Whose Backyard? Minority Population Concentrations and Noxious Facility Sites" (paper presented at the Annual Meeting of the American Association for the Advancement of Science, Chicago, February, 1991); D. R. Wernette and L. A. Nieves, "Breathing Polluted Air: Minorities are Disproportionately Exposed," *EPA Journal* 18 (March/April, 1992): 16-17; Robert D. Bullard, "In Our Backyards: Minority Communities Get Most of the Dumps," *EPA Journal 18* (March/April, 1992): 11-12; Bryant and Mohai, *Race and the Incidence of Environmental Hazards* (Boulder, Co: Westview Press, 1992).

2. Ibid.

3. *L.A.'s Lethal Air.*

4. See H. P. Mak, H. Abbey, and R.C. Talamo, "Prevalence of Asthma and Health Service Utilization of Asthmatic Children in an Inner City," *Journal of Allergy and Clinical Immunology* 70 (1982): 367-372; I.F. Goldstein and A.L. Weinstein, "Air Pollution and Asthma: Effects of Exposure to Short-Term Sulfur Dioxide Peaks," *Environmental Research* 40 (1986): 332-345; J. Schwartz, D. Gold, D.W. Dockey, et al., "Predictors of Asthma and Persistent Wheeze in a National Sample of Children in the United States," *American Review of Respiratory Disease* 142 (1990): 555-562.

5. Environmental Justice Resource Center, *Environmental Justice and Transportation: Building Model Partnerships* Conference Proceedings (Atlanta: Clark Atlanta University, 1996).

6. The 1996 "Just Transportation" video was co-produced by CAU-TV and the Environmental Justice Resource Center at Clark Atlanta University. Transportation issues are examined in major U.S. cities, including Atlanta, New York (Harlem), Chicago, Washington, D.C., Los Angeles, and San Francisco. The video running time is forty-five minutes and costs $20. Copies can be ordered by writing the Center at 223 James P. Brawley Drive, Atlanta, GA 30314.

7. For an in-depth discussion of these problems, see Robert D. Bullard, J. Eugene Grigsby, III, and Charles Lee, eds., *Residential Apartheid:The American Legacy* (Los Angeles: University of California Center for African American Studies Publication, 1994).